Property Boom and Banking Bust

Property Boom and Banking Bust

The Role of Commercial Lending
in the Bankruptcy of Banks

Colin Jones
Professor of Estate Management
The Urban Institute
Heriot-Watt University

Stewart Cowe
Formerly Investment Director
Real Estate Research and Strategy
Scottish Widows Investment Partnership

Edward Trevillion
Honorary Professor
The Urban Institute
Heriot-Watt University

WILEY Blackwell

This edition first published 2018
© 2018 John Wiley & Sons Ltd

The right of Colin Jones, Stewart Cowe, and Edward Trevillion to be identified as the authors of this work has been asserted in accordance with law.

Registered Offices
John Wiley & Sons, Inc., 111 River Street, Hoboken, NJ 07030, USA
John Wiley & Sons Ltd, The Atrium, Southern Gate, Chichester, West Sussex, PO19 8SQ, UK

Editorial Office
9600 Garsington Road, Oxford, OX4 2DQ, UK

For details of our global editorial offices, customer services, and more information about Wiley products visit us at www.wiley.com.

Wiley also publishes its books in a variety of electronic formats and by print-on-demand. Some content that appears in standard print versions of this book may not be available in other formats.

Limit of Liability/Disclaimer of Warranty
While the publisher and authors have used their best efforts in preparing this work, they make no representations or warranties with respect to the accuracy or completeness of the contents of this work and specifically disclaim all warranties, including without limitation any implied warranties of merchantability or fitness for a particular purpose. No warranty may be created or extended by sales representatives, written sales materials or promotional statements for this work. The fact that an organization, website, or product is referred to in this work as a citation and/or potential source of further information does not mean that the publisher and authors endorse the information or services the organization, website, or product may provide or recommendations it may make. This work is sold with the understanding that the publisher is not engaged in rendering professional services. The advice and strategies contained herein may not be suitable for your situation. You should consult with a specialist where appropriate. Further, readers should be aware that websites listed in this work may have changed or disappeared between when this work was written and when it is read. Neither the publisher nor authors shall be liable for any loss of profit or any other commercial damages, including but not limited to special, incidental, consequential, or other damages.

Library of Congress Cataloging-in-Publication Data

Names: Jones, Colin, 1949 January 13– author. | Cowe, Stewart, author. | Trevillion, Edward.
Title: Property boom and banking bust : the role of commercial lending in the bankruptcy of banks /
    Colin Jones, Stewart Cowe, Edward Trevillion.
Description: Hoboken : Wiley-Blackwell, 2017. | Includes bibliographical references and index. |
Identifiers: LCCN 2017031759 (print) | LCCN 2017043453 (ebook) | ISBN 9781119219200 (pdf) |
    ISBN 9781119219217 (epub) | ISBN 9781119219255 (paperback)
Subjects: LCSH: Real estate investment. | Commercial real estate. | Mortgage loans. |
    Financial institutions–Real estate investments. | Banks and banking. |
    Global Financial Crisis, 2008–2009. | BISAC: BUSINESS & ECONOMICS / Real Estate.
Classification: LCC HD1382.5 (ebook) | LCC HD1382.5 .J666 2017 (print) | DDC 332.109/0511–dc23
LC record available at https://lccn.loc.gov/2017031759

Cover Image: © MarianVejcik/Gettyimages
Cover Design: Wiley

Set in 10/12pt Warnock by SPi Global, Pondicherry, India
Printed and bound in Malaysia by Vivar Printing Sdn Bhd

10 9 8 7 6 5 4 3 2 1

To Fiona and Louyse for their patience and understanding during the preparation of this manuscript.

For Margot for her constant support over many years and to Adriana who encouraged me to put pen to paper.

Contents

List of Figures

Acknowledgements

We thank MSCI for permission to use its data on worldwide property trends. We also thank Property Data for permission to use their UK transactions data. Both of these data sources represent the essential empirical base for the book. We also acknowledge the support of CBRE, the De Montfort UK Commercial Property Lending Survey, the Investment Property Forum and Real Capital Analytics in giving permission to reproduce figures from their reports.

Glossary

APUT Authorised property unit trust – a means by which personal investors can access and invest in the property market.

BASEL III The Basel international agreements relate to common global standards of capital adequacy and liquidity rules for banks. These were first introduced in 1988. Since 2013, the amount of equity capital that banks are required to have has been significantly increased by BASEL III.

Fannie Mae Fannie Mae is a US government sponsored enterprise originally set up in 1938. It operates in the 'secondary mortgage market' to increase the funds available for mortgage lenders to issue loans to home buyers. It buys up and pools mortgages that are insured by the **Federal Housing Administration** (see below). It finances this by issuing mortgage-backed debt securities in the domestic and international capital markets.

Federal Housing Administration The Federal Housing Administration is a US government agency created in 1934. It insures loans made by banks and other private lenders for home building and home buying.

Freddie Mac Freddie Mac is a US government sponsored enterprise established in 1970 to provide competition to Fannie Mae and operates in the same way.

lending margins The difference between the rates banks charge to borrowers and that paid (usually) on the wholesale markets or to savers.

limited partnership A partner in a limited partnership has limited liability but normally has a passive role in management. There is also a manager who decides the investment policy of the partnership.

liquidity Liquidity is the ability to transact quickly without causing a significant change in the asset's price. Property tends to be considered illiquid, not least because of the time taken for a transaction.

NAMA The National Asset Management Agency was established in 2009 by the Irish government as one of the initiatives taken to address the crisis in Irish banking. It took over the bad property loans from the Irish banks in an attempt to improve the management of credit in the economy.

OECD The Organisation for Economic Co-operation and Development (OECD) comprises a group of 34 countries that includes all Western countries. It was set up in 1961 to promote policies that improve economic and social well-being in the world.

off balance sheet It refers to the ability to place assets and liabilities off a company's balance sheet.

open ended funds A collective investment vehicle where the number of shares or units can be increased or decreased according to cash flow into and out of the fund.

pre-let A pre-let is a legally enforceable agreement for a letting to take place at a future date, often upon completion of a development.

REIT A Real Estate Investment Trust is a listed company which owns and manages (generally) income producing real estate and which is granted special tax measures (i.e. income and capital are paid gross of tax with any tax being paid according to the shareholder's tax position).

retail fund An open-ended fund that invests funds which are derived from selling units primarily to individual investors.

rights issue A rights issue occurs when a company issues more shares and its existing shareholders have the initial right to purchase them.

securitization This is the practice of pooling assets (often commercial/residential mortgages) and selling, usually bonds, with interest payments to third party investors. The interest payments on these securities are backed by the income from the mortgages.

sovereign debt crisis The failure or refusal of a country's government to repay its debt (interest payments or capital) in full is a sovereign debt crisis.

upward only rent review A typical lease may have points in time in the future when the rent is due for review. An upward only rent review is the term used to describe a situation in which the rent payable following a review date cannot be reduced (even if market rents have generally fallen since the last review).

1

Introduction

Two shots from Gavrilo Princip's semi-automatic pistol at Sarajevo set in train a complex chain of events that lead to the First World War (Taylor, 1963). Commentators writing on the assassination of Archduke Franz Ferdinand of Austria-Hungary and his wife Sophie on the 28 June 1914 could not have imagined that this 'local difficulty' would rapidly escalate, develop into the world's first global conflict and cost the lives of an estimated 17 million combatants and civilians. It would also sweep away the remnants of three empires, bring about the decline of monarchies, instigate the rise of republicanism, nationalism and communism across large swathes of Europe and change the social fabric forever (Strachan, 2001; Taylor, 1963).

Almost a century later, financial commentators reviewing the failure of New Century Financial, one of the largest sub-prime lenders in the United States, which filed for Chapter 11 bankruptcy protection on the 2 April 2007, could not foresee that that this local problem would escalate and develop into the world's first truly global financial crash and almost see the ending of the capitalist system as we know it. It was to cost unprecedented billions of pounds, euros, dollars and just about every other major currency in attempts to address the issue.

The Great War had a defined start and conclusion. It formally began with the Austro-Hungarian declaration of war on Serbia on 28 July 1914, which then drew in other countries owing to a series of alliances between them. Hostilities formally ceased on Armistice Day on 11 November 1918. But despite that cessation of hostilities, not all the contentious issues were addressed at the ensuing Versailles peace conference. Many consider the outbreak of the Second World War two decades later to be a direct consequence of the flawed decisions made at Versailles (Strachan, 2001; Taylor, 1963).

Fast forward a century and the timing of the global financial crisis (GFC) cannot be quite so precisely stated. There was no single action or event that one can say triggered the crash, nor has there been a point in time – so far – when we can say that the crash is now finally behind us. We can certainly agree that not all financial hostilities have ceased, even a decade on, and we still remain years away from a complete return to normality. Austerity still lingers on for millions, and many governments are still printing money in an attempt to kick-start growth while the living standards for those in the worst affected countries remain at depressed levels. And in a striking comparison with the Great War, one wonders whether decisions made in the heat of the financial battle will not create a lasting peace but merely represent unfinished business prior to another major financial crisis erupting.

Property Boom and Banking Bust: The Role of Commercial Lending in the Bankruptcy of Banks,
First Edition. Colin Jones, Stewart Cowe, and Edward Trevillion.
© 2018 John Wiley & Sons Ltd. Published 2018 by John Wiley & Sons Ltd.

The banks were at the forefront of criticism over the scale of the crisis – and justifiably so – with their lax underwriting standards and their ineffective weak response to the crisis. But at the heart of the problem was the banks' interaction with commercial and residential property, their questionable lending practices, their almost casual disregard for risk and their creation of complex and barely understood financial products which pushed the risk out into an unsuspecting world.

This book seeks to lay bare the role of property – primarily commercial – in what became known as the global financial crash, explaining the rationale behind the banks' lending decisions and highlighting the changing emphasis on property on the part of both investors and lenders. While many excellent books have been written extolling the faults of the banking system and exposing the gung-ho policies of the bankers, fewer have looked at the specific role real estate played in the crash. This book addresses that omission.

This chapter begins by looking at how sub-prime lending evolved and not only led to the demise of the lenders of this product in the United States but also brought the international banking system to its knees in the GFC. It then explains the historical commercial property market context to the banking collapse and in particular the dynamics and role of property cycles. The next section discusses the role of commercial property in the macroeconomy, highlighting the interaction between the two. In the following section, the emergence of investment short-termism is considered with its potential consequences. The penultimate section explains some prerequisites for the analysis of property market trends presented in subsequent chapters. Finally, the book structure is explained in detail.

Sub-prime Lending Enters the Financial Vocabulary

While the housing market downturn in the United States was the critical event which ultimately lead to the onset of the global financial crash, the residential property markets played a less significant role in the rest of the world. As we will read in later chapters, it was exposure to the commercial property markets and an over-reliance on 'wholesale' funding via global capital markets that precipitated the crisis in the United Kingdom and other Western economies. However, to set the scene on the contributing factors to the global crash, it is important to explain why sub-prime lending was such an issue and how problems in that market spilled over to the derivative markets and thence to the wider world.

Prior to 2007, few commentators beyond the United States had heard of the term 'sub-prime'. Events would soon propel the term into the forefront of common usage, but in a less than flattering way. Sub-prime lending, at the outset, was the consequence of a genuine attempt to broaden the scope of mortgage provision in the United States and promote equal housing opportunities for all. Unfortunately in their quest to engage the wider population, lenders targeted more and more inappropriate customers: those with a poor credit history, those with job insecurity or even those without a job. Not for nothing were these loans called NINJA loans (no income nor job nor assets). It is useful to look at the US experience in some detail.

These sub-prime mortgage loans generally took the form of a '2–28' adjustable rate mortgage involving an initial 'teaser' mortgage rate for two years followed by a upward resetting of the mortgage rate for the remaining 28 years. The mortgages were sold on the premise of rising house prices and customers were offered the prospect of refinancing the mortgage (possibly with a mainstream lender) at the end of the initial two-year period if they could demonstrate an improvement in their financial position and credit rating. Regular repayment would support the household to rebuild its credit rating. Not all could, of course, and borrowers in that category would remain on a sub-prime mortgage but at considerably higher mortgage rates.

It was the sheer scale of the sub-prime market that propelled the crisis into one of major proportions. Sub-prime mortgages were relatively rare before the mid-1990s but their use increased dramatically in the subsequent decade, accounting for almost 20% of the mortgage market over the period 2004–2006, and that percentage was considerably higher in some parts of the United States (Harvard University, 2008). But it was not just the volume of sub-prime mortgages in force that was the problem: it was the number of mortgages which were due to have reset rates in 2007 and 2008. Not only would these mortgagees face higher rates from the reset but general interest rates were rising, compounding the problem.

Even before the full impact of the housing market downturn became evident, defaults on the sub-prime loans were rising. By the end of 2006, there were 7.2 million families tied into a sub-prime mortgage, and of them, one-seventh were in default (Penman Brown, 2009). In the third quarter of 2007, sub-prime mortgages accounted for only 6.9% of all mortgages in issue yet were responsible for 43% of all foreclosure filings which began in that quarter (Armstrong, 2007).

The effect on the US housing market was profound. Saddled with a rising number of mortgage defaults and consequential foreclosures by the lenders, house prices collapsed. Once these house price falls had become entrenched in the market, further defaults and foreclosures occurred in recently originated sub-prime mortgages where the borrowers had assumed that perpetual house price increases would allow them to refinance their way out of the onerous loan terms. A growing number of borrowers who had taken out sub-prime mortgages and/or second mortgages at the peak of the market with 100% mortgages found themselves carrying debt loads exceeding the values of their homes. In other words they had *negative equity* in their homes, meaning their homes were worth less than their mortgages, rendering refinancing impossible. It also made selling the homes difficult because the proceeds would fall short of outstanding debt, forcing the sellers to cover the shortfall out of other financial resources, which many did not have. If they tried to sell and were unable to make good the deficit, the loan was foreclosed and the house sold. Sub-prime default rates had increased to 13% by the end of 2006 and to more than 17% by the end of 2007. Over the same period, sub-prime loans in foreclosure also soared, almost tripling from a low of 3.3% in mid-2005 to nearly 9% by the end of 2007 (Harvard University, 2010).

By September 2008, average US housing prices had declined by over 20% from their mid-2006 peak. At the trough of the market in May 2009, that fall had increased to over 30% (Jones and Richardson, 2014). This major and unexpected decline resulted in many borrowers facing negative equity. Even by March 2008, an estimated 8.8 million borrowers – almost 11% of all homeowners – were in that category, a number that had increased to 12 million by the end of the year. By September 2010, 23% of all US homes were worth less than the mortgage loan (Wells Fargo, 2010). As the housing and mortgage markets began to unravel, questions were being asked about whether the damage would be confined to the housing market or whether it would spill over into the rest of the economy. No one knew at that stage just how the rest of the economy would suffer.

There was not long to wait for the answers to these questions. The reduction in house prices, bad as it was, had a consequential hit on the financial system through its impact on a process known as securitization that expanded significantly in the decade leading up to the GFC. Securitization involves the parceling together of many mortgages to underwrite the issue/sale of bonds to investors whose interest would be paid from the mortgage repayments. Securitization has three benefits for an issuing bank: it generates fee income by selling the resultant bonds to other institutions; it creates a secondary market out of what were illiquid mortgage assets; and, just as importantly, it moves these mortgages 'off balance sheet', which lowers the banks' capital requirements. This in turn allows the income generated from the sale of the bonds to expand a bank's lending.

Mortgage lending banks and companies sold bond packages of mortgages, known as residential mortgage-backed securities (RMBSs), to whichever institution its marketing team could attract as a way of raising funds on the wholesale market. These purchasing institutions were not just US domestic institutions, they were global, and so the seeds of the global financial crash were sown. These securitized bonds were structured so that the default risks attaching to the underlying mortgage loan and the originating lender were transferred to the bond holder. To make them therefore more marketable bond issuers usually arranged further add-ons in order to reduce the risk to the purchaser by improving the credit standing of the bond. These extras were default insurance providing credit enhancement. Incorporating these into the bond allows them to be granted a positive credit rating by specialist ratings agencies. This in turn allows companies to issue the bonds at lower interest rates, that is, at higher prices.

The purchasers of the bonds were provided with reassurance that the borrower would honour the obligation through *additional collateral*, a third-party guarantee or, in this case, insurance. In the United States this was undertaken by guarantees from insurance companies known as 'monoline insurers' (the United States only permits insurers to insure one line of business, hence the term). Because of their specialism these companies were typically given the highest credit rating, AAA, defined as an exceptional degree of creditworthiness. These monoline companies provided guarantees to issuers. This credit enhancement resulted in the RMBS rating being raised to AAA because at that time the monoline insurers themselves were rated AAA. Any RMBS these insurers guaranteed inherited that same high rating, irrespective of the underlying composition of the security.

These practices were considered sufficient to ensure that default risks were fully covered, and during the boom years leading up to 2007 few investors paid much regard to the risks, anyway. By the end of 2006, these mortgage securitization practices were beginning to unravel. It was finally dawning on investors that their portfolios of subprime mortgages and the derivatives created from them were not as 'safe as houses' and that they could well be sitting on significant financial losses. The truth was that subprime lending was not adequately monitored in spite of many senior people at the Federal Reserve and the Treasury having commented that this was a disaster waiting to happen (Penman Brown, 2009). Indeed, consumer protection organizations and university sponsored studies had repeatedly produced critical surveys of the practice from as far back as 1995 (Penman Brown, 2009).

The security provided by default insurance also proved to be illusory. The size of this insurance market was huge and the insurers were undercapitalized. At the end of 2006, Fitch (one of the credit ratings agencies) estimated that the largest 10 monoline insurers had over $2.5 trillion of guarantee insurance on their books, compared with cumulative shareholder funds of less than $30 billion (Fitch Ratings, 2007). These figures included all insurance business and not just mortgage bond insurance, although the latter would have accounted for a sizeable proportion of the total. The reserves of the insurers were grossly inadequate to cope with the volume of claims that emerged from 2007. The result was that the confidence in many of these financial products that had been created was decimated and valuations collapsed. The resale market of these bonds became moribund and new sales impossible.

It had become apparent just how damaging the downturn in the US housing market had come to be, not just in terms of the human misery and hard cash of the American households affected but also for the banks. And it was not just the US financial institutions which were affected; the process of selling on these securitized bonds to any interested buyer had ensured that the risk was pushed out to the wider world. The RMBS structure resulted in a transfer of the credit risk from the originating lender to the end investor – a critical factor in the credit crunch that was to ensue. That transfer of risk would not have been quite so problematical were these end investors actually able to identify, assess and then quantify the risks. But such were the complexities of these securities that it was almost impossible for anyone to do so, and no one could differentiate between the 'good' and 'bad', so all were tainted.

We know now the recklessness of some of these securitization practices. In monetary terms, they proved to be far more serious and far-reaching than the recession that could have resulted from merely a housing crisis. Not only did they magnify the extent of the problem but they moved the financial consequences away from the original players, turning the local US sub-prime problem into one of global proportions. And the biggest concern of all was that the securitization processes embroiled hundreds of financial institutions, none of which actually knew what their exposures (or potential losses) were.

The Global Extension

When evidence of the financial crisis first emerged in the summer of 2007, followed by the collapse of the Northern Rock bank in the United Kingdom in the September of that year, many (in particular, Continental European commentators) believed that the crisis created in the United States was a problem that would be confined only to the United States and to the United Kingdom. For a while, European institutions and regulators denied the existence of any problems in their markets. But as evidence grew of the increasing nature of the troubles, particularly through widespread participation in the securitization markets, it became clear that few countries across the world would be unscathed from the financial fallout. In fact most European countries were affected as the GFC took hold.

In quick succession, the European Central Bank (ECB) was forced into injecting almost €100 billion into the markets to improve liquidity, a Saxony based bank was taken over and the Swiss bank UBS announced a $3.4 billion loss from sub-prime related investments. The news from the United States was equally grim. Citigroup and Merrill Lynch both disclosed huge losses, forcing their chief executives to resign, while in a truly depressing end to 2007, Standard and Poors downgraded its investment rating of several monoline insurers, raising concerns that the insurers would not be able to settle claims. If anyone had any doubts as to the severity of the crisis, the events in the closing months of 2007 surely laid them bare. The banking authorities responded by taking synchronized action. The US Federal Reserve, the ECB and the central banks of the United Kingdom, Canada and Switzerland announced that they would provide loans to lower interest rates and ease the availability of credit (see Chapter 3 for how the story subsequently unfolded).

The later, but connected, sovereign debt problems encountered, initially and most severely, by Greece, but also by Portugal, Italy, Ireland and Spain, were a direct consequence of the crash. At the time of writing, the Greek debt crisis remains unresolved despite the harsh austerity demanded by the 'troika' (the European Commission, the IMF and the ECB) in exchange for the release of 'bailout' funds. The Greek economy in 2016 had shrunk by quarter from its pre-GFC level and unemployment was 24% after three funding bailouts. At the same time the nation's debt continues to grow (Elliot, 2016).

Commercial Property Market Context

The GFC is at the core of the book, with a focus on the associated commercial property boom in the lead up to the crisis and the subsequent bust, including the role of the banks and its consequences. The book takes an international perspective but draws heavily on the UK experience. This section sets the scene by considering the historical commercial property market context, including property's role as an investment and the significance and dynamics of cycles.

Traditionally, commercial property was regarded as primarily a place to conduct business. It was only in the 1950s that commercial property became a key investment medium (Scott, 1996; Jones, 2018). By the early 1970s, the commercial property investment sector consisted of not much more than city centre shops and offices, town shopping centres and industrial units which accommodated the many manufacturing operations around the country. These segments reflected the localities and premises of conducting business at that time. But the nature of cities was about to see a dramatic upheaval.

The period from the mid-1970s onwards witnessed major economic changes in the United Kingdom, seen in the decline of manufacturing and the growth of services and a major urban development cycle stimulated by the growth of car usage and new information communication technologies (ICTs). This led to the rise of alternative out-of-town retailing locations and formats such as retail warehouses along with the advent of retail distribution hubs and leisure outlets (Jones, 2009). Developments in ICT in particular have resulted in the obsolescence of older offices, replacement demand and provided greater locational flexibility (Jones, 2013). These changes brought property investors new classifications of property, such as retail warehouses and retail parks, out-of-town shopping centres, distribution warehouses and out-of-town office parks. Many firms, both large and small, also elected to invest cash flow into their business activities rather than in the bricks and mortar supporting them by effecting sale and leaseback deals or even full sale of their premises, thereby providing further opportunities for outside investment in property assets.

Property as an investment class differs from the mainstream classes of equities and bonds on several counts, one of which is its liquidity, or more precisely, its lack of liquidity. Unlike its equity and bond cousins, transactions in which can be completed at times almost instantly, buying and selling property (both residential and commercial) can take an age. Equally, it is not easy to switch off the development pipeline when conditions deteriorate. At times these two attributes do not lie easily with investors, and they often give rise to extremely volatile investment performance and cycles. This volatility was never more evident than during the run up to the global financial crash and during the subsequent bust. But that commercial property boom and bust period was not the first in recent memory, nor will it be the last!

Commercial property has a long history of cycles. Much of property's volatility is down to variations of supply and demand during an economic cycle. In times of economic growth and when confidence is high, occupational demand for new space rises, which in turn pushes up rents because of lack of suitable supply. This in turn attracts investors and stimulates new development, but because of development time lags continuing shortages see further rises in rents and capital values. However, as has been the way over much of the past, if too much new development (particularly of a speculative nature) coincides with an economic slowdown or a recession, these new buildings fail to find tenants and so the next property downturn begins (Barras, 1994; Jones, 2013).

Investment activity and the variability in the accessibility of finance is a critical element in this classic model of a property cycle. The ready availability of borrowing and equity capital amplifies the upturn supported by relaxed lending criteria that enables investors by being highly geared to make large profits. The availability of credit also contributes to stimulating speculative bubble effects that inflate capital values and transaction activity. Liquidity in the property market increases during this period with rising values and positive investment sentiment, so that selling will be relatively easier, encouraging profit taking (Collett, Lizieri and Ward, 2003; Jones, Livingstone and Dunse, 2016). Some, at least, of the initial unwilling sellers will be assuaged by the rising values. The downturn is similarly exaggerated as banks become more risk averse as properties they have funded in the boom lie empty and hence property developers default on their loans. The consequence is that there is a famine of credit for a number of years following the downturn (Jones, 2013, 2018).

An important dimension of investment is the relationship between gearing, risk and return. The concept of gearing, called leverage in the United States, is basically using other people's money to invest and make a profit, or to be more precise, borrowing other people's money to invest. This is a key concept in explaining the dynamics of a commercial property cycle.

Two types of gearing can be distinguished – income and capital. Income gearing relates to the proportion of trading profit accounted for by interest on loans. Capital gearing measures the proportion of total capital employed that is debt capital. The two are clearly related as higher capital gearing means greater interest payments. Essentially, if an investor is highly geared, when the economy/property market is growing and interest rates are relatively low, the returns will be high. However, the investor's position changes dramatically when the economy/market turns down as the gearing effect is magnified in the reverse direction, and profits are often turned into losses. The chapter now reviews property cycles in practice, beginning with a detailed examination of the United Kingdom, where they are well documented, before then considering the wider global context.

Past UK Experience

In the United Kingdom there have been a number of boom and busts since the Second World War. A significant property boom occurred in the 1950s with Britain in critical need of new commercial premises following the devastation of the war. With the physical rebuilding of the country, the United Kingdom was also moving away from an economy rooted in heavy engineering to one more linked to the service sector. New office space was urgently needed, especially in London, and to a lesser extent modern retail space was also in short supply. In the initial years of this boom there was little development risk as bomb sites were plentiful, contracts were invariably tendered on a fixed price basis and both interest rates and inflation were low, while on completion there was a high demand for office and retail space.

Developers typically obtained short-term finance for the site purchase and for the cost of construction from the major banks (who equally regarded this form of lending as virtually risk free). Once the property was completed and let, the developers generally replaced the short-term finance with longer term fixed-rate finance from the insurance companies. As explained in Chapter 3, the banking model at that time focused on the provision of short-term finance only, hence the requirement to look elsewhere for this longer term finance. At that time, the rental income of completed properties was typically above the cost of borrowing, so these projects were mainly self-financing. In the early years, development profits were generally high as development gains were free from tax (Fraser, 1993; Jones, 2018).

The construction boom lasted for almost a decade, but this highly profitable period for the developers came to a natural conclusion at the beginning of the 1960s. The low barriers to entry attracted a raft of new players, increasing competition for the dwindling stock of available sites, which increased acquisition costs and lowered profits. The changing balance between supply and demand also brought an end to the excessive profits. A recession in 1962 further cut demand, and the office development boom in London was brought to an end two years later when Harold Wilson's new Labour government banned any further development in the Greater London area (Marriott, 1967). The advent of higher inflation also bid up construction costs and ultimately changed the dynamics of investing in commercial property during the 1960s.

As inflation became entrenched, lease lengths and more importantly rent review periods were reduced, in stages, to five years, which became the norm in the United Kingdom for decades to come. So inflation brought the prospect of future increases in rental income from an investment in commercial property at periodic rent reviews. It altered the nature of commercial property from a fixed-income to an equity-type investment (Fraser, 1993). This changed the attitude of the life assurers. They had been merely passively involved in providing long-term finance, but now they wanted a stake in the upside; that is to say, they started to take an equity stake in the entire development project. From that position, it was but a small step to undertaking the entire development project alone and even to broadening their exposure by directly investing in any form of commercial property. It was the beginning of life assurance funds acting as both financiers to and direct investors into commercial property (Fraser, 1993).

In the early 1970s the liberalization of the financial markets (which are referred to in depth in Chapter 2), rapid economic growth and the expectation of membership of the European Economic Community (now the European Union) in 1973 brought about significant increased demand for office space, and not just in London. Obtaining accurate commercial property data for that period is not easy, but average commercial property values are reported to have increased by over 23% in both 1972 and 1973, with office properties delivering by far the greatest growth (MSCI/IPD, 2014a). Fraser (1993) notes that the increases in values during this period far exceeded those of any year within living memory. That may well be so, and certainly, no nominal capital value rise in any calendar year since has ever exceeded those witnessed over 40 years ago. Even stripping out inflation reveals that the real rates of capital growth were pretty exceptional too. Real capital growth, as shown in Figure 1.1, in 1972 and 1973 was 14.8% and 11.4% respectively (MSCI/IPD, 2014a). The 1972 real capital growth figure has since been exceeded just the once at the peak of another boom in 1988.

With economic fundamentals positive during these boom years there was rising tenant demand justifying the invigorated investor interest in the asset class. However, the boom was the first one in the United Kingdom to have been markedly affected by the use of debt to support investment (a topic that is further explored in Chapter 3). From 1967, the flow of funds into property increased substantially until 1973 (which also was the peak year of growth in property capital values and in the country's GDP) but then reversed quickly as a recession impacted. It is intriguing to note that although property companies were net disinvestors from 1974, financial institutions such as life assurance companies were actually still investing (Fraser, 1993). That dichotomy is not as strange as one may initially think. The life assurance funds and pension funds were in the midst of strong fund inflows at the time, so strong in fact that even cutting the overall allocations to the commercial property asset still resulted in funds being invested in property. Equally, these institutional funds, which used less debt (if any) to assist purchasing, were also not under the same selling pressure as the property companies were when the

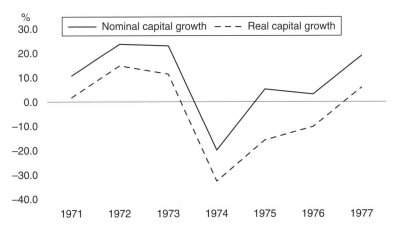

Figure 1.1 Nominal and real capital value growth 1971–1977. *Source:* MSCI/IPD (2014a). Reproduced with permission.

property market turned. We look into the position of the life assurers in more detail in Chapters 2 and 3.

The property bust came as UK inflation reached 20%, the balance of payments continued to deteriorate and there was a series of sterling crises. A new Labour government was forced to obtain a loan from the IMF and hike interest rates. Coupled with a tight fiscal policy, there were sharp falls in the stock market and in commercial and residential property values. Banks' balance sheets were weakened, particularly those whose assets were secured on property. And in a striking resemblance to events more than 30 years later, bank deposits began to be withdrawn in what became known as the 'secondary banking crisis', which is considered in more detail in Chapter 2 (Fraser, 1993).

Property companies were faced with rising debt interest payments as interest rates rose coupled with at best static income as the overheating economy contracted by a cumulative 4% over the two years from 1973. Many highly indebted property companies were forced to sell to address their debts. Much of these companies' debt had been borrowed from what was known as the secondary banking sector, whose future was by then looking precarious. Not only were these property companies unable to obtain new loans, they were faced with the difficult task of either having to refinance maturing loans or having to sell property in order to remain solvent. As more and more property was placed on the market, buoyant 1973 gave way to an altogether different couple of years. A hard landing was the inevitable consequence (Fraser, 1993).

In nominal terms, the fall in commercial property values was recorded only over one calendar year (1974, when average values fell by 18%). But in inflation-adjusted terms, the downturn was much more acute, covering three years (1974–1976) and cutting values by an inflation-adjusted 49% (see Figure 1.1). In all likelihood, the actual duration of the fall would have been longer and its magnitude would certainly have been even more acute had more frequent valuation data been available then, rather than only the annual figures. Nevertheless, the above 49% fall in real capital value was just as severe as seen in the commercial property crash of 2007–2009 (MSCI /IPD, 2014a).

The government continued through the 1970s to struggle with reducing inflation in the economy and its consequences for real incomes. In 1979 a Conservative government was elected led by Margaret Thatcher. The early years of the government were accompanied by high interest rates (in an effort to defeat inflation), higher indirect taxation but lower personal rates of taxation, public spending cuts and recession. Together with the arrival of income from North Sea oil, which prompted sterling being given 'petro-currency' status, the value of the pound rose, damaging the country's exporters and reducing the price of imports. The impact on the labour force was severe, with unemployment reaching 13%, or a total of 3 million – the highest since the great depression of the 1930s.

The unemployment story was critical for the performance of commercial property. Large tracts of the Midlands, the North of England and Scotland were laid waste by the closure of factories as de-industrialization accelerated through global trade. The resultant high rates of unemployment, and the threat of future unemployment for those in work, plus the very high mortgage rates, subdued consumer spending in the early part of the 1980s. It was not a positive backdrop for commercial property to perform against, and it did not. At the same time investors were presented with alternative competing investments through the introduction of index-linked government bonds, and the removal of exchange controls by the government opened up investment opportunities overseas.

It took three years before the 'battle' against inflation could be said to have been 'won', but finally, by August 1982, inflation was down to 5%, allowing interest rates to fall. The fall in inflation was a defining step change for the economy, but the benefits took some years to crystallize. A cut in interest rates finally prompted some good news for the hard-pressed homeowner while manufacturing (or what was left of it) was regaining its competitiveness. Economic growth returned, and from the mid-1980s a consumer spending upturn contributed to commercial and housing property values beginning to rise again in nominal and real terms (Fraser, 1993; Jones and Watkins, 2008). Alongside the surge in house prices there was also a commercial property development boom that centred especially on London offices and was stimulated by a combination of ICT improvements and increased demand resulting from financial deregulation. Fainstein (1994) estimated that new development during a 1980s boom contributed a net addition of nearly 30% to the office stock of the central area of London (including the new docklands office area).

Over the whole decade, average total commercial property returns were 11.6% per annum, or 4.9% per annum when adjusted for inflation – both highly creditable levels of returns. But that decade encompassed three distinct growth phases: the first two years were years of very high inflation and commercial property's return was equally high; the middle five years reflected lower inflation and similarly property returns were low; and two of the last three years provided exceptional total returns of over 26%, significantly ahead of the increasing inflation rate.

The seeds of the end of the property boom began with the 1987 stock market crash. The government's concern about its impact on the economy led to fiscal loosening, but this fuelled the existing consumer spending and house price inflation booms. To address the subsequent inflationary pressures, interest rates were raised to record levels. The economic recession which followed was deep and accompanied by another property downturn. Residential values fell substantially, and with a rise in unemployment, the result was that foreclosures reached record levels. Commercial property capital values fell in nominal and real terms through 1990 to 1992, as shown in Figure 1.2. As the recession took hold, tenant demand withered and the property market was further adversely affected by the development boom pipeline that continued after demand had disappeared.

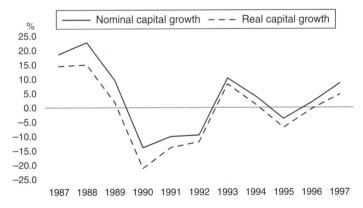

Figure 1.2 Nominal and real capital value growth 1987–1997. *Source:* MSCI/IPD (2014a). Reproduced with permission.

The recession was exacerbated by the exceptionally high interest rates in double figures as part of the government's strategy to control inflation. High interest rates were designed to increase the value of sterling. The plan was for the value of sterling to shadow the German Deutschmark, the currency of a low-inflation economy. Following a wave of speculative sales of sterling, suddenly, in October 1992, on what became known as Black Wednesday, the United Kingdom abandoned its Deutschmark policy, which immediately allowed UK interest rates to fall and base rates tumbled to 6%. The cut in the interest rates prompted economic recovery and a rise in property values (see Figure 1.2). But the recovery proved temporary. It was to be another two years before property generated meaningful long-term rental growth and capital growth. Like the economy itself, commercial property then generated high rates of growth consistently until the onset of the GFC.

Overall since the 1970s, the United Kingdom has experienced four major property booms and crashes prior to that caused by the GFC. All four of the booms were associated with periods of strong economic growth, all were characterized by the increasing use of debt by property investors and each was followed by a severe property recession. The property downturns occurred over 1974/76, 1979/85, 1990/92 and 1995/96. There is an argument that the two years 2001/02 should also be included, but the total fall in average capital values was modest, less than 1% in real terms. This modern era of cycles since the Second World War is only the latest chapter of the history of development/property cycles in the United Kingdom that can be traced back to before the Industrial Revolution (Lewis, 1965).

A Worldwide Phenomenon

Property cycles have similarly occurred around the world through history, although they are less well documented. In the late 1960s through to the early 1970s there were development booms, for example, in New York, Sydney and Dublin (Daly, 1982; MacLaran, MacLaran and Malone, 1987; Schwartz, 1979). The data on the United States is best verifiable, for example Jones (2013) charts office property cycles of New York back to the 1920s. Wheaton (1987) reports on the US office market between 1960 and 1986, and based on vacancy rates identifies three distinctive cycles with market peaks in 1961, 1969 and 1980. In addition Dokko *et al.* (1999) study 20 metropolitan areas in the United States and find that cities had different cycles.

The growth of financial services and the emergence of global capital markets since 1980 have stimulated a strong pressure toward creating 'interlocking' markets, especially of major cities. The underlying trends have been the liberalization of capital movements that has resulted in the global co-movement of share prices and real estate investment strategies (Lizieri, 2009). There are indications that this has contributed toward property cycles occurring simultaneously around the world, although the evidence at least until recently is incomplete. Goetzmann and Wachter (1996) argue that there is clear-cut evidence of office markets moving up and down with global business cycles based on an analysis of rents and capital values in 24 countries.

More contemporary research by Barras (2009) detects three global office cycles since the 1980s, starting with the late 1980s, followed by a more subdued upturn in the late

1990s and the speculative-driven boom of the mid-noughties. He plots in some detail the similarities and differences of the office cycles of 25 'global cities' – 9 in the United States, 9 in Europe and 7 in Asia-Pacific – based on rent and vacancy levels. This globalization of property cycles is undoubtedly a manifestation of the three-way interdependence between the property sector, financial services and macroeconomies (Pugh and Dehesh, 2001).

The degree of volatility in property cycles between countries can be explained by a number of factors, including differences in the supply response to rising demand that in turn is a function of planning controls. Another factor may be the differential approaches to the valuation of property. This can be seen in the use of 'sustainable' valuations adopted in some European markets which are designed to smooth changes in individual asset valuations. That means that valuations in countries adopting that approach rarely show much volatility even in times of deep market stress.

Commercial Property's Role in the Wider Economy

Commercial property stock is essential to a nation's economy and the production of goods and services. A macroeconomic perspective on property also views it as a component of the fixed capital stock of a nation. Property development, whether it is residential, commercial or industrial construction, is then considered to be expanding the capital stock of a country. It is essential to the working of the economy. The proportion of capital investment accounted for by real estate development will vary from country to country and from year to year as a result of property cycles. However, a country's changing capital stock is not just the result of additions but is also a function of the depreciation of the existing stock so that it is important to assess additions in terms of the net impact. Part of the space created in the upturn of a property cycle may be replacing obsolete buildings, that, for example, no longer meet current needs in terms of size or structure, say, because of ICT innovations. From this macroeconomic standpoint, we can view the cyclical supply of buildings as central to the business cycle, not simply as a distinct property cycle.

Besides cyclical influences, there are also long-term effects on property investment. One long-term force, as noted above, is technological change, for example flexible working enabled by ICT may reduce total office space requirements. It is also seen in the rapid reduction in the number of banks as cash machines replace tellers and online sales vie with high street shops. Other long-term influences include the decentralization of economic activity within cities and the rise of out-of-town retail centres and business parks (Jones, 2009). Where population is rising there is a need for additional housing while increasing real incomes can lead to the demand for more shops. The shift to a services based economy in many developed countries over the last 50 years has been reflected in a growth of offices and a decline in factories.

There are therefore overlapping short- and long-term economic influences on the property market. The performance of the property market is interwoven with the economy and business cycles, and this means that there will forever be property cycles. However, property cycles have their own internal dynamics, and the booms and busts are more amplified than the business cycle. The longer the economic upturn the greater the property boom.

Property Investment and Short-termism

In addition to the various economic, social and property market changes over the years, there has also been a marked change in the attitudes of investors (see Chapter 2). It is not that long ago that investors were content to buy an investment 'for the long term' – a period of time which was never defined but which could be generalized as certainly being more than five or even ten years. It was not uncommon for institutions (and particularly life funds) to hold property assets almost indefinitely that is, their individual asset business plans did not include sales.

It can be argued that what was partly responsible for changing investors' approach was the advent of fund performance measurement. At first property suffered from the lack of market statistics when compared with bonds and shares, but from the early 1980s this was addressed with the evolution of new databases discussed below. Not only did this lead to the monitoring and comparison of the overall performances of investment funds' portfolios with those of their peers but also the performances of each asset (Hager, 1980). This measurement was ultimately being conducted over shorter and shorter periods.

This process has been bolstered by the emergence of external fund management. Prior to this development property was generally managed internally by financial institutions. Now many fund managers are under competitive pressures to deliver target returns for their clients, and to do so over short periods. When the management contract period is nearing completion they know they may face competition from other fund managers for the renewal of the business. There are also a vast number of new property investment management companies and funds that depend for their existence on attracting (new) investment funds (Forster, 2013). The result is that in the middle of the 2000s properties churned over much more rapidly in the United Kingdom, and the average holding period fell to around five years (Gerald Eve, 2005).

Part of the reason for this was the rapidly rising capital values in the mid-noughties that meant that substantial profits could be made by trading properties with little effort on the part of the owner. This was rendered even more profitable if borrowings were used. However, there were also property market forces at work that challenged the traditional long-term passive investment model. Cities were experiencing a long-term upheaval in the spatial structure of the property market that brought new property forms such as retail warehouses, and many buildings needed to be refurbished or indeed redeveloped to meet modern requirements (Jones, 2013). This was also reflected in shorter lease terms as tenants sought flexibility to respond to the pace of change (Office of the Deputy Prime Minister, 2004).

The commercial property market conditions of the noughties were probably at their most vibrant compared to its past. The combination of short-termism and dynamic change provided greater scope for profit but also greater scope to make bad commercial property decisions.

Measuring Commercial Property Market Performance

Information on the commercial property market has traditionally been weak. Part of the reason is that the heterogeneous nature of properties makes it difficult to compare the price of individual properties. The scale of turnover in the market in any given locality is not sufficiently significant either, unlike the housing market, to use the evidence from transactions as a basis for the derivation of statistical trends. Instead commercial property databases have been developed primarily based on the regular valuations of properties usually undertaken for large owners, the financial institutions. These valuations are then embedded into an aggregate property database. This model is applied in many countries, although the introduction of these databases has been phased in from the early 1980s. In the United States the main database of this kind is constructed by the National Council of Real Estate Investment Fiduciaries (NCREIF) while elsewhere in the world MSCI (IPD) is the primary publisher. These databases are available on a paid subscription basis.

The valuations in these databases are derived from valuers or surveyors who use, in the main, a comparative approach to estimate property values. In other words they compare the capital or rental values of similar properties (in terms of type/location) sold or let. However, capital values *per se* are not used to compare the value of properties, instead yields or capitalization rates (in the United States) are applied. The reason is that the use of capital values on their own cannot determine which of two properties that are very different is the more expensive. Yields resolve this by standardizing for the different rental incomes of the properties. The (initial) yield is calculated as

$$\frac{\text{net rental income}}{\text{capital value}} \times 100$$

By comparing yields it is possible to assess which of the two are more expensive given their current rental income. The higher the yield the lower is the value, and vice versa. More importantly, it is changes in yields, how much investors are prepared to pay for a given rental income (including future expected growth), that determines the capital value of a property. For these reasons property market price trends are usually quantified not by using capital values but by yields. This approach is followed in this book.

In the book the analysis of commercial property trends in the United Kingdom is primarily based on annual or quarterly data from the MSCI/IPD Digests (2014a, 2014b). Overall commercial property yield and rental market trends are taken as the "All Property" indices/values from this source. In some cases the analysis is disaggregated to the retail, offices and industrial sectors as well as by region or property type (e.g. shopping centre). There are a few points where necessary where the research employs monthly data but this is based on a smaller sample size (MSCI/IPD, 2015). The research also draws on equivalent data for other countries produced by the same company from its Multinational Digest December 2014 (MSCI/IPD, 2014c). Commercial property returns in the United States are derived from NCREIF data. The book also utilizes information from a relatively new source on transactions collected by a private company, Property Data. Since 2000 the company has recorded over 34 000 UK investment transactions.

In addition to yields, the book also examines how the risk premium for commercial property varies over time. The risk premium is the additional return an investor expects from holding a risky asset rather than a riskless one – in essence the difference between the total expected return on an investment and the appropriate estimated risk-free return. For property it will encompass an allowance for the risk associated with property as an asset class – for example, uncertainty regarding the expected cash flow (both income and capital), illiquidity, management and transaction costs (Baum, 2015; Fraser, 1993). Investments with higher risk will normally attract a higher risk premium. Baum (2015) estimates the expected long-term risk premium for the property market at 3%, the mean of an historic range covering the period 1921–2011, although there has been considerable variation over the period (Jones, Dunse and Cutsforth, 2014).

To calculate a risk premium it is necessary to start with a risk-free rate. In UK commercial property investment calculations the risk-free rate is usually taken as the redemption yield on a 10-year government issued bond (gilt). Although these are not riskless they provide a better comparison than do treasury bills (government bonds or debt securities with maturity of less than a year) because

- they are a closer substitute for property for the long-term investor;
- there is a closer relationship between their yields and property yields over time;
- the market in long-dated gilts is larger and less speculative and their redemption yields are believed to provide a better indication of the opportunity costs of long-term investment capital.

Book Structure

The subject of the book is the commercial property boom of the noughties and its implication for banking. In the succeeding chapters, we look at the commercial property market in the build-up of the boom and then during the post-crash period. Figure 1.3 gives a sense of the historic scale of the boom and bust of the commercial property market in the United Kingdom over that decade, not only in terms of its dramatic rise in real capital values but also in the subsequent fall. To fully understand the phenomenon the book takes a step back by first examining the evolving investment landscape and the changing lending practices of the banking sector over previous decades.

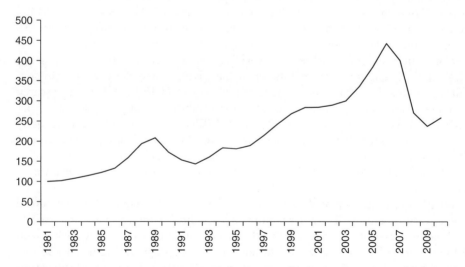

Figure 1.3 Real commercial property capital values 1981–2010 (1981 = 100). Figures deflated by the retail price index. *Source:* MSCI/IPD (2014a). Reproduced with permission.

Chapter 2 Long-term Changes to Property Finance and Investment

This chapter provides the historical context to the book by explaining recent trends in the landscape of banking finance and commercial property investment. With the role of banking finance critical to the property market through its support of investment purchases and the funding of development activity, the starting point for this chapter is bank lending. It outlines the evolution of the banking sector in the United Kingdom, emphasizing the role of deregulation and globalization in transforming a once restrained industry to one encompassing high-risk 'casino' businesses. The chapter uses this outline to provide a stage to explain banks' entrepreneurial motives during the property boom of the noughties.

The financing of, development of and investment in commercial property is explained within the short-term framework of property cycles and the long-term evolving economics of life assurance funds and pension funds since the 1960s. The arrival of overseas investors and their motivations are also reviewed. The backdrop is the continuing transformation of cities that has brought redevelopment and decentralization together with new property forms such as retail and office parks. The overall property investment outcome of these combined influences is shown to be the emergence of niche property funds, the growth of indirect investment via first limited partnership funds, new property investment vehicles, the emergence of 'retail' investors and short-termism.

Chapter 3 Economic Growth, Debt and Property Investment through the Boom

In this chapter we develop building blocks to explain the key underlying forces that influenced the property boom. In particular it profiles the predominant financial attitudes of the time supported by the positive macroeconomic climate that held sway in the build-up of the boom. These attitudes were common to most Western economies as the world experienced an unprecedented long economic upswing. The chapter stresses that this macroeconomic environment provided the basis for the boom and coloured views about the inherent risk of property investment, lending and borrowing. It further draws out the role of finance and debt, tracking the changing cost, scale and availability of bank-lending finance including lending criteria in the United Kingdom through the decade.

The chapter then considers the implications for investors, showing how gearing enabled very high profits to be made in the boom thereby expanding the funds wishing to purchase property. It looks at the extent to which the availability of finance and the attractive investment conditions translated into development activity. Finally, Chapter 3 examines the implications of the vast weight of investment money attracted into the property market in terms of the spread of values.

Chapter 4 The Anatomy of the Property Investment Boom

This chapter examines the scale and timing of general global property upturns, both housing and commercial, around the world beginning in the mid-1990s and gathering pace in the first part of the last decade, setting the UK experience in a wider context.

The chapter then examines the anatomy of the investment boom in the United Kingdom by reference to the relationship between capital and rental values as the boom develops. It asks what proportion of the rise in capital values can be attributed to rental growth and examines the premise that this time the boom years really were different from what had happened in previous cycles.

Chapter 4 considers the scale of investment funds and the growth of transactions during the boom. It also reviews who was purchasing (and selling) and the impact this had on capital values. A particular focus is the large inflow of cash via retail funds (funds that are derived from selling units to individual investors) as property returns rise in the fervour of the boom. The role of bank lending in supporting the weight of money into commercial property is reprised from the previous chapter.

Ultimately the chapter assesses the rationality underpinning the investment boom. It reviews the fundamentals of pricing and how investment behaviour in the boom arguably distorted a proper assessment of price, value and worth, thereby encouraging a disconnect between rental value growth and capital value growth. In this way it considers to what extent the boom represented a bubble.

Chapter 5 The Global Financial Crisis and its Impact on Commercial Property

In this chapter the timing of the financial events that collectively gave rise to the GFC are set out as the preface to an analysis of its worldwide impact on the commercial property market. It includes the unravelling of banking liquidity and its impact on lending and ultimately on commercial real estate investment markets globally. The chapter focuses on the detailed consequences for the UK property market in terms of falling capital values/rising yields, forced sales, falling liquidity and transactions and the collapse of bank lending. The study is placed in the context of the dysfunctional market and the irrational behaviour discussed in Chapter 4 and the mismatch between capital value growth and rental value growth. Finally it examines the market responses in the context of changing perceptions with regard to property risk premium.

Chapter 6 Property Lending and the Collapse of Banks

This chapter tells the story of the growth of commercial property lending by banks through the boom and the consequences for the banks of the subsequent fall in capital values. It distinguishes between the short-term liquidity problems caused by the collapse in credibility of mortgage-backed securities during the GFC and the impact of the falling commercial (not residential) property valuations on their loan books. The chapter demonstrates how this decline in values undermined the capital bases of many banks and ultimately challenged their fundamental economics much more than a short-term liquidity problem.

The chapter describes the paths to disaster of a number of major banks through commercial property lending in the United Kingdom, Ireland and the United States. In the process it examines attitudes to risk, the failure of predictive models and the impact of banking behaviour on property market trends. It encompasses in-depth case studies of RBS, HBOS, the Dunfermline Building Society and the Co-operative Bank, and Irish banks.

Chapter 7 Aftermath and Recovery

The property market recovery from the GFC around the world suffered not only from the legacy of debt owed to the banks but also from the vast overhang of consumer credit. Many banks faced massive challenges to their fundamental viability, only part of which was the resolution of the bad debts in their commercial property loan book. Chapter 7 chronicles the steps selected banks took to address these debts. The backdrop to the banking system's attempts to deal with its overhang of commercial property debt is the macroeconomic environment. The chapter therefore begins by examining the international macroeconomic policy reactions to the GFC, including the recapitalizations/nationalizations of banks, the timing of the recessions in the different countries, and the initial international fiscal stimuli followed by austerity policies.

The trends in housing and commercial property markets in various countries, and the differential impacts of the GFC in the short and medium terms, are also mapped out for different countries as a prelude to examining the processes of recovery. But the ramifications of the GFC stretched further than the problems of the banks so the chapter also reviews the impact of the GFC on property investors such as financial institutions, property companies and the specialist property funds explained in Chapter 3. Finally the chapter examines the overall impact of the boom and bust for attitudes toward commercial property as an investment class and in particular how investors view the risks involved.

Chapter 8 Conclusions

Individual chapters consider different aspects of the lead up to the GFC and the commercial property boom and bust followed by the consequences for banks, investors and the property market. To address the complexities individual chapters have dealt with particular issues, although in reality many of them are interrelated. The conclusion examines the important cross-cutting themes that sum to the boom, bust and recovery.

These themes include the role of globalization in terms of the international commonality of macroeconomic cycles and world capital markets that entwined banks in a labyrinth of debt instruments. It also considers the impact of greater international competition for commercial property lending between banks. A second theme relates to the implications of the use of valuations rather than actual prices to principally describe the property boom and bust. The responsibility of the banking sector through the boom, bust and recovery is then assessed, following which, the property sector's irrational exuberance is evaluated, first through over-optimism in the boom and then to the reverse, over-pessimism, in the bust. The final sections look to the future in terms of whether it could happen again and what can be done – for example, how debt should be managed in the future.

2

Long-term Changes to Property Finance and Investment

The role of banking finance is pivotal in the operation of the property market, supporting investment purchases and the funding of development activity. This chapter focuses on the United Kingdom and charts the evolution of the behaviour of the banking industry with regard to lending, highlighting the various regulatory changes which propelled a previously sober sector into the risk-taking entrepreneurial model of the noughties. Although the focus is on UK banking, parallel processes were occurring around the world as banking became more international with the emergence of global capital markets, bringing greater cross-border competition and more deregulation. By tracing the history of UK banking over the last half century, the analysis provides a platform for the reasoning behind the banks' motives during the latest boom in their quest for ever greater market share and bottom-line profits.

From there, we turn our attention to commercial property, and in particular the financing of development and investment in this sector of the economy. We start by looking at the provision of finance by banks by taking a historical and evolutionary perspective focusing on the influence of property cycles. The next section examines the changing economics of life assurance funds and pension funds since the 1960s and the implications for their role as key investors in property. The arrival of overseas investors and their motivations are then considered. The final part of the chapter concentrates on recent innovations in institutional investment. These innovations were initiated by the transformation of cities as a result of a combination of the car and new information communication technologies bringing a long urban development cycle with obsolescence of existing properties and new property forms/locations. This urban upheaval contributes to a reappraisal of property investment seen in the emergence of first niche property funds, the growth of indirect investment via limited partnership funds, new property investment vehicles and the emergence of short-termism and 'retail' investors.

The Changing Role of the Banks in the United Kingdom

The role of the UK banks in the years leading up to the boom altered markedly from that of the sleepy institutions that had existed in the immediate post-war years. No longer were they mere lenders of finance, they were now offering a huge range of products to a wide range of clients and had become experts in marketing products that many

Property Boom and Banking Bust: The Role of Commercial Lending in the Bankruptcy of Banks, First Edition. Colin Jones, Stewart Cowe, and Edward Trevillion.

purchasers (and quite a few lenders) did not fully understand (Gola and Roselli, 2009). Strange as it may now seem, it is less than 50 years since the main UK banks started offering long-term loans *of any nature*. Back in the 1960s, they offered little long-term finance for commercial property as their business models favoured the short-term provision of finance and this clashed with the generally longer term nature of property lending (Pike and Neale, 2006). That is not to say that the clearing banks were not involved in any lending on the back of commercial property at that time. But any lending on property tended to be predominantly short-term development finance (Gola and Roselli, 2009). On completion of the project, this finance was replaced by longer term finance, either from the life assurers or from 'secondary banks', small specialist banks that did not take part in the clearing system of cheques and other financial transactions.

In the 1960s the clearing banks relied on a large branch network, offering them economies of scale and allowing them to spread lending risk nationwide. They operated conservatively, mainly offering short-term loans. However, critics argued they did little to contribute to the needs of the country's industrial companies and consumers. All that changed in 1971 with the Competition and Credit Control (CCC) reform and the abolition of the interest rate cartel (Fletcher, 1976); deregulation then began. Its purpose was to transform the way in which the sector conducted its business, and its primary focus was on lending – to ensure that the banking industry was sufficiently competitive in order to give customers a 'good deal'. To that end, the abolition of the interest rate cartel and the opening up of the lending market to participants other than the mainstream banks were fundamental. Over the following decade the UK banking system changed from an oligopolistic structure within a rather protected environment into an industry exposed to high competition, and regulation and supervision of its activities became more articulate and statute-oriented (Gola and Roselli, 2009).

Besides the main retail banks, known at that time as 'clearing banks', 'secondary banks' emerged during the 1960s. Many of these secondary banks were subsidiaries of foreign banks. In contrast to the clearing banks, these secondary banks had no direct access to the payments mechanism and clearing arrangements, and having little access to retail deposits they took the bulk of their funds from the wholesale market rather than from the retail market approach more commonly used by the clearers. In other words, they borrowed money primarily from other financial institutions, and they often specialized in offering loans on commercial property. In addition to the short-term development finance that was also provided by the clearers, they offered longer term loans for commercial property (Gola and Roselli, 2009).

As noted above, this was a relatively new area of lending for banks in the United Kingdom as this group's business models were generally more flexible than those of the clearers. But lending to commercial property did have attractions. As observed in Chapter 1, in the 1960s, the perception of property as an investment was being transformed from that of a bond-type investment into one offering equity-type characteristics. Many investors believed that the asset class could potentially provide a hedge against the steadily pervasive effects of inflation (the belief being that rents, and hence capital values, increased roughly in line with inflation). This in turn attracted new investors into the asset class as well as occupiers wishing to own their own premises. Some of these would finance the purchase partly or wholly through the use of debt.

The deregulation in 1971 removed the barrier between the clearing banks and secondary banks and allowed the full entry of the former into wholesale banking – previously they had only been able to use the wholesale market through subsidiaries (Gola and Roselli, 2009). Combined with a relaxation of the government's macroeconomic policy bringing economic growth, these regulatory changes led to a swift increase in bank lending, rises in consumer spending and stock market prices, and a significant commercial property boom (Fraser, 1993). Property companies went on an investment spending spree assisted by debt. Analysis by Fraser (1993, Figure 26.2) of government statistics show that the amounts outstanding to property companies remained fairly constant in the late 1960s and early 1970s at around £350 million – £400 million. By mid-1973, total outstanding loans had soared to around £1.5 billion, and by then the clearers had been overtaken as the prime source of lending by secondary banks.

This period is known as the Barber boom after the Conservative Chancellor of the Exchequer at the time, and as Chapter 1 notes, the economy overheated bringing inflation, high interest rates and a subsequent bust. The sharp rise in the minimum lending rate (a form of bank base rate) in 1973 (Bank of England, 2016) was the catalyst for a marked fall in share prices and an end to commercial property's bull run. Coupled with the ending of the consumer boom, both tenant and investor demand disappeared, leading to sharp falls in commercial property valuations (see Chapter 1).

The falls in the value of their property assets hit the lenders hard, causing major bad debt problems for a whole raft of banks, particularly the secondary banks. As the first whiff of the problem filtered out, depositors rushed to withdraw, producing the first banking crisis for some time. Initially it was assumed that this problem was one of liquidity, not solvency (shades of the initial denial of the solvency problems in 2008). Ironically, most of the funds withdrawn from these secondary banks had then been deposited with the clearing banks, so the Bank of England's neat solution, in what became known as the 'lifeboat' operation, was to arrange for the clearing banks to recycle these funds back into the banks with liquidity problems. A total of 26 financial institutions ultimately received support from the 'lifeboat'. It is estimated that the cost to the Bank of England was £100 million, roughly 10% of the total bailout (Reid, 1982).

The secondary banking crisis can be seen to stem directly from the relaxation of regulation in 1971, which increased competition but also, in the short term, brought instability. The subsequent bailout of the secondary banks was the first systematic exercise of its kind by the Bank of England. It also marked a sea change in the way banks were monitored by the Bank: reporting requirements to the Bank were strengthened and the scope of supervision broadened (Gola and Roselli, 2009).

1979 – A New Direction

The 1979 Banking Act extended the supervision of the Bank of England to the then secondary sector (which included licensed deposit takers) and formalized supervision in the primary sector (the mainstream banks) (Gola and Roselli, 2009). It thus created a two-tier system. It was a revolutionary Act as before then bank supervision was conducted on an essentially non-statutory basis. Nevertheless, financial deregulation became the mantra of the 1980s with the election of governments wedded to monetarist policies in the United Kingdom and United States. The abolition of exchange controls and the United Kingdom's entry into the EEC had increased cross-border capital flows and attracted foreign banks (Gola and Roselli, 2009). It also led to British banks taking a more global outlook (Davies *et al.*, 2010).

What became known as investment banking was another facet of the financial markets that would feel the winds of change in this decade. Up to this point in banking, business had been cosily segmented with clearing banks concentrating their activity on short-term lending, while longer term loans were granted by specialist intermediaries, in particular merchant banks, specialist lenders and building societies (Gola and Roselli, 2009). Meanwhile, much of the business which we now regard as 'investment business' was conducted by institutions on a 'club' basis with little risk and with a high degree of protection. Prior to 1986, there were relatively few participants in the investment business market. However, in that year 'Big Bang' completely changed the way in which this type of business operated. The term 'Big Bang' relates to a collection of reforms that were designed to remove anti-competitive practices from the London Stock Exchange. In the process it placed London's financial markets on an equal competitive footing with its international rivals, especially the United States. In the process it contributed to the establishment of a global capital market and universal banking (Davies *et al.*, 2010).

The most important change was the abolition of the rule that firms conducting business had to be members of the London Stock Exchange, which ushered in a raft of new players – many of whom were foreign banks. The system of fixed commissions was abolished, cutting costs by as much as 75 to 90% (although the subsequent increase in business did compensate for this). But perhaps the most significant physical change was the move from open outcry (in which actual business was conducted on the floor of the stock exchange) to an electronic screen-based system which almost at a stroke ended the need for a physical presence in the exchange. Soon, the floor of the stock exchange had become redundant (Gola and Roselli, 2009).

The deregulation brought diversification, greater competition for household savings and reduced margins on retail banking activities. In 1988 the Basel Accord initiated international regulation of the banks and as a by-product provided an incentive for banks to expand by requiring an extra fixed cost of meeting regulatory capital requirements and an additional tier of reporting and supervision (Davies *et al.*, 2010). The overall result was also a transformation in the way corporate business was conducted. Gone was the rather quaint approach of building relationships with clients. In came a more aggressive transaction-driven approach. It arguably ultimately led to a more short-term, bottom-line driven approach, often with scant regard for the risk involved.

From 1980 onwards banks began lending mortgages in the housing market and entered the long-term preserve of building societies (Jones, 1984). Building societies are specialist financial institutions that trace their history back to the late eighteenth century, borrowing primarily from personal customers to provide residential mortgages. They are mutual societies owned by their members, savers and borrowers. The societies are constrained in the manner in which they can grow their business, having to place greater reliance on customer deposits, monthly mortgage payments and retained profits to generate the funds for further lending (HM Treasury, 2010). Up until reforms in the 1980s they could not offer overdrafts, thereby restricting their ability to compete with banks (Jones, 1984).

Although building societies gained more freedoms in the 1980s, the increased competition from banks and the constraints on their activities were the key reasons that many building societies decided to demutualize and convert to banks (HM Treasury, 2010). The first to convert was the second largest, the Abbey National, in 1989. The largest building society, the Halifax, followed in 1997, and in the same year further large societies, the Alliance & Leicester and Northern Rock, changed status. As a consequence over half of building society assets, equivalent to 15% of GDP, were transferred out of the sector in the 1990s (Davies *et al.*, 2010). Many of these new banks were subsequently taken over by larger banks or amalgamated with other banks as part of a consolidation in the sector (see Chapter 6). The remaining building societies also continued their long trend of amalgamation so that by the turn of the millennium the number of UK financial institutions offering credit/debt finance to households, industry or the property sector was much smaller than it had been 30 years previously.

By 2010 the four largest banking groups, Barclays, Lloyds, Royal Bank of Scotland/ NatWest and HSBC, plus Santander Bank and the Nationwide Building Society accounted for almost 80% of UK customer lending and deposits (Davies *et al.*, 2010). However, the banking transformation from the 1980s had not just led to a more concentrated structure it had also changed the culture of banking and the scope of the services banks offered. The largest banks could now be described as international, with branches in many countries, and their activities encompassing not just consumer and business banking but also securities underwriting and trading, fund management, derivatives trading and general insurance. The awakening of competition between banks also stimulated a wave of innovation in financial products. One of these was the extensive use of mortgage-backed securities to raise money on the wholesale markets as explained in Chapter 1. It is to this backdrop of fundamental change that we now review the evolution of the financing of commercial property development and investment in turn.

Property Development and Investment Finance

Commercial real estate development can be undertaken on a speculative basis or bespoke for an owner occupier. Property companies who build on a speculative basis do so with a view to finding a long-term investor to purchase and occupiers to let to. Preferably, the property would be let or sold before, or at an early stage during, the development period (practices known as pre-letting and pre-selling). Speculative development in this way is typically financed by borrowing. This short-term finance could cover all aspects of the process, from site acquisition through to the periodic payments for construction, and ultimately up to the point at which the property is built and let. The traditional model for short-term lending is to roll up interest incurred during the development phase and to repay the entire principal plus the built-up interest on completion. This is referred to as a 'construction loan' in the United States (Fergus and Goodman, 1994).

Once the property is completed (and let), it can either be sold with the loan being repaid out of the proceeds or kept as an investment property, and the development loan repaid by taking out a longer term loan/mortgage with the completed building as security (Jones, 2018). Some commercial property companies undertake development usually only with the intention of supplementing their existing investment portfolios. These are usually large companies that are listed on the stock exchange, including Real Estate Investment Trusts (REITs), but could embrace smaller private companies that tend to operate at a provincial rather than a national level.

While speculative development can be traced back to the nineteenth century with the building of office blocks it was very limited except for housing until after the Second

World War (Jones, 2018). It is therefore appropriate to consider the evolution of development finance for commercial property from the 1950s. In the United Kingdom, the rebuilding of London after this war and the emergence of a more services based economy stimulated an office property boom that has been well documented and is a useful case study of this time. The financial equation facing property developers at that time was very attractive given low interest rates, high demand/supply shortages and readily available finance. As Oliver Marriott noted in his book *The Property Boom*, 'Since all the money to buy the site was usually lent by the banks, all of the construction costs paid for by the contractor or the bank, and the total repaid from a long-term mortgage borrowed from an insurance company, the developer seldom had to find any money at all, once his credit was established' (Marriott, 1967, p. 5).

Interest payments on the mortgage finance were at that time less than the rent received. In other words the whole process was 'self-financing': a very lucrative business stemming from the specific market conditions of that time. That enabled developers, in theory, to conduct development projects without recourse to any of their own equity – an extremely profitable exercise. In other words, the developer kept 100% of any upside while the banks did not participate in any of the upside but covered 100% of the downside. Until the 1970s, this longer term finance was generally obtained from life assurance companies, but the banking sector then became the prime financier of completed developments.

The traditional model for short-term lending that rolled up interest incurred during the development phase evolved with the changing economics of development. In the absence of such beneficial financial circumstances in the 1950s, and in particular when mortgage interest payments exceeded the initial rental income, the short-term loan from the 1980s was often extended by, say, five years to the time of the first rental review on the property. At that point it would be expected that with inflation the new higher rental income would be sufficient to cover the interest. More recently, however, the strict segregation between short-term and longer term finance has become even more blurred. Short-term debt finance in the latter half of the 1980s became more complex through the arrangement of general credit facilities that provided a developer with the opportunity to draw on funds at prior interest rates up to agreed limits. These credit facilities were often syndicated across a group of banks. A bank's risk could be shared with other banks, not all of which were in the same country as the development, thereby reducing specific risk of each project (Lizieri, 2009). These arrangements could also last up to 35 years.

A further innovation initiated during the 1980s was 'limited recourse' or 'non-recourse' finance loans (Fraser, 1993). Under these loans a bank lends only to the development project or investment vehicle which has been set up as a subsidiary company, known as a single or special purpose vehicle (SPV), or as a fund, usually by a group of investors. The latter can include limited partnerships (LPs) and property unit trusts explained later in this chapter. The security for such a loan is linked to the assets of the fund or SPV with no recourse to the investors/owners or to their other assets if the project/fund fails. The benefits to the bank are that the loan is sheltered from any wider problems that may occur with the parent investors. From the investors' perspective the loan will not normally appear in its balance sheet.

A further evolution was the emergence of asset securitization of properties owned by an SPV. Essentially the arrangement involves the issue of bonds secured against the rental income of the assets. These bonds are placed by a bank with investors, usually with other banks, supported by a risk grading from rating agencies. An SPV can also raise up to 90 or even 100% of real estate value compared to a bank loan of up to 75% (Lizieri, Ward and Lee, 2001). An extreme example of the use of securitization is provided by Olympia and York, a private Canadian property company that had non-recourse loans with 91 international banks in 1992. More than $1 billion was securitized against the Canary Wharf office development in London alone (Ghosh, Guttery and Sirmans, 1994). The 1990s saw the continuing rise of these asset-backed securitizations, often on trophy office buildings let to a blue chip company with an excellent credit rating (Jones, 2018).

The motivation for these innovations was simply one of competition, with the banks wishing to provide the finance for longer than they hitherto would have done. That change was to the detriment of the security of the loan and to the solvency of the lenders. There was no shared interest in seeking a profitable outcome. A financial failure would cost the developer/investor nothing (apart from their reputation) while the banks would be left with a property asset worth less than the loan secured on it.

The reason is that finance for property development incurs greater risk than lending on investment properties. The risk is not simply that associated with letting. In times of weak markets even a newly completed and let property can detrimentally affect the lender. That can be shown in the followin very simplistic valuation model, which looks at the potential capital value of a new office development. Let us assume that the lending institution lends 80% of the expected completed capital value of the project – which is based on a rental assumption of £80 per square foot and a competed valuation yield of 5%. For a property of 10 000 square foot, that would equate to (roughly) a capital value of £16 000 000. Hence the lender would lend, say, £12 800 000, which would be expected to cover the purchase of the site, the construction and the rolled-up interest.

Given that the decision to proceed with the development and the loan negotiations would have taken place some years before the completion of the development, there would be no way of knowing what the property market conditions would be when it was completed. For example, it only takes rents to be £10 per square foot lower than had been forecast and a 1 percentage point increase in yield to render the valuation of the completed building below that of the loan. Some developments are speculative, in that there is no tenant signed up. Extending the example to a newly completed but vacant property could easily see its valuation hit by another 50 basis point (0.5%) outward yield movement, producing a valuation of around £10 750 000 (and that is without any further weakness in rents), which is significantly below the amount borrowed.

That simple example shows just how the viability of any scheme to both developer and financier depends on the assumptions used in the appraisal adopted at the outset of the scheme and the reality when the project is complete. In good times, as witnessed during the early 2000s, tenants looking for space were plentiful, and in many locations the actual rent obtained was ahead of that expected at outset, while the asset also benefited from rising investment demand increasing values generally (which lowered the valuation yield). Many developments would have then been particularly profitable given the combination of strong tenant demand, higher rents and lower yields.

The example also highlights how such profitability can evaporate very quickly. A typical development completing during the first half of 2007 (pre-crash) would have earned the developer healthy profits; one completing just a few months later (and certainly after the Lehman Brothers collapse in September 2008) is unlikely to have generated much profit at all, and in all probability it would have been loss making. Crucially, owing to the financial model typically adopted, the property development company would have lost most or all of its (relatively small) equity component and the lenders would be liable for virtually all of the valuation shortfall. We look at the costs and financial implications of development for the banks in Chapter 3.

The availability of bank finance varies according to the economic and property cycle. Development finance from banks is more readily available during an upturn in the property cycle while the opposite occurs in a downturn. Banks that lend up to 75% of development costs with low markups over base rates in a boom become risk averse as the cycle turns down. In property market downturns the lenders suffered major losses from the fall in property values. That weakens their balance sheets, requiring them to augment capital and limit lending (or to refuse to lend any) on new development.

Debt finance, if it could be found, would be subject to strict conditions, for instance requiring developments to be pre-let with tenants signed up. Even in these circumstances banks may be only prepared to advance less generous sums based on a lower loan-to-cost ratio, in the order of, say, around 60%. In property market downturns there is what amounts to a short-term development finance 'famine'. The early 1990s' property downturn was one case in point, where the large scale of property development continued well after the economy had gone into recession, causing property values to decline significantly and hurt banks' viability. That resulted in these banks reigning in further lending until, at the earliest, the surfeit of empty properties had been let.

Aside from development finance, banks have contributed over the years to financing the buying of completed and let properties (in investment terminology, those properties are called 'standing investments'). Given the risk involved in development finance, lenders pay great attention to the financial standing of the developer and its ability to service and repay the loan on the project's completion together with the likely terms that would be achieved on letting. On the other hand, bank lenders for investment properties pay far higher attention to the property's fundamentals, that is to, say, its location, age, specification, tenant and lease length. They understand that the continual servicing of the loan interest, which may be over a period of 10 years, 15 years or even longer, and then the repayment of the loan depends on the property's ability to retain its value over the long term.

The amount lent for standing investments usually exceeds the amount lent on developments by a considerable factor, and consequently the state of the economy, and through that the state of the commercial property market, has a significant bearing on banks' profits. The early 1980s, for example, saw a marked increase in property development, but at that time only just over 20% of loans committed to property went to developments (SG Warburg, 2000). A substantial majority of funding went into standing investments, even during the period when the percentage allocated to development was at its highest. Similarly, Chapter 3 indicates that, despite the strength of the economy and of the property market in the boom of the noughties, property debt for development remained at a relatively low amount – less than 10% of all money loaned on property. Again, by implication, that indicated that around 90% was placed in standing investments.

The Changing Investment Landscape of the Non-banking Financial Institutions

The banks were not the only financial entities transforming themselves over the second half of the twentieth century: financial institutions that had been traditionally regarded, like the banks in the 1950s and 1960s, as safe and solid were also changing. In contrast to the banks, their investment policies, and consequently their investment objectives, were generally of the long-term variety. These institutions invest directly and indirectly in property as part of a mixed portfolio of assets including shares and government bonds. It is apposite to explain precisely what these institutions are by looking at the products they offered and how they have evolved.

The most significant in terms of longevity are the life assurance funds that manage and invest billions on behalf of their policyholders and whose policies generally include some form of life cover. Typical policies include whole-life and term assurance (where proceeds are paid out in the event of death) and endowment assurance policies, which were savings plans that also paid out on the earlier of death or the maturity of the policy. With-profits endowment policies in the United Kingdom can trace their origins back to the late eighteenth and early nineteenth centuries (Institute and Faculty of Actuaries, 2014) and became important savings vehicles in the mid-twentieth century. Rising inflation and the need to offer investment products that delivered inflation-beating returns was a further boost (Fraser, 1993). Endowment mortgages were common in the 1970s, 1980s and early 1990s and were bought by home owners taking an interest only 'endowment' mortgage. These endowment mortgages were sold as incorporating a monthly savings plan, known as an 'endowment policy', that was designed to pay off the home loan at the end of the, say, 25-year term. The endowment element was called 'with profit' as only a basic level of cover was guaranteed, which would then increase annually on the declaration of bonus rates by the assurer. There was also a 'terminal bonus' applied on the maturity of the policy.

They were criticized for being too complex and for having maturity values that did not meet their marketing claims. The main problem was that forecast profits were based on extrapolating the high returns from investing in shares and commercial property during the boom years of the 1980s. By the mid-1990s it was evident that these forecasts were widely over-optimistic. At the end of that decade, regulators instructed insurance companies to write warning letters to policyholders to spell out the potential shortfalls. Many people received compensation for having been mis-sold such policies (Peachey, 2013). As a result of these problems the proportion of endowment mortgages fell from 50% in 1995 to 4% in 2004 (Building Societies Association, 2010). More generally endowment policies are now difficult to sell and have effectively been consigned to history.

More recently, newer forms of policies, such as unit-linked assurance, unit-linked pension funds and unit trusts have become key selling points (see later in the chapter under Unit Trusts and Indirect Investment for detail). These additions to their armoury have become important profit earners for the assurers with the decline of the 'with profit' element of the assurance portfolio. These assurers typically also offer pension provision, either group pensions (where they manage the pensions of the entire workforce of a company, so-called segregated funds) or individual pensions where (typically) self-employed people could effect a pension plan. They can be focused on providing income or capital growth, depending on investors' wishes.

The second type of institutional investor is the private pension funds themselves. These company-based pension funds expanded significantly in the period immediately following the Second World War. The pension funds of large companies have sufficiently large assets to independently provide investment services internally without recourse to external fund managers. Smaller pension funds use external management but they need not be particularly large as some relatively small firms may also run discrete funds. The primary objective is to generate capital growth from regular payments by individual employees of a company's pension fund to offer pensions on retirement historically linked to their final salary and their years of membership. More recently private pension schemes have moved toward a defined contribution approach whereby members receive a pension based on the sums they have paid in and how their contributions are invested.

These changes have had implications for the choice of investment assets by financial institutions. The growth of inflation from the 1960s on in particular was a watershed with a reappraisal of their financial investment models. Inflation was rising to such an extent that no one could ignore its consequences in portfolio construction. As inflation rose, so did interest rates, and with increasing interest rates came falling bond prices. Not a happy position for institutional fund managers, most of whose assets were invested in these fixed-interest securities. The 1950s saw institutional investment turn their backs on bonds (which had long been the asset class of choice) and invest more and more in equities. There was also a theoretical driver for change in the form of the then ground-breaking work from the Nobel Laureate Harry Markowitz, who, in his modern portfolio theory work (1952), demonstrated that a diversified portfolio of equities could generate a higher rate of return with lower risk than a portfolio of bonds.

The general move into equities encompassed not just company shares but also commercial property. It was encouraged by the shortening of lease lengths on shops and offices and the introduction of rent review periods every five years – innovations which, themselves, were nurtured by inflation. Commercial property became more akin to real assets than fixed-interest bonds. With these features financial institutions began investing both in direct property and in property companies. At the same time the number of property companies being formed also increased.

Just like the banks, the financial institutions too have therefore gone through a host of changes since the 1960s. They have extended and adapted their range of products, evolving from companies predominantly investing in fixed-interest securities into fund management companies investing in a wide range of asset classes. In the process they have also successfully attracted many new classes of investors. In particular there was a major shift into investing directly in commercial property as an equity asset in tandem with company shares (including property companies) as institutions moved away from depending solely on fixed-income investments such as government bonds and mortgages (Scott, 1996).

The Other Main Players in Commercial Property

The other main investors in commercial property are the property companies (both listed and unlisted). This group tended to use debt in contrast to the life and pension funds. We read in Chapter 1 of the profitability of redeveloping Britain in the post-war years. That gave rise to a raft of new property companies being formed specializing in either property development and/or property investment. Land Securities, the largest UK property company, can track its history back to 1944, but Slough Estates (now Segro) can trace its roots back to the 1920s. Many property companies have been users of debt from banks, and listed companies have the ability to raise further capital through the stock exchange. The number of unlisted property companies, which also go by the name of private property companies, family trusts and funds of high net worth individuals, has mushroomed over the last two decades, and in particular during the property boom after 2000. Most of the largest property companies in the United Kingdom converted to real estate investment trusts in 2007 following enabling legislation (see Chapter 4).

It is only relatively recently, from the 1990s, that overseas investors have become involved in UK commercial property, although foreign banks were actively involved in offering debt finance during the 1980s boom. In much the same way UK commercial property investors have only recently invested abroad. Part of the growth of overseas investment has been down to the formation of the European single currency bloc, which led to concerns over insufficient economic diversification, even if investment were to be spread across the different countries of the eurozone. The other main reason for overseas investment into the UK market is the 'institutional lease' in place in many UK properties (i.e. a relatively long lease – by European standards – with five yearly, upward-only rent reviews), which confers greater income security than is available in Continental Europe. There is also greater liquidity of UK commercial property, and investment in London in particular is seen as a safe haven for international investors (BNP Paribas, 2015, 2016).

Investment in UK commercial property by overseas investors increased in the boom years (see Chapter 4). Part of this was down to the need for diversification away from their domestic economy but it was also down to the perceived diminution of risk that was underway in the early to mid-2000s. Overseas investment does pose greater risk than domestic investment, if for no other reason than the effect of comparative currency movements, yet the risks associated with both property and currency were almost ignored in the rush to invest. At the height of the boom, overseas investment into the UK market is estimated to have accounted for well over one-third of all transactions (information provided by Property Data).

Commercial property also attracted the interest of the hedge funds. This is a disparate group of investors which is difficult to describe, but hedge fund managers and traders took advantage of the growing importance of the asset class in the boom. Their activities in the post-GFC period are considered in Chapter 7.

The Changing Face of Institutional Property Investment

The growth of pension schemes offering 'final salary' pension benefits, which required constant additional funding as pension liabilities increased with rising salaries, led to increasing commercial property investment. Similarly, the huge amounts of premium income generated by 'with profit' endowment policies of the life assurance companies demanded more investment assets. Premiums exceeded outgoings for these products through the 1990s for both pension funds and insurance funds, and so all these inflows required investment. In fact, some funds were growing at such a pace that at times it was difficult for the property manager to 'keep up' with these investment demands. As funds grew, so did the number of properties in these funds. While the benefits of port-folio diversification were by then well known, many funds just had too many individual assets. One of the most challenging aspects for a property manager is managing a fund during a period of rapid growth or of rapid decline. The latter would happen two dec-ades later, but the challenge in the 1990s was still one of investment.

As funds grow, fund managers tend to increase the average size of the funds' assets (known as the average lot size). For funds investing in equities or bonds, that poses no great problem as it is fairly easy to 'top up' an existing holding by buying more shares or more of the bond. With property, that is not possible. Property is indivisible: simply buying larger properties commensurate with the larger fund size still leaves a tail of small properties; the only way one can satisfactorily adjust the size of all the assets in the portfolio is by selling the original (smaller) assets and buying larger ones: a very costly exercise, even in the early 1990s when stamp duty was still pegged at 1% since the 'round trip' or the cost of selling and reinvesting property assets was even then around 4%. Nevertheless, many funds did go through regularly thorough reviews of their assets and rebalanced their portfolios. Many of the smaller properties were sold and the proceeds invested in larger properties. Some of the more enterprising funds 'packaged' up these unwanted properties and placed them in a separate fund, offering other institutions access to these assets through an indirect vehicle approach. The management of these funds was either done in house (despite the house not really wanting to keep them in the first place) or subcontracted out to some other manager who could devote more management time and effort to the task than its larger rival. It was the start of institu-tions using their property assets to create funds for outside investment as a means of generating fee income – both from the annual management fee and from the perfor-mance related fee.

The 1980s also saw a period of rapid change to the spatial structure of cities, as dis-cussed in Chapter 1, with significant ramifications for property investment (Jones, 2009). The change to the mix of a typical institutional property portfolio can be seen in Table 2.1, which gives the average composition of a portfolio in the MSCI/IPD annual index from its inception in 1981 and in 1995. In 1981 a typical institutional portfolio consisted largely of city centre shops, central business district offices, industrial sheds, perhaps the odd industrial estate and possibly a city centre shopping centre. By the mid-1990s stand-alone retail warehouses or retail warehouse parks, business parks, distribution warehouses, hotels and leisure assets (such as cinemas, bowling rinks and bingo halls) together with out of town shopping centres were very much part of the investment landscape.

These new property forms, often in decentralized locations, reflected the ways in which the social environment and commercial economy of cities and towns were chang-ing. It also brought obsolescence to existing property investment with subsequent rede-velopment. The motor age had begun to see the long-standing dominance of the high street under threat from the new, emerging retail formats of out-of-town/edge-of-town shopping centres and retail warehouses while increasing leisure time and increasing spending power was further altering the composition of the traditional high street (Jones, 2014). Roll on 20 years and the property market has also experienced the increas-ing influence of new information communication technologies as 'traditional' ways of

Table 2.1 Average sectoral structure of institutional property investment funds in 1981 and 1995.

	1981	1995
	%	%
Standard shops	14.9	16.6
Shopping centres	9.2	17.1
Retail warehouses	0.5	7.7
Other retail	2.9	5.0
City centre offices	53.5	35.4
Office parks	0.0	2.8
Standard industrial	14.7	10.9
Distribution warehouses	0.5	2.3
Miscellaneous	3.7	2.1
Total	100	100

Source: MSCI /IPD (2014a).

conducting business are rethought, most notably in retailing that faced ever-increasing Internet sales (Jones and Livingstone, 2015) but also in logistics and services more generally.

Not every fund management house was equipped with the skill base or knowledge that allowed them to invest in these new submarkets as they appeared or to make informed decisions. A new breed of sector or segment specialists grew up – the so-called niche players – offering to invest institutions' money prudently (so the theory went) and for a modest management fee plus a performance fee. The final move into indirect property vehicles was a combination of two of the above elements working in tandem. A group of like-minded institutions would pool their resources in one particular submarket and elect which particular house would manage the fund. All parties would then benefit from the presumed better and more dedicated management offered by the fund management house, which was able to commit more resources thanks to the larger fund size. Management fees were usually cut to the bone and performance fees were rarely involved.

These initiatives whereby financial institutions invested in a fund managed by another financial institution meant that there were a growing number of indirect property vehicles as we moved through the 1990s into the new millennium. However, there was little marketing of them as most of the funds that were created either for internal purposes or for external marketing purposes were limited partnership structures. A few others were also used, for example Luxembourg SICAVs (Société d'Investissement à Capital Variable), where the fund was domiciled in Luxembourg and so appealed more to Continental European investors, but they were not as commonly used. These SICAVs had a variable amount of capital, i.e. they were open-ended, so that the fund could grow and contract. The closed-ended variant was the SICAF (à Capital Fixe). Given their prominence the next section explains how a limited partnership (LP) works.

Limited Partnerships

LPs had been around for decades before their more general application to property investment from the 1990s. They had been used in the private equity market for some years, and their existence goes back as far as the Limited Partnership Act 1907. An LP is a partnership formed between at least two partners. There must be at least one general partner with any or all of the other partners being termed 'limited partners'. The general partner is usually the manager of the partnership and is the one making decisions. The limited partners can be regarded as passive partners; they cannot be seen to be 'influencing' decisions, but in return, they are granted limited liability – by which is meant any losses are capped at the amount they have invested in the partnership (plus any uncalled for capital). Should a limited partner be found to be participating in the partnership's management, the LP would lose its limited liability status and would thereafter be treated as a general partner. By contrast, the general partner has unlimited liability for the debts and obligations of the partnership if things go wrong.

To address this issue the general partner is usually established as an SPV with negligible assets – a limited company is often used – and is thus protected against possible adverse financial consequences. The term of the partnership is stated at the outset in the LP agreement, which covers the nature of the LP business, the role of the general partner, the rights of the limited partners, the funding of the LP, the appointments of managers, corporate governance (voting, accounting and reporting), the distribution of profit and transfers of interests. The assets of an LP are acquired by the general partner acting on behalf of the partnership. Any property is held by the general partner and/or nominee companies. LPs are funded by capital advances from partners and by borrowings from third parties, the security for which will usually be a charge on the partnership's assets.

There are two distinct forms of LP in the United Kingdom: the English Limited Partnership and the Scottish Limited Partnership. They differ not only according to where the partnership was formed – through the application of the different legal systems in the countries – but also in that under Scots Law, a partnership is considered to be a distinct legal entity and therefore can borrow money from a bank in the name of the partnership. Under English law, a partnership is not a distinct legal entity and therefore borrowing would be in the names of the individual partners (Luck, 2011). English LPs are not precluded from buying Scottish-based properties, nor are Scottish LPs precluded from buying property south of the border. A third type of LP, the Delaware Limited Partnership, was occasionally used in the 1990s and early 2000s. Its attraction was the unlimited number of partners it permitted (as opposed to the maximum number of 20 then in force in the British equivalents) and the fact that one could in theory avoid paying stamp duty on the purchase of a property by the LP.

A crucial attraction of these LPs was that of the payment of tax. For UK tax purposes, an investor 'looks through' the partnership structure to the actual assets in which the partnership has invested. The taxes paid on income profits and capital gains by a partner in an LP were therefore the same as if the investor had invested directly in the assets – a key point for commercial property investors. Rental income is paid (and received by the investor) gross – that is, without the deduction of tax – and the LP structure replicates that feature (Luck, 2011). In contrast, investors in property company shares would be paid dividends from the company's profits only after tax is paid, and then this income would be subject to tax again at a personal or corporate level. LPs clearly had an advantage.

These LPs had a fixed capital base with a fixed term, often 10 years. Most would have an extension period built in, often two years, which the manager could invoke if market conditions were unfavourable for selling at the stated time of expiry. A few did manage to raise additional capital during their life, but it was normally for specific projects (for example the purchase of a neighbouring asset offering marriage value benefits). These new partnership interests would be offered first to the existing investors and only if they did not want to, or could not, invest their full pro-rata allocation would the manager seek new investors from outside the existing investor base. That apart, the original limited partnership structure was not conducive to aggressive marketing.

With institutions as the most dominant group of investors in these LPs it ensured that few risks were taken with the portfolio. Consequently, gearing was fairly conservative in the early 2000s. Gearing ratios were rarely above 60% loan to value and in many cases well below that. For funds such as LPs the usual way of measuring the amount of borrowing was through the loan-to-value (LTV) ratio, the total loan divided by the total value of the assets. In contrast the equivalent measure for companies listed on the stock market (e.g. REITs) generally used the loan-to-equity ratio.

As the industry began to use these structures more and more, there was a change to the restriction on the number of limited partners that were allowed. Since its creation over a century ago, the limit had been 20, but that restriction was becoming outdated. A feeder limited partner, while legally one limited partner, but representing more than one investor, was becoming more and more common, thereby in theory allowing many more than the maximum of 20 to join the partnership. So in 2002, the UK government rescinded the limit of 20 and allowed an indefinite number of partners to invest in an LP.

However, by far the more fundamental change in the management and indeed viability of these LPs occurred in 2004. It was a change in the operation of stamp duty which had ramifications far wider than its intention. Prior to 2004, stamp duty had been payable on a transaction's consideration, which for direct property was the purchase price, and for LPs it was the transaction price which was based on the LP's net asset value. The problem occurred because of the closing of a particular loophole which was being used by some investors and LPs to avoid or minimize the stamp duty that was due on a purchase. Through this scheme, it was possible to deem a purchase of land for investment or development a non-land transaction by incorporating debt into the transaction. By offsetting an amount of borrowings (almost) equal to the value of the land, the net asset value of the transaction was next to nothing, and consequently no, or minimal, stamp duty (later stamp duty land tax – SDLT) would be payable on the transaction. The government closed that loophole in 2004 so that from then on SDLT payable was not to reflect the consideration paid but was to be based on the proportion of the market value of the partnership land being acquired – that is, in the government's words, to reflect the substance of the investment. The substance referred to was the gross asset value of the entity, not as it had been previously, the net asset value after debt was included. Consequently, SDLT was to be charged on gross assets not on net assets as had been the case before.

Examples given in Table 2.2 show how LPs were particularly adversely affected by the change to the SDLT rules. The table sets out three instances where a partnership's net asset value is £60 million but its gross assets vary according to the extent of the partnership's borrowings. In each case we consider the sale or transfer of a partner's 10%

Table 2.2 Tax obligations by LPs for different levels of debt gearing before and after 2004 SDLT reform.

	LP with no debt	LP with debt	LP with debt
		(LTV 40%)	(LTV 80%)
Gross Partnership Assets	£60 m	£100 m	£300 m
Less debt	Nil	£40 m	£240 m
Net partnership assets	£60 m	£60 m	£60 m
Transferring percentage	10	10	10
Market value of consideration	£6 m	£6 m	£6 m
Market value of partnership land	£6 m	£10 m	£30 m
SDTL payable			
Previous method	£240 000	£240 000	£240 000
New method	£240 000	£400 000	£1 200 000

holding in the LP, which is based on its net asset value of £6 million. In the example shown of an LP with loan to value (a measure of the fund's gearing or leverage) of 40% (i.e. 40 divided by 100), the SDLT would have risen from £240 000 under the previous rules to £400 000 under the new. Another way of looking at the tax payable is to equate the amount of tax (£400 000) as a percentage of the consideration (£6 m), which comes to an effective SDLT rate of 6.67%. It can readily be seen that the greater the gearing, the greater the effective SDLT. For instance, were the gearing percentage 80% (share of gross assets of £30 m, debt of £24 m and net assets the same £6 m), the total SDLT would now be calculated on the appropriate percentage of a much larger gross assets (£30 m) but payable on a transfer of the same £6 million consideration, effectively increasing the rate of SDLT payable on a transfer to 20%.

That position not only impacts potential buyers of an LP interest, it can also impact on the valuation of an institution's LP interest throughout ownership. Under the various valuation rules that govern the valuation of assets of life assurance funds, which were large investors in LPs, such assets have to be valued at 'readily realisable value', even if there is no real intention to dispose of the asset before maturity. It is therefore necessary to take into account in any valuation of that asset the likely achievable selling price of that type of asset. For these life companies to be able to sell their interest there has to be a potential buyer. And if that potential buyer has the choice of either buying the LP interest in question or buying an individual property for the same consideration, the argument goes 'why should I pay more in SDLT?' (and potentially a lot more, as we have seen). The potential buyer would then, in all likelihood, start negotiations around an *overall* purchase price, where

overall purchase price = [consideration plus standard rate of SDLT].

This equation can be reconfigured as

overall purchase price offered = [*discounted consideration* plus increased rate of SDLT].

A cautious actuary is likely to take on board this arithmetical sleight of hand and reduce the value of the investment in the life company's accounts throughout its ownership. Using the example of an LP geared at 40%, a life fund may wish to reduce the value of its holding in its books of the LP's net asset value by almost 3% (6.67% less 4%). A fund with 80% loan to value would similarly face calls to reduce the value of its holding by a much larger 16% (20% less 4%). At a time when actuaries were counting every penny under tight solvency rules, these potential reductions in life funds' assets were not what they wanted.

Jersey Rides to the Rescue

It is often the case that the solution to what was likely to become a major headache for the property investment industry would arrive from the most unlikely of places. With the introduction of the new SDLT regime fast approaching, and the industry desperately trying to seek a solution to mitigate this potential increase in stamp duty, legal and accounting brains came up with the idea of taking these limited partnerships offshore and converting them into Jersey Property Unit Trusts (JPUTs). There were parallel but marginally different Guernsey property unit trusts with similar features, but for simplicity the focus here is on JPUTs. As with many of the neat solutions found to cope with sudden and adverse changes to tax, the answer was in a form of a decades-old entity but one which had rarely been used.

A unit trust is a legal structure in which the legal ownership of its assets is vested in a trustee who holds these assets on trust for the benefit of the unit holders. A trust instrument sets out the terms on which the trustee holds the trust assets. The trustee usually appoints a manager who will manage the day-to-day business of the trust, for example concerning matters of tenancies, rent collection, etc. (Alonzi, 2015).

One advantage of converting to a JPUT is that, like LPs themselves, the trust may be structured so that neither the income nor any capital gains deriving from it are taxable in Jersey. That is to say, a JPUT is transparent for UK income and capital gains tax purposes, in the same way that LPs were. But note that this tax transparency only applies to non-Jersey resident investors. The key consideration for this tax transparency is that it must be a 'Baker Trust', one where the trustees are deemed not to be the beneficial owners of a trust's income as it arises – instead this is the unit holders. If that is the case, the trust is deemed transparent for the purposes of income tax and corporation tax purposes (Alonzi, 2015).

But the real bonus, and the main reason why the JPUT route was chosen, was that, at that time, property could be transferred to a JPUT trustee without UK SDLT being incurred. In addition, no stamp duty was payable either in Jersey or in the United Kingdom on the transfer of units in a JPUT – precisely the issue that they were trying to mitigate. Establishing these JPUTs for institutional investors seemed to have addressed fully the increases in SDLT on LPs by the UK government, but the conversion was not that simple in practice.

The first issue was that the time to set up a new JPUT and convert the LP into it was very tight. Few property managers had adequate knowledge (if any) of the legal points, and the deadline for conversion was rapidly arriving while there were only a very small number of companies and individuals in Jersey with the necessary experience. One of the key restrictions in forming a JPUT was that the trust had to have a majority of its trustees resident in the island. The manager was nominally based in Jersey, but the trust often subcontracted day-to-day routine work back to the United Kingdom where the former management team that managed the former limited partnership undertook the work. However, the legal position was that the manager was based in Jersey and all decisions had to be made 'offshore'. That required the actual managers attending management meetings in Jersey while all decisions on how to run the trust – whether that entailed changes to the trust deed, changes to the level of gearing to be employed, or whatever – had to be made 'offshore'.

A reminder here that neither Jersey, the Isle of Man nor Guernsey nor any of the other Channel Islands are in the United Kingdom, and therefore they are not subject to UK tax. They are Crown dependencies and form part of the British Islands (not to be confused with the British Isles). In order to satisfy the rules on managing the trust, decisions must be taken offshore, which means anywhere outside the United Kingdom. While that would obviously include Jersey itself, many investor meetings (or meetings of the unit holders) often take place on the Continent, at locations more accessible for all investors and managers.

Despite all the hurdles, a substantial number of high-value UK commercial properties were transferred to JPUTs without any SDLT being incurred. Although this SDLT exemption was abolished in 2006, JPUTs retain many features attractive to investors, namely:

- no stamp duty being payable (in Jersey or the United Kingdom) on transfers of units in a JPUT;
- income tax purpose 'transparency' for UK investors;
- exemption from UK capital gains tax on the sale of UK property by the JPUT (Olsen 2012).

Another key difference in the JPUT structure compared to LPs is the fact that the former is open-ended in that new units can be created when required. That factor was not the one that drove the industry offshore, but once conversion had taken place it was a short step to the property investment houses catching on to the idea of first issuing new units to grow the unit trust (by offering these new units to existing unit holders) then inviting subscriptions from totally new investors. Almost overnight, the institutional indirect property market went from one that was passively run to one seen as having the ability to generate the investment house high levels of fees, which themselves could be increased through the introduction of new units.

Another sea change was the concept of fixed lifetimes. Initial JPUT documentation did still include a stated termination date, but unit holders were often keen to accept extension plans put forward by the manager. Investors were obviously wary about extending the life of a poorly performing fund, and many of those would be wound up at the earliest possible time. But many of the well-managed and better performing funds were successfully extended, often at a cost of a 'modernization' of the trust deed that was demanded by unit holders as a quid pro quo for accepting the extension. Given that the trusts had been extremely rapidly converted from LPs in 2004, it was fair to say that the trust deeds in many of them were in dire need of updating.

The benefits of fund extensions were not simply confined to the management house, which obviously benefited from the extended management contract. Investors benefited

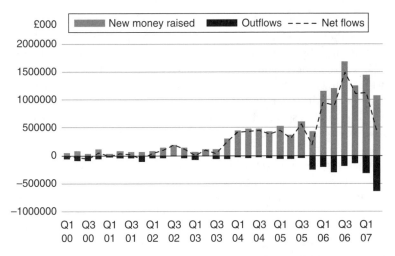

Figure 2.1 Quarterly cash flow into specialist (retail) real estate funds, 2001–2007. *Source:* Association of Real Estate Funds.

too through improved liquidity provisions introduced as part of the negotiations between manager and investor and often through lower fees that were also negotiated at the same time. Investors had become concerned about the reducing lifetimes of many of the JPUTs. Not only does significant management time need to be spent on exit strategies (which often produces conflicts of interests between manager and investors) but also the liquidity of the units reduces as termination approaches. Why would an investor wish to buy units in a JPUT which has only a couple of years left to run? By voting to extend the life of the trust, investors could remove uncertainty over the trust's strategy (for some years, at any rate) and allow investors to seek exit on more favourable terms if they so desired.

Property managers are always at pains to point out the merits of the properties they manage. So too with indirect property managers, and particularly those investing in a niche part of the market. 'We understand the market', goes the cry, 'and we can make further gains for you by buying more property if you give us the money'. If existing unit holders did not wish to, or could not, invest in the new units being offered, they were offered to the wider investment community. Consequently, these JPUTs, already a significant part of the indirect property landscape in 2004, became major players in the next three years of the property boom as it reached the peak of a crescendo. The other reason that existing unit holders sanctioned the increase of the size of the unit trust was that increasing the number of property assets in the fund improved the fund's diversification. The larger the fund means the greater the underlying liquidity of its units, assuming, of course, that its performance remained good. The precise scale of the dramatic rise of money into specialist retail funds after 2003 is shown in Figure 2.1.

Unit Trusts and Indirect Investment

This extension of the unit-holder base had huge ramifications in the way in which the indirect property investments sector was run, although it was not appreciated fully at that time. Historically, unit trusts had been one of the most successful types of products available to retail investors in equities. These have been a popular means of investment for small investors since their introduction in the 1930s. The property equivalent, however, was not as well received by the market. Firstly, there are fundamental differences between equity indices and property 'indices'. The latter is a valuation based index, with all the subjectivity that brings, as opposed to a pricing index (see Chapter 1). The other key variation is that equity indices can be replicated by buying exposure, in the correct percentages, in every constituent segment of the market. That is not possible with property indices because by its very nature it is a heterogeneous market and difficult to replicate the constituent parts.

Unit-linked funds had grown to become an extremely important part of life companies' sales. We have already discussed the decline of the life companies' with-profits business and its replacement with unit-linked contracts. Part of this move came about because of the state of life companies' balance sheets. Unlike the with profit policies which had been the life companies' main sources of new business for much of the twentieth century, these new variants became progressively more important sources of new business for these companies. From an actuarial point of view, unit-linked policies consume less capital than their with-profits brothers. New business strain occurs when the initial costs of writing a new policy – payment of commission, administration costs, the early years' cost of life cover plus the reserves set up – exceed the early years' premiums. This position reverses in subsequent years as these policies become profitable on their books. Writing unit-linked policies requires much less capital in the early years and hence is more attractive in the short term.

A unit-linked policy is basically a combination of an investment element coupled with a life assurance component. Many life assurance companies will offer both unit-linked life funds and unit-linked pension funds, but the concept is the same. Each year, the costs for life insurance and administration are deducted from the premium with the residual amount – often a constant percentage. Investors choose the particular types of assets or 'asset class' into which their money is to be invested from a range of specialist funds. Individual policy holders can invest in the management house's mixed or balanced fund, or they may elect to choose to invest in one or more of the range of market specialist funds they offer.

Life companies are usually at pains to explain to customers that life policies are long-term commitments and that policy holders should not make short-term decisions which invariably cost policyholders (and companies) money. Much of this is down to the new business strain in the early years, but in both with-profits and unit-linked policies, early years' surrender values are invariably below the amount of premiums that have been paid.

The turnover of unit-linked policies tends to be higher than that of with-profits policies. Also, policy holders do not act rationally at all times, and crucially, they tend to act in unison, as they do in the unit-linked and unit-trust markets. The unit-linked funds can find simultaneous weight of requests from savers either to withdraw cash from their policies or to switch out of, say, property into another fund specializing in a different type of asset class (which has the same effect in that the fund will have to find the necessary cash).

The unit-linked funds contributed to a significant change in investors' approach to liquidity and short-termism. In addition while the life assurance funds at the turn of the millennium were still nominally long-term investors, many of their component funds were declining as policy maturities exceeded premium inflows. The result was that they had also become concerned about liquidity provisions. This emergence of institutions' shorter horizon funds as unit holders in the JPUTs removed the previous consensus on the trusts' investor base's decision making. But it was the short-term funds which had the bigger demands on improving liquidity rules, in particular to ease exit provisions when they wanted to exit the trusts.

The launch in 2002 of mutual listed funds based and managed in Guernsey therefore revolutionized property investment. In the first few years post migration to Jersey, the property market performed strongly. Inflows into commercial property remained strongly positive. Another contributory factor to the rise of investment by small investors in retail funds was the use of authorized property unit trusts (APUTs). Investment guidelines were changed in 2003 to allow these APUTs to invest up to 100% of the fund's assets in property, and, indeed, they were permitted to utilize gearing of up to a further 10% to assist with liquidity. These APUTs were investor friendly and could deliver property performance not weighed back by non-property assets.

Investors warmed to these new investment vehicles and a completely new breed of commercial property investor appeared – many seeking profits over much shorter time frames than had been seen previously. The rapidity with which yields were falling and the consequential sharp growth of capital values was the driver. The entry of these short-term funds and the extension of the unit-holder base had huge ramifications in the way in which the indirect property investments sector was run although it was not appreciated at that time.

Conclusions

The UK banking industry was a radically different animal at the end of the century than it had been in the early 1970s, having been transformed from a sleepy, staid industry into one that competed often on a global stage. In the 1970s a combination of the advent of inflation and deregulation led to banks deciding to break with the past and lend long on commercial property. Further deregulation and increased competition between banks and building societies in the 1980s led to the largest of the latter institutions converting to banks but ultimately to greater consolidation in financial services sector as banks merged.

The banking ethos had become entrepreneurial and the range of their services had been extended to embrace securities underwriting and trading, fund management, derivatives trading and general insurance. The basis of the banking business was also fundamentally reappraised by the use of wholesale funding such as mortgage-backed securities. The use of wholesale funding on a global basis removed the constraints on banks from a simple reliance on domestic saving and supported the banks' desire to lend extensively on the perceived lucrative lending on commercial property (see Chapter 6). The banks had a short memory of the difficulties such lending had created in the property downturns of the 1970s and 1980s. Commercial property was seen in the millennium as a safe place for lending.

Non-banking financial institutions, such as life assurance companies, were also subject to historic re-evaluations of their core business as inflation meant a dramatic rethink of the business model with the selling of with-profits endowment policies.

Within 20 years these were to fall from favour with households as they did not deliver their promised financial returns, and many were deemed to have been mis-sold. Life assurance companies then turned to offering unit-linked pensions and life assurance. In this journey of adjustment financial institutions turned to investing directly in commercial property as a real asset that would keep pace with inflation.

While the banks and financial institutions were experiencing arguably a revolution in their businesses, so cities and the property market were also undergoing their own transmutation in the form of an urban development cycle. City centres were rebuilt and decentralization of shopping and offices occurred as a consequence of the motor age and new information communication technologies. Many existing properties suffered obsolescence and new property forms emerged such as retail parks in out-of-town locations. Lease terms also shortened.

The pace of urban and property market change, together with the restructuring of the business models of financial institutions toward unit-linked savings plans, underpin a rethink of property investment and the rise of indirect property investment. It is manifested first in the establishment of niche property funds and the use of limited partnership funds. With modifications to UK tax legislation these are replaced particularly by JPUTs, which offer tax transparency to investors and the ease of ability to grow in size if necessary. The long-term consequence of these processes is that the investment environment has been restructured. In particular a major innovation is the creation of 'retail' funds investing in property that depend directly on the funds attracted from selling units to individual investors. Short-term return horizons have also emerged. Chapter 3 charts the parallel rapid increase in debt as the peak of the property boom was reached.

3

Economic Growth, Debt and Property Investment through the Boom

The lending and property investment environment at the beginning of the noughties in the United Kingdom was strongly influenced by the prevailing financial ambiance of the positive macroeconomic climate of the times. It was also the product of the past 60 years or so of the evolution of the financial system set out in Chapter 2. Banks had been offering long-term loans on commercial property for some time but had become more entrepreneurial and innovative in their lending approaches. Commercial property, too, had become a mainstream equity investment class within the portfolios of financial institutions. At the same time property companies quoted on the stock exchange had grown and had become established as major investors supported by a combination of borrowing from banks and equity/share capital owned primarily by financial institutions.

Many of these phenomena were common to Western economies. From the mid-1990s, too, the long upswing in the global economy provided the platform for an apparent classic property cycle. As Chapter 1 emphasizes, a central element of the dynamics of such a cycle and the associated investment activity is the role of finance. Extravagant, arguably excessive, use of debt is a key contributing factor to a boom, and this chapter will highlight its role in the boom of the noughties. In particular this chapter tracks the changing cost, scale and availability of bank lending finance, including lending criteria in the United Kingdom through the decade. It then considers the implications for investors, development and the property market. It begins by quantifying the global economic upturn and the contribution of debt.

Global Economic Upturn and Debt Accumulation

The period from the early to mid-1990s to the global financial crisis (GFC) was characterized by a long period of global economic growth. In the United Kingdom, for example, the 15 years or so immediately preceding the GFC witnessed the country enjoying low unemployment and inflation, high economic activity and improving standards of living. From 1992 to 2006 inclusive annual GDP growth had averaged around 2.8% per annum, only slightly lower than the global growth rate of 3.1% per annum (World Bank, 2017). Such was the spirit of the time that following the election of a new UK government in 1997, Gordon Brown, the Chancellor of the Exchequer, in his first budget statement vowed that he would do away with 'boom and bust'. Indeed for over

Property Boom and Banking Bust: The Role of Commercial Lending in the Bankruptcy of Banks,
First Edition. Colin Jones, Stewart Cowe, and Edward Trevillion.
© 2018 John Wiley & Sons Ltd. Published 2018 by John Wiley & Sons Ltd.

15 years from 1991, the United Kingdom enjoyed times of plenty, not just consistent economic growth but low unemployment and inflation and improving standards of living for many (Office of National Statistics, 2016a). The problem was that this period of calm had put the country into a hypnotic trance. In fact this Goldilocks economy, which also went by the acronym NICE (non inflationary, constant expansion) had lasted since the third quarter of 1992 (Office of National Statistics, 2016a). It not only represented the longest unbroken period of growth in living memory, but, as Brown pointed out in a speech in the House of Commons in March 2004, was the longest for over 200 years, or as he also proudly stated, 'the longest period of growth since the beginning of the industrial revolution' (Brown, 2004).

But it was not just the United Kingdom that was experiencing a long upswing in the macroeconomy, parallel economic growth occurred in most Western countries. The United States and many European countries were in broadly similar positions (although for some a small recession in 2000–2001 resulting from the dot-com crash interrupted it – see later in the chapter under The Cost and Role of Debt). While one cannot say that the global economy was firing sweetly on all cylinders in the early to mid-2000s, global growth of 5.3% in 2004, 4.9% in 2005 and 5.5% in 2006 (International Monetary Fund, 2005, 2006 and 2007) represented a consistent buoyancy. This lengthy period of growth had engendered in governments and in companies – financial and non-financial alike – a false sense of security.

In the United States the Chairman of the Federal Reserve, Ben Bernanke, highlighted in 2004 the 'Great Moderation' – the fact that statistically traditional business cycles had declined in volatility across the world in recent decades. Theories explaining this phenomenon included structural changes that have occurred in the international economy and improved macroeconomic policies, especially monetary policy. Structural changes included the use of ICT to manage business inventories, the shift to services in developed economies, the greater sophistication of financial markets helped by deregulation and the increase in international trade as a result of globalization. An alternative explanation was the 'good luck' hypothesis that held that recent shocks to the global economy had by chance been limited. Bernanke was of the view that the 'Great Moderation' was primarily the consequence of the success of monetary policy and particularly short-term bank base rates controlling inflation expectations (Bernanke, 2004).

Global interest rates, especially in the earlier part of the decade, were down to levels that were arguably inappropriate given the robust state of the global economy. These low interest rates were a direct result of the surfeit of cash that was in the market in the early to mid-2000s, much coming from the Far East. A significant proportion headed for the United States and into government bonds in particular – the safe haven investment. This inflow of money pushed down US bond interest rates, triggering similar falls in the yields of other state bonds around the world. The lowering of bond yields then further reduced interest rates. In the United Kingdom the bank base rate fell from 6% in 2000 to less than 4% in 2003. These reductions encouraged further borrowing. The demand for home mortgages increased on the back of low mortgage rates and buoyant house price growth. Money into commercial property increased significantly post 2000 too (see Chapter 4).

What few commentators were pointing out during these good years was that much of this growth was being built on foundations made of 'sand', and that if conditions were to deteriorate, the growth edifice could come tumbling down. The sand in this metaphor was debt. As Chapter 1 notes, high debt gearing brings substantial returns in a boom but potential financial disaster in a downturn. Reinhart and Rogoff express it well in *This Time It's Different*, as, 'Unfortunately, a highly leveraged economy can unwittingly be sitting with its back at the edge of a financial cliff for many years before chance and circumstance provoke a crisis of confidence that pushes it off' (2009, p. 1). The position was amplified because there was a build-up of debt across virtually the whole of the Western world.

Table 3.1 gives an overview of the accumulation of domestic debt in OECD countries. Denmark had the highest household debt-to-disposable income in all three annual snapshots. Norway, Ireland and the Netherlands complete the premier division of debt. The United Kingdom lies in the second division. Many countries exhibit a dramatic rise in personal debt from the mid-1990s. The exceptions are Japan and Germany where the proportion of debt is broadly stationary.

More generally McKinsey reported that global debt increased by 63% from the end of 2000 to the end of 2007 – from \$87 trillion to \$142 trillion (Dobbs *et al.*, 2015). Growth of debt in absolute terms is not unexpected, particularly during a period of strong global economic growth, but when measured as a percentage of global GDP, the amount of debt showed exceptional levels of increase. Total debt in 2000 represented 246% of global GDP and it rose to 269% seven years later (Dobbs *et al.*, 2015). Even more striking was the significant rise in debt levels accounted for just by financial bodies (companies plus financial institutions), whose debt rose from the equivalent of 56% of global GDP to 70%. In absolute terms this represented a staggering 85% from \$20 trillion to \$37 trillion over the seven years. (Figure 3.1)

Table 3.1 Household debt as a percentage of disposable income in selected OECD countries 1995, 2000 and 2009.

Country	1995	2000	2009
Italy	38	53	76
Germany	97	114	99
France	66	77	106
Finland	72	70	118
United States	92	101	128
Japan	130	135	132
Spain	59	86	141
Canada	103	113	148
Sweden	88	106	163
United Kingdom	110	117	171
Australia	89	122	187
Czech Republic	–	186	199
Norway	131	142	209
Ireland	–	98	222
Netherlands	104	164	284
Denmark	188	239	357

Source: Lunde (2012).

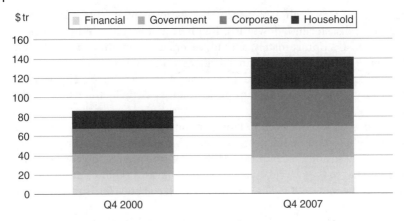

Figure 3.1 Global debt outstanding in 2000 and 2007 broken down by sector. *Source:* Dobbs *et al.* (2015).

The Property Boom and Escalating Debt

The global economic expansion provided the base for commercial property booms around the world. It fed through to increased commercial property demand and so rental and capital values rose. Capital values had begun to rise in many countries world-wide from 2003, as shown in Figure 3.2. However the graph also indicates differences between countries in the timing and scale of increases in capital values that partly reflect national valuation practices. This is considered in more detail in Chapter 4.

The low interest rates, particularly in the first part of the decade, together with the strong capital performance in the mid noughties had a significant impact on the financial attractiveness of property investment and development. The result was an explosion in the demand for borrowing from banks.

The build-up of debt levels occurred throughout the developed world, but nowhere more than in the United States and Europe. Figure 3.3, from DTZ's *Money into Property* publication of 2010, shows the inexorable rise of property borrowings over much of the 2000s. It can be seen that Europe and North America (which would be predominantly driven by borrowings by US investors) showed the greatest increase in borrowings, but that even in the Far East, where borrowing levels were more subdued than elsewhere, the amount lent on commercial property (including residential development) was also beginning to creep up by the mid-2000s.

The increase in borrowings seen in North America is quite remarkable. At a time when property valuations were rising strongly, the effective gearing percentage for these funds increased from below 55% to 65% by the end of 2007, at the top of the boom. The subsequent years' increase to over 70% mostly reflects the fall in property valuations after 2007 rather the impact of further borrowing. Europe showed a similar pattern of growth over the decade, increasing by around 10 percentage points to the end of 2007, but here, the further rise to over 60% was as much due to continued lending as it was to valuation falls (see Chapter 6). Over this period there was a dichotomy between the United Kingdom and the rest of Europe.

Focusing on the United Kingdom, Figure 3.4, from the Bank of England's paper on commercial property and financial stability (Benson and Burrows, 2013), shows the

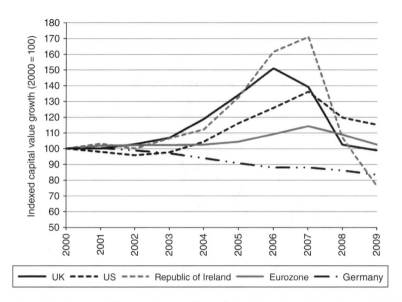

Figure 3.2 Commercial property capital growth in selected countries. *Source:* MSCI/IPD (2014c). Reproduced with permission.

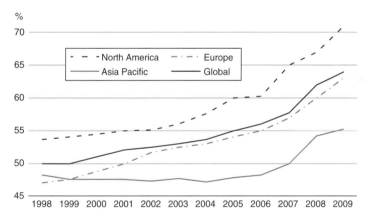

Figure 3.3 Total property debt as a percentage of invested stock in different parts of the world 1998–2009. *Source:* DTZ (2010). Reproduced with permission.

scale of bank lending on UK commercial property since the 1970s. This graph sets the amount of bank lending of the noughties in perspective, even accepting the figures do not account for inflation. One can readily see the relatively modest period of lending over the first half of that period and then the dramatic growth seen from the turn of the century. Nevertheless the pattern of lending over the whole period demonstrates the cyclical nature of bank lending. Outstanding loans ranged from around 4% to about 10% of nominal GDP until the turn of the millennium, after which the figure soared to over 20% of nominal GDP. While the downturns in the mid-1970s and at the beginning of the 1990s were not in the same league as the GFC, these sharp reductions in lending

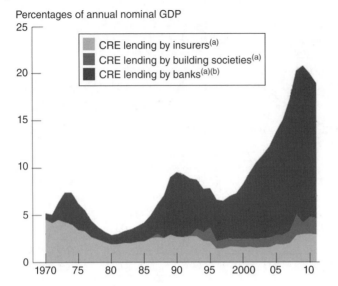

Percentages of annual nominal GDP

Figure 3.4 Commercial real estate lending as a percentage of annual UK GDP 1970–2011.
Source: Benson and Burrows (2013).
(a) end-year stock of outstanding lending.
(b) in 2010 and 2011 this includes an adjustment to include CRE loans transferred to the Irish National Asset Management Agency.

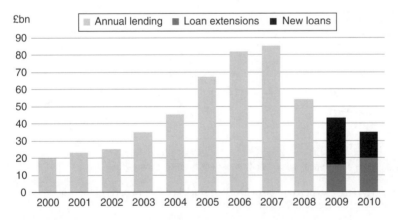

Figure 3.5 Annual bank lending for property in the United Kingdom 2000–2010. *Source:* Maxted and Porter (2014). Reproduced courtesy of Maxted and Porter.

availability highlight the vulnerability of property lending during recessionary periods in which property values were falling.

The real growth in bank lending in the United Kingdom occurred after 2000, just as it did in other countries (Maxted and Porter, 2014). Figure 3.5 shows the absolute amount lent each year, from which we see that lending increased each year from a relatively modest £20 billion lent on commercial property in 2000 through to its peak of £85 billion in 2007. It is sobering to realize that the amount lent over the course of 2005 alone (£67 bn) exceeded the total outstanding loans just four years earlier – and that over the course of the following two years annual lending increased even further.

This massive growth in annual lending obviously had a significant effect on the total outstanding loans. Figure 3.4 shows that from £49 billion of outstanding loans at the end of 1999, lending on property soared over the following decade – reaching an outstanding amount of £250 billion at the height of the boom. In comparison, the stock of commercial property owned by investors, often called the 'investable universe', was estimated by Mitchell (2015) at £363 billion in 2008 (out of a total stock value of £632 bn). This suggests a slightly higher level of gearing, 68%, compared with the figures by DTZ for Europe (Figure 3.3). The difference may be attributed to the fact that some of the lending by UK banks went overseas. Overall, with bank lending equivalent to approximately two thirds of the total value of the commercial property investment stock, the market was totally dependent on extremely high levels of debt (see also Chapter 4). To put these lending figures in another perspective, the total outstanding loans on property of £250 billion was equivalent to over 17% of the nation's 2009 GDP Office of National Statistics, 2016a).

By far the bulk of property lending came from UK banks and building societies as Figure 3.6 indicates. At the turn of the century, domestic lenders accounted for roughly two-thirds of all lending to property. It is perhaps surprising that despite the increasing presence of international lenders in the market place, the percentage of lending by British institutions actually increased in the build-up of the boom, rising to 72% by the end of 2005. And this at a time when property lending was growing rapidly, indicating that the amount of property debt outstanding that was accounted for by UK lenders increased from a mere £33 billion in 2000 to a peak of £165 billion in 2008 (Maxted and Porter, 2010). The lion's share of this increased lending is accounted for by the two banks based in Scotland, HBOS and Royal Bank of Scotland, both of which are considered in more detail in Chapter 6.

There were also significant contributions from German banks. However, lending by German banks as a percentage of the number of loans outstanding declined toward the end of the boom. Nevertheless measured by the amount outstanding, their exposure to

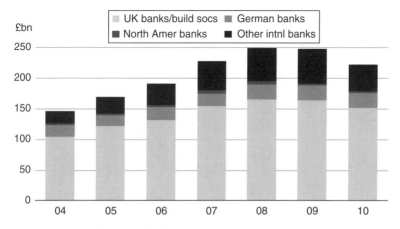

Figure 3.6 International sources of bank lending in the United Kingdom 2004–2010. *Source:* Maxted and Porter (2014). Reproduced courtesy of Maxted and Porter.

commercial property remained remarkably steady, rising only modestly from £15 billion to £25 billion in the eight years from 2000. Overall, as the boom progressed more lending from international banks (excluding German ones) was sucked in, and loans from these banks saw the biggest growth in 2007 and 2008 (Maxted and Porter, 2014). The share of lending by international banks more than doubled over the course of the decade. Measured by outstanding loans, the increase was an eight-fold one – from £7 billion at the beginning of the decade to £55 billion by 2008. At the peak of the market, international banks accounted for approximately a third of lending. These banks included a prominent group of Irish banks, all of which were to undergo severe problems when the financial music stopped and are detailed in Chapter 6.

Perhaps surprisingly, the year in which new bank loans on commercial property peaked was not 2007. It was not even 2008; it was 2009. So although the financial crisis had been raging for some months, bank lending still continued to grow, though admittedly by relatively small amounts. This is not as surprising as might at first be thought, however, given that many agreed loan facilities would not have been fully drawn down when the crisis broke. In fact, as Table 3.2 notes, there was still as much as £42.5 billion committed funds by banks as yet not drawn upon at the end of 2009. Maxted and Porter (2010) have estimated that in addition to the peak figure for outstanding lending to commercial property of around £250 billion in 2009, a further £50 billion had been lent by UK banks on products derived from other commercial or residential mortgage backed securities. We return to the securitized market later.

Table 3.2 includes a small proportion of lending on social housing, which at the end of 2009 totalled approximately £20 billion. Equity stakes taken by the banks are also a relatively small, at around £600 million. These equity stakes were part of a joint venture fund with a private investor, and it was not uncommon for a bank to lend up to 85% of the value of the property with the remaining 15% financed through capital from the investor (see Chapter 6). In return the bank would be entitled to a share of the profit from the joint venture. As well as receiving the interest on the loan, the value of the bank's equity rose through any increase in the property's valuation.

Mezzanine loans also represented a small proportion of bank lending. Such loans, an innovation of the late 1980s, were a way of addressing the traditional 75% ceiling banks

Table 3.2 Breakdown of outstanding property bank funding in the United Kingdom at the end of 2009 (£m).

	Loans including social housing	Mezzanine loans	Equity stakes	Outstanding funding	Committed funds not yet drawn down
UK lenders and building societies	158905	394	548	159847	32567
German lenders	25972	183	0	26155	8249
Other international lenders	57454	261	25	57741	1562
North American lenders	4556	22	40	4618	135
All lenders	246887	860	613	248360	42514

Source: Maxted and Porter (2010).

had on financing development costs. Mezzanine finance could permit developers to borrow up to 90% of their costs. This top slice of funding is more risky and so financiers charge a higher rate of interest and a share in any profit in the development. Mezzanine finance is the *junior* debt and repayments are made once the *senior* debt has received its repayment. The role of mezzanine finance in supporting development relates primarily to during a property boom, but it is also and more commonly used as supplementary finance by investors in standing properties (Giostra, 2011).

To Whom Were the Banks Lending?

There were six different categories of commercial property investors to whom the banks were lending from the turn of the century.

- Companies wishing to purchase the business premises they occupied. This form of lending had been banks' bread and butter for years, but decisions to purchase tend to vary according to the economic cycle, the cost of rent being paid and the cost and availability of finance. Although capital values were high, the ability to borrow at cheap rates swayed many potential owner occupiers' minds. Loans for these properties were traditionally standard loans up to a maximum of around 60% of the property value.
- Institutionally managed property funds, in particular the Jersey Property Unit Trusts (JPUTs) explained in Chapter 2. We have already read of their formation and subsequent growth in the mid-2000s. Although the ownership of many of these trusts was dominated by investors who were traditionally conservative in the management of conventional funds, it was remarkable how their attitude changed when they realized the accretive benefits of higher gearing. Consequently, borrowings did rise over the mid-2000s (PriceWaterhouse Coopers, 2012). Three factors were at work here. First, increases in property valuations had reduced the loan-to-value (LTV) ratios of many funds. Simply increasing borrowings to push these LTV ratios back up towards their upper limit accounted for some of this additional borrowing. Secondly, some funds were encouraged (sometimes this would be manager driven, sometimes, investor driven) to increase gearing to the maximum permitted according to the trust deed (as not all funds had borrowed the maximum permitted). And finally, some funds elected (with investor approval) to actively increase the maximum amount they could borrow (for example raising the LTV ratio from, say, 60% to 75%).
- Private and listed property companies. The former encompass a large range of funds from small private trusts to larger funds, many of which may have been investing in the asset class for the first time. In addition, there were the listed property companies (some of which converted to Real Estate Investment Trusts (REITs) in 2007). For many, the use of debt was paramount in their decision to invest in commercial property. It was not just a case of favourable debt-assisted returns, many investors just did not have sufficient capital to conduct any form of investment without using debt.
- Overseas investors taking advantage of Britain's safe haven status and the investor-friendly lease structures inherent in the UK property market. Many of these investors had been involved in the UK market for years. Often individual foreign investors move in and out of the United Kingdom, but in aggregate they remained net investors right through the boom years (and through the immediate post-crash

years too). Many were seeking to take advantage of the forecast stronger returns in the UK commercial property market relative to the poorer performing markets in Europe (Scottish Widows Investment Partnership, 2003, 2004, 2005, 2006)

- Hedge funds, the short-term speculators and other investors, many of whom were unfamiliar with property investment. For many in the mid-2000s, full appreciation of the nuances of property management was not essential when capital profits surfaced very quickly with little effort from the owners – buying, holding for a few months, riding the so-called yield curve then selling at a profit. And as we have touched on already and will look at in more detail later in the chapter, the use of debt magnified the rates of return from these already profitable assets.
- Developers. Developers are highly dependent on debt capital. Certainly from the 1950s, banks have granted loans for the financing of property development. Traditionally the availability and scale of development finance expands substantially in a property boom.

The one category of investor who eschewed the use of debt was the retail investor (see Chapter 2) who invested relatively small amounts that they pooled with other similar investors, allowing them to gain exposure to commercial property that they would otherwise have been unable to access. Part of their conservatism was attributable to the regulations in force at the time, which sought to protect retail investors from the effects of volatile markets and so they only allowed very limited borrowings. Few of these funds specializing in selling to the retail investor actually borrowed as property values accelerated upwards.

The Cost and Role of Debt

Global interest rates, as noted earlier, were very low in the years after the millennium. It made borrowing for commercial property investment very attractive. Figure 3.7 highlights the relatively narrow band in which UK base rates operated for much of the 2000s. They were within the 4% to 6% range, dipping below that from the beginning of 2003 to 2004. For borrowers, that marked a welcome change from previous decades,

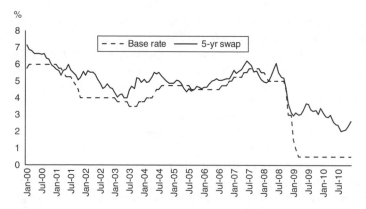

Figure 3.7 Bank base rates and 5-year swap rates 2000–2010. *Source:* Courtesy of Thompson Datastream.

when not only were base rates more volatile but were also much higher. The actual interest rate generally used when borrowing for property purchases is the '5-year swap rate', on top of which, an interest rate margin, arrangement fees and non-utilization fees are applied. As Figure 3.7 indicates, this swap rate also traded in a relatively narrow band. The 5-year swap rate was around 7% in 2000 and for much of 2005 and 2006 it was below 5%. Both base rates and the swap rate began to rise in the middle of 2006 as the peak of the boom approached.

Interest rate margins added to the 5-year swap rate vary with the state of the market and competition between banks. As Figure 3.8 demonstrates, margins of just over 1% (100 basis points) or so were available through 2002 to 2006 (Maxted and Porter, 2014). With swap rates between 4.5% and 5.5% from 2004 to 2006, that implied that funding was obtainable on a vast range of property types at around 5.5% to 6.75% – in some cases below the income return achievable.

There was little difference between the interest rate margins charged by banks over the course of the 2000s on loans for prime and secondary property (in less accessible locations or poorer quality) as Figure 3.9 shows for retail assets. So even lending on more secondary properties was keenly priced at that time at margins around 120–130 basis points. Offices and industrial properties show similar paths. It is noticeable that margins reduce over the course of the first half of the decade but increase in 2006 and more rapidly once the market turmoil began. It is also evident that the differential in the margins charged for secondary retail (as with the other sectors) over its prime counterpart remained relatively constant at about 20–25 basis points prior to 2007 but then increased significantly after 2007. The combination of both rising interest rates and margins from the middle of 2006 would have been a double whammy for the cost of borrowing.

Beside the falling interest rates there was an additional influence on the investment sentiment at the time. In 2000 the value of high technology shares on the American stock exchange (NASDAQ) collapsed dramatically after a rapid 650% rise from 1996 as

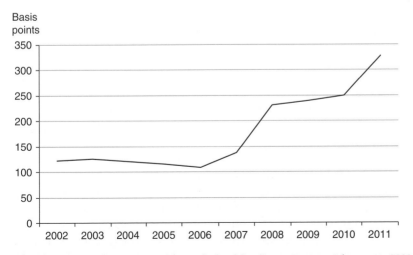

Figure 3.8 Average interest rate margins for bank lending to commercial property 2002–2011. *Source:* Maxted and Porter (2014). Reproduced with permission.

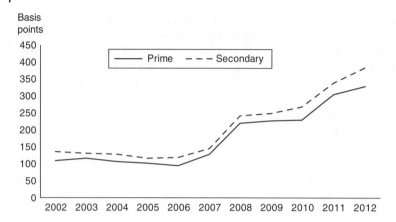

Figure 3.9 Average interest rate margins on prime and secondary retail properties 2002–2012. *Source:* Maxted and Porter (2014). Reproduced with permission.

the Internet began to take hold. This is known as the bursting of the 'dot-com bubble'. By August 2002 these shares were down 80% from their all-time high. This phenomenon occurred on a global basis. There were parallel if less spectacular rises in share values in other sectors over the same period of the late 1990s, followed by negative contagion effects across many other industrial sectors after the bubble burst (Anderson, Brooks and Katsaris, 2010). The consequences were that share prices in Western countries were deflated and investors looked to other types of assets for returns.

As part of this wider reappraisal of investment, money into commercial property increased significantly in the post-2000 era (see Chapter 4). The reasons were clear. Commercial property in the early 2000s was one of the highest yielding asset classes around, supported by the low borrowing rates reported above. New investment players were enticed into the market. No one concerned themselves with risk as property was perceived as harbouring next to no risk. This is reflected in the low interest rate margin differential between prime and secondary property previously noted.

The precise attractiveness can be seen by simply looking at two key financial variables. The relative differential between the initial returns on an asset (the yield) and the cost of borrowing is a good, if simplistic, indicator of the profitability of commercial property investment. If property yields are above the cost of borrowing then rental income would be more than the cost of paying off the loan to purchase (assuming a 100% loan). In these circumstances investment could be described as 'self-financing' as in the 1950s (see Chapter 1) and the attractiveness of the investment would be further enhanced by the prospect of rising rents and capital values as the boom proceeded.

Taking the cost of property borrowing as the 5-year swap rate plus a bank's margin, Figure 3.10 charts the relationship with the initial yields of prime 'institutional' grade commercial property from 2000. It illustrates that on average investment in these types of properties was marginally self financing from 2001 through to the middle of 2004. The financial equation then deteriorates a little but is still finely balanced for the next year. These figures relate to a typical property for the decade. The position could have been even more favourable in locations with low capital values and high initial yields. And of course not all properties offered yields above the all-in cost of debt. Nevertheless,

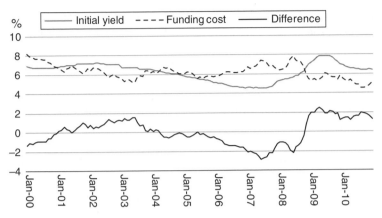

Figure 3.10 Differences between initial yield and funding costs 2000–2010. *Source:* MSCI/IPD (2014b) and Maxted and Porter (2014). Reproduced with permission.

Table 3.3 Indicative capital returns over the period 2004–2006 with different gearing ratios.

Gearing ratio	0%	20%	40%	60%	80%
Capital return	40.7%	50.9%	67.9%	101.8%	203.7%

Source: MSCI/IPD (2014b) and authors' calculations.

at a time when rents and capital values were rising, debt-assisted purchases were evidently very financially attractive, and augmented by the benefits of gearing on future capital returns.

The indicative impact of gearing can be examined by applying different gearing ratios to average actual capital returns over the period 2004–2006 at the height of the boom. The cumulative capital return over these three years was 40.7% based simply on commercial property values, but rental income would increase the total return. This is equivalent to zero gearing as it assumes no debt. Table 3.3 presents the results of modelling the impact of gearing assuming that funding costs are matched by rental income. This is not strictly true as borrowing costs increase as the amount borrowed increases. The approach is sufficiently accurate for illustration purposes as the increasing negative differential between borrowing costs and rental income with higher gearing is swamped by the capital gain as a percentage of the smaller equity capital invested. It should also be noted that the preceding paragraphs assume zero capital gearing when comparing initial rental income with the cost of debt. For simplicity, transaction costs are also ignored.

From the results given in Table 3.3 it is readily apparent just how capital returns increase exponentially as the amount borrowed increases. Capital returns would have doubled over these three years using a 60% LTV gearing and would have increased threefold at 80%. While most institutions would balk at using such high levels of debt, gearing ratios of this magnitude (and even higher) were commonplace during these heady years. Investors who incorporated debt into their business plans would have generated exceptional rates of return. The use of debt also enables a fund to invest in a larger number of properties than otherwise would have been possible and hence aids diversification.

The combination of the benefits of gearing and the just about 'self-financing' nature of commercial property at the start of the millennium was an important reason for investors utilizing borrowings. With these assets delivering such high rates of capital return an illusion of stability was created where it did not exist. And it also attracted investors with insufficient understanding of the ways of the property world. Why bother managing the asset when you could simply buy it with borrowed money, hold it for a short time, then sell it on for a 'guaranteed' profit? This 'pass the parcel' attitude was rife during the heady years prior to 2007.

Once the property market turned in 2007 and markets in general were reawakened to the risks inherent in the banking sector, bank interest rate margins rocketed (see Figure 3.8). By mid-2012 Maxted and Porter (2014) note the average margin had increased to between 330 basis points (for average prime retail and office properties) and 410 basis points (for average secondary industrial properties), depending on the type and quality of asset under consideration. With swap rates, though, having fallen by then, financing costs were still at relatively low levels. The availability of debt finance, or more precisely, the lack of it, though, was the problem now. This illustrates that a focus on the simple differential between rent and debt costs and the benefits of gearing in magnifying returns was only part of the story of the boom and the accessibility and terms of bank lending were also crucial.

A key variable in the accessibility of banking finance is the amount banks are prepared to lend as a percentage of the total value of a standing investment or the cost of a development. The amount lenders were willing to lend on individual deals increased as the boom progressed, as set out in Figure 3.11. Banks have historically been wary of lending more than around 60% to 70% of the value (LTV) of most properties (Fraser, 1993), but as Figure 3.11 shows, these LTV percentages began to creep up towards the 80% mark in the mid-2000s. Some of these decisions to relax lending criteria were based more on their desire to cement client relationships rather than on fundamental assessments of business risk (see Chapter 6). But what is interesting is that that the average maximum LTV percentage fell during 2006, even before any of the problems that were to lie ahead surfaced. Maybe the banks were indeed concerned that something amiss was about to happen.

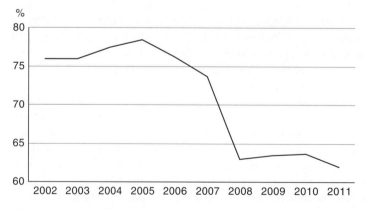

Figure 3.11 Average maximum loan to values on commercial property lending by banks 2002–2012. *Source:* Maxted and Porter (2014). Reproduced with permission of MSCI/IPD and Maxted and Porter.

Table 3.4 Indicative capital losses over the period mid-2007–mid-2009 with different gearing ratios.

Gearing ratio	0%	20%	40%	60%	80%
Capital return	−42.4%	−53.0%	−70.7%	−100%	−100%

Source: MSCI/IPD (2014b) and authors' calculations.

These LTVs are based on the valuation of properties at the time of the issue of the loan. The banks may have been comforted by the fact that the degree of risk would fall as values rose through the boom. Once property values began to fall after the GFC, these LTVs were historic; the actual ratio could be over 100% and very difficult to ascertain in a stagnant market. This represented a very different challenge for the banks, which is considered in Chapter 7.

For property investors the financial headache of falling capital values was amplified by the gearing that had brought vast riches in the boom. Gearing works well during the years in which property values are rising but conversely destroys equity when capital values are falling. Table 3.4 extends Table 3.3 by indicating capital losses over the period of stress using the same range of gearing ratios. Once again, we have ignored transaction costs and made the simplistic assumption that funding costs are matched by rental income. Average capital values fell by 42.4% between mid-2007 and mid-2009 (coincidentally a very similar amount by which they had risen over 2004 to 2006), and this figure is used to determine the extent of capital losses dependent on the level of gearing.

Table 3.4 shows that one's equity would have been completely lost even before the end of the property downturn had the fund utilized gearing of 60% or more. Not only would the investor's equity have been wiped out, the value of the property would have fallen below the amount lent, putting the bank at risk of at least partial loss (see Chapter 7). Remember that borrowing is normally given on a 'non-recourse' basis, which means that the loan is charged only against the particular asset (see Chapter 2). Consequently, the maximum potential loss that the lender could suffer is the full amount of the loan; the maximum loss incurred by the borrower is the initial equity input in the deal (the total purchase price less borrowings). Only when a loan had recourse to other assets could the borrower's loss exceed the equity amount.

So far this chapter has focused on the long-term economic growth, bank lending and the micro-implications for investors. The latter sections of the chapter turn to key dimensions of change in the property market of the noughties. First, the role and scale of development activity is considered in the light of rising capital values, low interest rates and the ready available of finance. Second, the impact of the reduction of interest rates and the narrowing of banks' lending terms between types of properties is examined in terms of the impact on the spread of property yields across the property market.

Development and its Finance in the Noughties Boom

Chapter 1 sets out the 'classical' theory of a commercial property cycle that revolves around demand shortages caused by an economic upturn and development lags. The consequent rises in rents and capital values are seen as the driver of development activity that takes off in the latter part of the boom, and often much of it is not completed until after the peak of the cycle. With this theoretical framework in mind the chapter now considers the time path of commercial development during the boom, distinguishing between use sectors. The scale of the commercial property development through the upturn of the noughties can be gleaned from Table 3.5.

Construction output of shops, offices and warehouses completed more than doubled in real terms between 1997 and 2007, the peak year. Factory development in contrast was not only more stable it was actually in modest decline. This trend probably reflects the restructuring of the economy over the period. Looking closely at the time paths of construction output there are significant differences between shops and offices over the boom. The expansion of shopping developments arguably occurred early in the boom with the main growth spurt over 2002 and 2003 when annual construction output overall rose by almost half, after which output stayed on a broad plateau until another stride up in 2007.

The office development path over the boom is more complex. Just like for retail development there is a relative spurt in construction that saw a step change in activity in 2000–2001; output rose by 46% over these two years. After a modest drop off in activity, office development again gathers pace and there is a mini-boom over the three years from 2005 to 2007 with output in 2007, 52% above that in 2004. In all four sectors

Table 3.5 Real value of private construction output by commercial property sector in Great Britain 1997–2015.

Year	Shops	Offices	Factories	Warehouses
1997	4505	6499	4243	1745
1998	5284	7212	4334	1978
1999	6680	8230	4313	2094
2000	5289	10074	3657	2373
2001	5625	12034	3698	2257
2002	7134	11801	3338	2044
2003	8249	10248	3585	2205
2004	8915	10319	3621	2584
2005	8612	11266	3296	3220
2006	8611	12876	3635	3528
2007	9144	15711	3664	3554
2008	8632	14769	3255	2420
2009	6297	8920	2121	1516
2010	5756	6857	2093	1574
2011	5877	6896	1798	1444
2012	4878	6188	2095	1311
2013	4559	7068	2147	1191
2014	5423	8432	2333	1684
2015	4929	9627	2559	2239

Source: UK Construction Statistics – nominal output (£m) revised to 2015 prices using Consumer Price Index.

construction output peaks in 2007 and is followed by a modest fall away in 2008 and significant reductions in the years from 2009 onwards.

These patterns of development activity represent two waves of expansion, first at the beginning of the noughties and the second towards the end of the boom. In terms of the theoretical model the first wave can be seen as a lagged response to the economic growth of the 1990s and the peak of development is just at the 2007 property market peak with an overhang into 2008. What is not clear is why development activity stutters between the two waves, albeit at a high level. Nevertheless, while the growth of development in the property boom is irrefutable it is useful to compare it with previous booms. Figure 3.12 demonstrates that office development in London during the last decade was not on a par with the level of development during the previous boom of the 1980s. In fact it is probable that in comparison with the 1980s less than half of the office space was built in London during the noughties.

The picture is more clouded for retail development as Figure 3.13 and Figure 3.14 reveal. The ongoing urban development cycle from the beginning of the 1980s had most impact on retailing. The peak decades for the building of retail warehouses were the 1980s and 1990s. And although these developments continue to be built through the noughties there is not an invigorated boom. On the other hand, while shopping centre development is more cyclical, the recent peak years are not the boom years of the noughties but 1999, 2000 and 2008. The intensity of development between 2001 and 2007 is above that of the 1980s and 1990s but less than in the 1970s when many towns and cities built covered malls in their centres.

Despite the strength of the economy and the relative abundance of debt in the boom years it can be argued that the property market did not experience an excessively large office development programme that has typified most previous boom periods. It seems

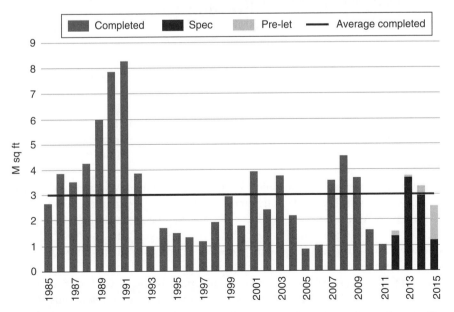

Figure 3.12 Office development in London 1985–2011. *Source:* Jones (2013), data from Savills Research.

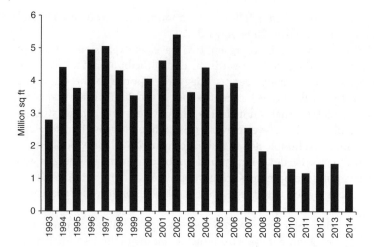

Figure 3.13 Annual retail warehouse space completed 1993–2014. *Source:* CBRE (2014a). Reproduced with permission.

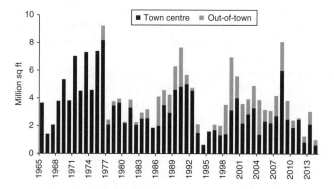

Figure 3.14 Annual completions of town centre and out-of-town shopping centres 1965–2014. *Source:* CBRE (2014b). Reproduced with permission.

that while there were ready funds at low interest rates available from the lenders to finance development during the mid-2000s, property investors/companies elected not to undertake as much development as might have been expected. It is probable that there is a range of explanations.

The institutional life funds, traditionally keen and successful developers in the past, for example, were beginning to see policy maturities exceeding premium income, and consequently their fund sizes were declining. Financing major developments in these circumstances raises issues for not just the fund manager but also the actuary. Consequently, large-scale developments were less common, many funds perhaps content to undertake relatively small developments or refurbishments.

For many of the shorter term funds, and certainly many of the newer funds, property trading was far more immediately lucrative than undertaking development where profits emerge only after completion that will take several years. The increased short-termism reflected in greater churn is supported by the research of Jones, Livingstone and Dunse (2016) that shows how trends in purchases as a percentage of the value of the stock increased by a factor of two for offices and two-thirds for shops between the booms of the 1980s and 2000s. They also find greater investment volatility in the noughties that they suggest can be attributed to a short-term sales/investment opportunity culture.

The historic muted office and retail development boom is also seen in the low percentage of the banks' loan books that went to commercial property development. At the peak of the boom only 7% of bank lending (around £17 bn) was in the form of loans for commercial property development. Loans for residential development for sale accounted for another 10%. By far the biggest share of bank lending, almost three-quarters (73%), went on loans for investment property (Maxted and Porter, 2010). The property boom of the noughties, it can be argued, was not fundamentally based on development activity but can be characterized as an investment-led explosion in real estate values supported by readily available and cheap credit.

The Weight of Money and Moving up the Risk Curve

We have already discussed the reasons for the reawakening of interest in commercial property investment at the beginning of the noughties. It was based on the low interest rates, the fallout from the bursting of the dot-com bubble and the high returns/secure income available from such assets together with much more relaxed bank lending criteria and its availability. New investment players were enticed into the market. Private property funds, private trusts, unlisted onshore and offshore funds, hedge funds and the 'man in the street' all discovered the benefits of commercial property investment. In addition, many enhanced their returns by gearing up by taking advantage of the lending readily available. Not all the newcomers employed debt – indeed the retail investor, as noted above, was one class that shunned borrowing (although rules were changed to permit some of the funds they did invest in to do so). But almost all the others were voracious in their use of debt.

The increase in investors and money into the commercial property market inevitably had consequences in terms of the level of capital values. The financial institutions, and other investors who did not use debt, found that they were being outbid in the market as those funds that did use borrowings were able to pay more for a building. Given the low cost of debt the simple arithmetic outlined above shows that geared funds could outbid ungeared investors yet still obtain the same level of returns. The result was that prices were bid up, and in particular, historically cheaper properties gained more in value than the more expensive ones. The former could be in localities that had previously been less favoured or of poorer investment quality, often described as 'secondary' rather the prime properties financial institutions targeted for their investment. This distinction between prime and secondary has been referred to above, but it is useful to consider it in more detail here.

The division between prime and secondary is a fuzzy line and actually one that changes over time. Prime properties can be defined as those invested in by risk averse financial institutions. The differences relate to a combination of location, quality, (large) size, the lease structure and the type/mix of tenants (often referred to as 'covenant'). One way to think of prime is those properties for which there will always be a demand – because of their location in the city centre, say, or in a prestigious area. Given that these properties/areas are more highly sought after by occupiers and that their supply is restricted, it is a certainty that there will always be excess demand for them. This means that any vacancies should be short lived and limited. This in turn means that prime properties are a less risky investment compared with secondary (Jones, 2013). The value of prime properties is therefore based on a lower risk premium (see Chapter 1). The increasing demand pushing up property values was in effect a rethinking of the appropriate risk premium to be applied to property investment as a whole and to different types of property and locations. This issue is discussed in a more theoretical framework in Chapter 4 and Chapter 6.

The expansion of investment in the noughties posed dilemmas for the long-term institutional investors as they were being outbid: either they must pay more than they would normally have considered prudent for properties in their 'normal' target investment range or move up the risk curve and seek to buy properties that had a lower prime status than their traditional investments. Should they, for example, purchase those in more secondary locations, those with a shorter leases remaining or those offering potential development opportunities, or walk away? The problem with moving into the less prime space was that soon even the geared funds were being forced to compete for these properties as competition for the ever dwindling number of prime properties increased.

The difficulty with electing to walk away and not bid was that the mandates of many funds required the manager to invest in commercial property; the individual investors had made the asset allocation decision (to invest in the asset class) – they would not take kindly to the fund manager sitting on the cash, especially in the mid-2000s when property values were increasing. But equally, those funds that did buy properties that could be called 'non-institutional' did manage to adhere to the fund mandate by investing in commercial property, but they did so at the cost of buying what was arguably 'second rate' property. Did the property fund managers in these cases properly inform their clients that they had moved up the risk curve? And were the investors aware of the fund's higher risk profile? These issues would prove paramount during the property collapse. Funds that needed to sell found the values of these less than prime properties were tumbling much more than their prime counterparts.

Notwithstanding the problems that would emerge after the global crisis, the weight of money undoubtedly saw the differences between the capital values of prime and secondary properties narrow during the boom (see Chapter 4). More precisely, as it is easier to compare the values of properties by their yields (see Chapter 1), what was happening was a convergence of yields. But it was not just the yields of prime and non-prime properties that were converging: so also were the yields of different types of prime properties. This convergence covered sectors such as offices and retail but also different cities.

This phenomenon was demonstrated by an analysis of the impact of the weight of money on city office markets undertaken by Dunse *et al.* (2007). The higher the level of investment funds flowing into a city the more positive the sentiment toward risks and returns in property investment which in turn means lower property investment yields generally (higher capital values). This occurred in the boom in many provincial cities in the United Kingdom as the real value of transactions in these cities achieved record levels (Dunse *et al.*, 2007). The result was a narrowing/convergence of the absolute

Table 3.6 Initial yield differentials of prime offices between UK provincial cities and the City of London 2001–2009.*

City	2001	2002	2003	2004	2005	2006	2007	2008	2009
Edinburgh	0.1	−0.1	−0.3	0.4	0.4	0.8	0.9	0.7	0.3
Glasgow	1.1	−0.1	0.1	0.7	0.4	0.4	1.0	0.9	1.3
Bristol	2.4	1.1	0.3	0.9	0.5	0.7	1.5	1.7	2.1
Birmingham	0.9	0.5	0.0	0.5	0.1	0.5	0.9	0.9	1.8
Manchester	1.2	0.3	−0.1	0.5	0.3	0.1	1.0	0.5	0.3
Leeds	0.9	0.3	−0.1	0.3	0.4	0.8	1.1	0.8	1.0

*at the end of year.
Source: MSCI/IPD (2009) and Jones (2013).

spatial spectrum of prime office yields as all the risk premiums for cities fell (except Edinburgh).

More perspective can be garnered by applying the analysis here of Dunse *et al.* (2007), whereby a city risk premium is expressed as the difference between the yield on prime office buildings in a given location and that of the City of London yield. The City of London is taken as the benchmark as the premier investment market with the highest liquidity albeit with the greatest volatility (Dunse, Jones and White, 2010). The changing pattern of prime office risk premiums across six major British provincial cities over the period 2001–2009 is shown in Table 3.6. These risk premiums in the early 2000s overall were at their lowest (as well as the range of values) level since records began in the 1980s, although 2006 marks the end of this phase.

In summary, the property mania of the early 2000s saw not only a rise in capital values but also a restructuring of relative capital values in the commercial property market. Part of the reason was general downgrading of the risk (premium) associated with such property. In the euphoria of the property boom arguably no one concerned themselves with risk as property was perceived as harbouring next to no risk. Certainly the risk premium for poorer quality properties was eroded with banks for example requiring only slight additional margins on loans for secondary property. Overall the differences between capital values as defined by yields, between different types of prime or between prime and secondary property, narrowed. There was convergence of investment yields across the breadth of the commercial property market.

Conclusions

This chapter has highlighted the long global upswing from the mid-1990s though to the GFC. Policy makers began to believe that a new world economic order had been achieved, and theories such as the 'Great Moderation' sought to explain the phenomenon. In hindsight the significant role that debt played in this economic growth was substantially underestimated. Debt also fuelled the commercial property boom as banks dramatically expanded their lending by offering very generous terms. The willingness of banks to lend would not alone have caused the explosion of lending that occurred; this was the result of the simultaneous rising demand from investors. In the early 2000s, in the aftermath of the burst of the dot-com bubble, historically low interest rates and sustained economic growth investment in commercial property took off.

The ensuing investment spending spree on commercial property was based on the attractive financial equation at the beginning of the decade. On average, investment from 2001 through to the middle of 2004 was almost self-financing in the sense that the costs of borrowing (a notional 100% of) for the purchase were broadly equivalent to the initial rental income. Not only were investment outlays all but covered by revenue but capital values were rising in percentage terms year on year in double figures, with a cumulative growth of 41% from 2004 to 2006. But this was only the basic return for this three-year period if the investor paid cash; whereas borrowing 60% of the cost would produce a return of 100% over this period, and 80% would give 200% on the capital outlay (ignoring loan repayments).

Highly geared investment supported by the readily available bank lending was extremely attractive – but only as long as the commercial property market bull run lasted. It only takes a relatively small fall in the value of the collateral to wipe out all the equity invested. The gearing that supported and accelerated the property boom had the reverse effects when the GFC brought a collapse in values. Gearing had supported not only the property market but the broader economy upswing through consumer debt, and it contributed to a hidden fragility.

Nevertheless, commercial property investors, encouraged by the record period of economic growth and continuing capital growth, arguably underestimated the inherent risks. Similar criticisms can be laid at the feet of banks in their lending decisions. An avalanche of investment funds led not only to commercial property's risk premium falling but also a restructuring of property values. In particular the spectrum of yields across the market, both in terms of quality and locations, narrowed or converged.

At the same time, property development experienced a parallel boom. However, the scale of this development acivity was in general less than that in the 1980s' boom. The dominant influence on property values during the noughties was not the shortage of commercial property but the weight of investment funds supported by a short-termism opportunity driven culture. This chapter has examined underlying mechanics and themes that have contributed to this boom and represents building blocks for the next chapters on the dynamics of the boom and the bust.

4

The Anatomy of the Property Investment Boom

The drivers of property booms, as Chapter 3 explains, are fundamentally macroeconomic. Inevitably, real estate performance is closely linked to the overall performance of a nation's economy. This is true for both the occupier (rental) and investment markets. Commercial property is an essential factor of production; without factories, offices, shops and leisure facilities, the productive activities of business would not be possible. Over the last 200 years, though, commercial property has also become a significant financial asset; its value now reflects its importance as an investment medium as well as its importance as a factor of production. This chapter concentrates on the former investment role.

The chapter sets the boom in property market values of the first decade of the millennium in this wider economic and financial framework. It examines property market trends in the build-up of the boom and analyses these trends in terms of behaviour and the impact that irrational exuberance may have had on capital value trends. It examines the premise that this time the boom years really were different from what had happened in previous cycles. It reviews the fundamentals of pricing and how investment behaviour in the boom arguably distorted a proper assessment of price, value and worth, thereby encouraging a disconnect between rental value growth and capital value growth. To achieve this task the chapter goes back to basics to discuss in detail the quantification of the changing risk premium attached to commercial property, noted in the Chapter 3.

This chapter starts with a brief reminder of the links between national economic health and property market performance and the importance of globalization. It then looks at the scale and timing of general global property upturns, both housing and commercial, around the world, beginning in the mid-1990s and gathering pace in the first part of the 2000s, setting the British experience in a wider context. The chapter then examines in detail the relationship between capital and rental values as the boom developed. It asks what proportion of the rise in capital values can be attributed to rental growth. The next section considers the scale of investment and the growth of transactions during the boom. It also reviews who was purchasing (and selling), and the impact this had on capital values. A particular focus is the large inflow of cash via retail funds (funds that sell units to individual investors) as property returns rose in the cauldron of the boom. The chapter next considers the role of bank lending in supporting the weight

Property Boom and Banking Bust: The Role of Commercial Lending in the Bankruptcy of Banks,
First Edition. Colin Jones, Stewart Cowe, and Edward Trevillion.
© 2018 John Wiley & Sons Ltd. Published 2018 by John Wiley & Sons Ltd.

of money into commercial property in terms of gearing as the boom proceeded. Finally, the rationality underpinning the investment boom is assessed as well as the extent to which it represented a bubble.

Commercial Property, the Macroeconomy and Globalization

Before undertaking the analysis it is useful to flesh out again the nature of some of the conceptual ideas of the dynamics of the property market outlined in Chapter 1. There is a close correlation between commercial property performance and a nation's economy. This is true both of the use and investment markets, and recent economic history indicates that when property market forces interact with cyclical macroeconomic factors, real estate fluctuations can be significant in both amplitude and duration (Tiwari and White, 2010). This is illustrated in Figure 4.1 and Figure 4.2, which compare property market performance (total returns) and economic performance (GDP growth) in the United States and the United Kingdom over the last 30 years.

The similarities between commercial property performance and the economy is not really surprising given that property is a derived demand and companies feel more optimistic in times of plenty, are more cautious in times of uncertainty and downsize in times of recession. A growing economy, one where confidence is high, unemployment is low and raw materials are plentiful sees rents rising, which in turn attracts other

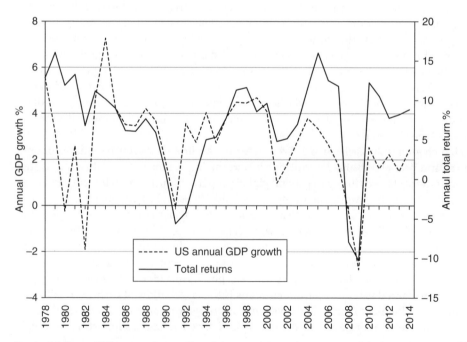

Figure 4.1 Annual US economic growth and commercial property returns 1978–2014. *Source:* World Bank (2016) and NCREIF (https://www.statista.com/statistics/376854/ncreif-index-returns-usa/). Reproduced with permission.

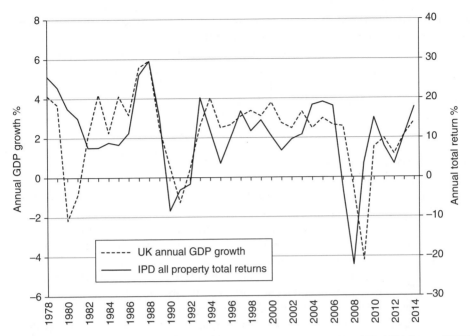

Figure 4.2 Annual UK economic growth and commercial property returns 1978–2014. *Source:* MSCI/ IPD (2014a) and Office of National Statistics (2016a). Reproduced with permission.

investors and developers and in turn produces a new supply of buildings. This can ulti- mately produce too much new or speculative space which fails to find a tenant, more so if the economy is stalling or moves into recession. However, as Chapter 3 demonstrates, the force of speculation in the noughties was more concentrated on property invest- ment, particularly with the assistance of gearing. The dynamics of these processes, and their interaction, are the focus of this chapter.

The added dimension is that real estate markets in different global cities are linked by common economic factors. A fundamental driver of international real estate market activity is economic growth and development. So as real incomes have grown and economies have developed there has been an increasing demand for real estate assets across all property sectors, retail, office, industrial and residential. The globalization of business activity pre-2007 was a continuing process driven by the desire to command global presence through organic growth and/or acquisition. It led to the conversion of ownership of successful companies from domestic to multinational concerns and the increasing opportunities offered to corporations, institutional investors and banks to own overseas assets through globally traded stock markets.

Financial deregulation and economic integration across national economies have played their part and have caused property cycles to be influenced by international eco- nomic events. Over the last 40 or so years, global economic change and growth, financial deregulation, and increasing flows of international financial capital have resulted in an increased synchronization of world economies and, it can be argued, in a synchroniza- tion of property market behaviour giving rise to global cycles (see Chapter 1). Economic integration has meant that property cycles can almost simultaneously occur in distant cities in different parts of the world. We might expect, in particular, that cities with similar economic structures in different parts of the world would have more synchronized property cycles than other locations (Barras, 2009). The implication, though, is that countries integrated into international capital will be destined to suffer from common 'boom and bust' scenarios. Importantly, strong user demand has been correlated with investor demand for property as an income-producing asset, and so both user and investment markets can be affected by global events.

Global Property Upswing

From the early to mid-1990s through to the global financial crisis (GFC) there was a long period of global economic growth. Chapter 3 provides detail on these trends. There were variations between countries, but by the early 2000s virtually all Western economies were experiencing consistent growth from one year to the next. The foundation of this economic growth was partly the low interest rates across the globe during this period, but the ready availability of finance also played its part. A consequence was the accumulation of a vast personal and commercial debt mountain, as chronicled in Chapter 3. Much of this debt was utilized to buy property.

In the housing market this was seen in a long upturn in prices for many Western countries from the middle of the 1990s, although for some it occurred earlier (Ireland, 1992, and Scandinavian countries, 1993) and others later (Canada, 1998; Italy, 1998; New Zealand, 1998; Switzerland 2000). Statistics for selected countries are given in Table 4.1. The longest upswing occurred in the Netherlands, where real prices rose by 217% over the 23-year period from 1985 to 2008. The Netherlands was not the only country to the experience the doubling of real prices. Acute real increases were also found in Ireland (302%), Norway (199%), Denmark(177%) and the United Kingdom (157%). In contrast the United States and Canada saw relatively modest real rises of only 61% and 72% respectively, and in Switzerland the rise was only 20%.

Table 4.1 Real house price growth in selected countries.

Country	Upturns	Duration (quarters)	% Change
Australia	1991Q2–2010Q2	76	+139.5
Denmark	1993Q2–2007Q1	55	+177.7
France	1997Q1–2007Q4	44	+117.7
Italy	1997Q3–2007Q4	41	+59.2
Netherlands	1985Q3–2008Q4	89	+217.6
Spain	1996Q3–2007Q3	44	+121.5
United Kingdom	1995Q4–2007Q4	48	+157.8
United States	1995Q1–2006Q4	47	+60.5

Source: Jones (2012a).

Not all countries participated in this international upswing, with Japan as the most notable example, where, instead, there were two decades of prices declining in real terms over the same period. Germany also exhibited a long downward trend in real house prices from 1994 to 2008, seeing an overall real fall of 26.5%. The explanations for these variations can be seen in the weak economic performance of Japan over this period while for Germany major factors were the reunification of the country and a declining population (Jones, 2012a).

The global economic expansion similarly fed through to increased commercial property demand, and so rental and capital values rose with yields falling. Many countries experienced a common commercial property boom, especially those that were more intimately linked in with the global capital cycle. This phenomenon is linked to long-term changes in the nature of cities and the growth of financial and business services that has resulted in similar property market trends. However, the commercial property boom began generally later in the first years of the millennium and was ultimately briefer than in the housing markets.

Inevitably there are differences in the scale of the upturn in commercial property values as despite economic globalization international markets are not homogeneous and not all countries were starting from the same base at the beginning of the economic upswing. Different countries also have different institutions and different legal systems which, with different informational property market efficiencies (information quality *and* interpretation) and transparency, moderate behaviour. In this context, while yields fell and capital values increased across many countries in the boom years they did so to different extents and over different timescales and they were inevitably mediated by local market conditions and institutions.

Capital values had begun to rise in many countries worldwide from 2003 but the United Kingdom had shown positive growth from 1996 with strong growth from 2002 (see later in the chapter under Market Trends in the Property Boom). In the United States there was no growth in commercial property values in 2001 or 2002 but capital growth was seen from 2003 and had reached 11.4% per annum by 2005. Ireland had experienced a sustained growth in capital values from the early 1990s, and this resumed in 2003 after a year of contraction. Growth reached double figures by 2005 and a staggering annual 21.9% by 2006 (MSCI/IPD, 2014a). Geographical differences in both the onset of capital value growth and the extent of growth during the boom years are illustrated in Figure 4.3 (repeated from Chapter 3). Taken as a whole the eurozone average values did not show any real growth until 2005, but there are considerable differences beneath this average.

The capital values of commercial properties rose by 70% from the millennium to the peak of the boom in Ireland. The equivalent figures for the United Kingdom and United States were lower, just over 50% and almost 40% respectively. The aggregate statistic for the eurozone is much less, just 15%, but this is substantially influenced by falling valuations in Germany. Figure 4.3 also clearly illustrates the completely different growth (contraction) pattern in Germany compared with other mature property markets, a difference that is paralleled in the housing market noted earlier. In Germany values actually fell during the whole period in which values boomed in other countries, but this may be down to valuation practices in that country. Crosby (2007) found that German valuations have been much less volatile than UK valuations, and the different time path for capital values could well be a result of these different valuation approaches.

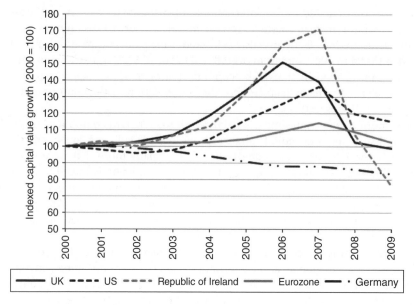

Figure 4.3 Commercial property capital growth in selected countries 2000–2009. *Source:* MSCI/IPD (2014c). Reproduced with permission.

Valuation approaches more generally vary from country to country (Baum, 2015), so a precise international comparison of the increase in capital values is difficult. With these caveats it is interesting to note that the climax of the boom varied across countries. Capital growth in Ireland and the United States peaked a year later than in the United Kingdom (the United Kingdom is discussed in detail later in the chapter as a separate case study).

An alternative way of illustrating some of the value trends in these boom years of the early to mid-noughties is to look at trends in yields. As we noted in Chapter 1 the (initial) yield is calculated as the ratio of net rental income to capital values (as a percentage). By comparing yields it possible to assess which are more expensive given their current rental income. It is how much investors are prepared to pay for a given rental income (including future expected growth) that determines the capital value of a property. The higher the yield the lower is the value, and vice versa. For these reasons property market price trends are often quantified not by using capital values but by yields. A lower yield means that the price paid for a property is increasing for the rental income stream being purchased.

In general a lowering of yields across a country's property market means that the differences between yields for different sectors (e.g. shops and offices) becomes more compressed. As Chapter 3 demonstrates, it is useful indicator of a property boom. Table 4.2 uses end of year 'All-Property Yields' from the MSCI Multinational Digest to illustrate the trends in the boom years prior to the GFC. Year-end yields are used because for most countries quarterly data is not available, but inevitably they do not necessarily show the total peak to trough compression, for example in the United Kingdom, where yields bottomed out in mid-2007 and increased slightly by the end of the year. Despite these difficulties the data demonstrate the general downward trends in

Table 4.2 Yield compression from the end of 2000 to end of 2007.

Country	Yield compression 2000 to 2007 (bps)*
Australia	99
Canada	242
Denmark	146
France	80
Germany	26
Ireland	172
Netherlands	100
Norway	171
South Africa	391
United Kingdom	158
United States	250

Source: MSCI/IPD (2014c).
*100 bps (basic points) = 1% change in yield.

yields over the period 2000–2007 across most Western economies. What is particularly interesting here is that this yield compression was not limited to the more mature property markets of the United Kingdom, the United States and Ireland. Emerging markets such as South Africa also experienced a strong increase in values over this period, as did Canada. German yields hardly moved, again a probable consequence of valuation approaches in that country.

In summary, global property markets have become increasingly synchronized but trends are to a degree mediated by local market conditions and practices. The upturn in Western economies from the mid-1990s was mirrored by rising house prices and a commercial property boom in the noughties stimulated by an increase in demand for space leading to rising values as property yields fell. The United Kingdom was clearly part of this global movement and events. Trends in the United Kingdom up to the point that values began to fall in mid-2007 are now considered in more detail and placed in the longer term context of the nation's economy and property market behaviour.

Market Trends in the Property Boom – Was Something Different this Time?

In turning our attention to the events and trends that comprised the anatomy of the commercial property boom in the United Kingdom, we also ask the question 'Was anything different this time?'. There were five or so years from 2002 of a commercial property bull market, although the market had been experiencing capital value growth more or less since the mid-1990s. The period was typified by increasing transaction volumes, increased bank lending into property, increasing investment, all driven by improving total returns. There was a continuing perception that property returns would continue to deliver favourable (or stronger) returns compared with other asset classes, and towards the end of that period there was an over-optimistic expectation of rental value growth. These are now considered in detail.

The bare facts are that between December 2001 and the peak in capital values in June 2007, commercial property values increased by 53% while rents improved by only 8.2% (MSCI/IPD, 2014b). Interestingly, rents actually peaked in September 2008 at 10.9% higher than in December 2001 but still well below the growth seen in capital values and a full 15 months later than the peak in capital values growth. This inevitably raises questions about the fundamentals of the boom.

In a rational and efficient market, long-term capital growth ought to be determined mainly by rental value growth and pricing by the income streams generated by the investment. If we compare indices of the long-term pattern of commercial property capital and rental growth back to 1975, given in Figure 4.4, we see that this has been largely true over the last 40 or so years. Trends in rental value growth have been mostly matched by similar trends in capital value growth with capital values leading, presumably by investors anticipating rental value growth. *Clearly though, something different was happening over the period 2002 to 2007.* Over this period capital value growth gradually outstripped rental value growth and pricing appeared not to be determined by property fundamentals. There had been at least one period prior to that when there was an imbalance between rental growth and capital growth (over the period 1977 to 1986) but there had never been such a sharp difference or so great a disconnect as seen between 2002 and 2007.

In order to understand more about what was happening over this period it is useful to breakdown the components of capital growth and to look at this in the context of longer term trends. Figure 4.5 breaks down capital growth by yield impact and rental growth from 1981 as calculated by MSCI. There are other ways of undertaking this calculation. Yield impact here measures the effect of yield change alone on capital growth. It is calculated periodically by MSCI in their indices as the ratio of the period-start to period-end yield with the sign reversed, so that a rise in yields is shown as a negative impact and vice versa (MSCI, 2014). Figure 4.5 includes the residual term from the

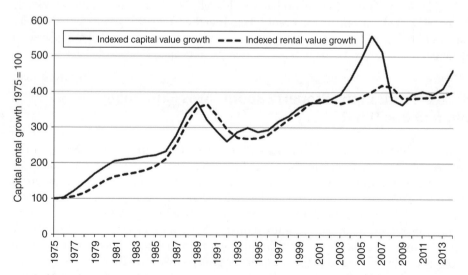

Figure 4.4 Long-term capital and rental value growth patterns 1975–2015. *Source:* MSCI/IPD (2014a). Reproduced with permission.

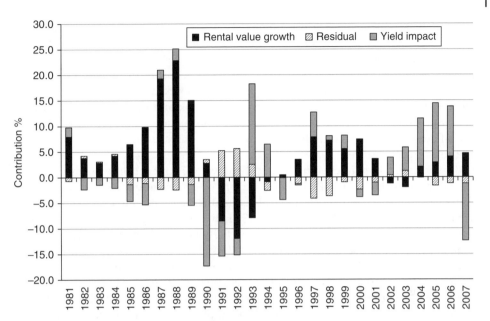

Figure 4.5 Annual contributions to capital growth 1981–2007. *Source:* MSCI/IPD (2014a). Reproduced with permission.

index. In the analysis of capital growth, the residual is that part of the change in value that is not attributable to either rental value growth or yield impact.

Approaching capital value changes in this way highlights starkly the relationship between rental value growth, which has traditionally driven capital value growth, and capital value growth overall, and it illustrates how post-2001 rental value growth was not the main driver of capital growth. From 2002 to 2007 capital growth was dominated by yield impact. In general, the behaviour after 2001 was completely different from that in the years 1981 to 2001 where, apart from the year 1990 and the period 1992/1993, capital growth could be mainly attributed to rental growth, as one might expect in a rational market. It suggests some kind of structural shift in the market that can be explained by the increasing attractiveness of commercial property as an investment driving yields down and values up. Baum (2015) also notes that some extreme market movements have been strongly yield driven, in particular over the periods 1973–1974, 1993–1994 and of course the period post 2002.

The evidence supports some kind of structural shift over this period. The five-year period of the boom was heavily influenced by exceptionally high liquidity in world financial markets. But from the early 2000s trends in property investment mirrored, and were shaped by, conditions in other investment markets (CBRE, 2008). The investment landscape was changing. The dot-com bubble that characterized much of the previous decade was well and truly burst (see Chapter 3). Equity markets across the developed world tumbled over the period 2000/2003. Many company dividends were cut, hitting the incomes of private investors, insurance funds and pension funds alike.

The challenges facing investors to maintain a high level of income explain to some extent the way that many turned to property. Returns from other established asset classes fell as central banks cut interest rates to very low levels. At the same time, high volumes of savings in the world economy attempted to secure the highest possible returns and what can be described as a 'hunt for yield' developed which pushed down bond yields. This global 'hunt for yield' by investors pushed values up in a range of markets as money chased alternative investments capable of delivering a higher return, including emerging market debt, corporate bonds and property. Investors in effect, as Chapter 3 notes, were accepting a lower risk premium than the (property) market previously endorsed. It was based on the expectation that low interest rates, low inflation and importantly higher returns and increases in capital values would continue into the future.

What is particularly interesting is that there were significant differences in performance between the main UK property sectors over the period. This is reflected in Figure 4.6, Figure 4.7 and Figure 4.8, which quantify indexed capital value growth and rental value growth from 2000 using the MSCI Quarterly Index for the three main sectors: retail, offices and industrial. Retail property showed the largest increases in capital value between December 2001 and June 2007 of 68.5% compared with 36.9% for the office sector and 43.8% for the industrial sector (MSCI/IPD, 2014b). What is perhaps more remarkable is that rents in the office sector actually *fell* according to this index by 3.6% over this period compared with increases in the retail and industrial sectors of 18.8% and 5.6% respectively. While clearly all of the sectors considered showed a significant degree of disconnect, offices showed the greatest degree of misalignment of fundamentals in the sense that rents were falling as capital values were increasing! Offices also come late to the party, with capital values actually falling over the year to December 2003 before levelling off and then starting to rise from early 2004.

The commercial property boom was therefore not uniform and there were significant variations across sectors. Although the boom can be traced back to the mid-1990s the disconnect between capital and rental value growth only started in 2002 as property was seen in a more favourable light with the ramifications of the dot-com bubble

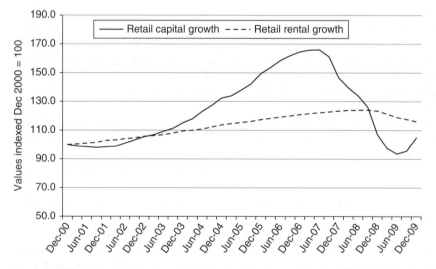

Figure 4.6 Quarterly capital and rental value growth in the retail sector 2000–2009. *Source:* MSCI/IPD (2014b). Reproduced with permission.

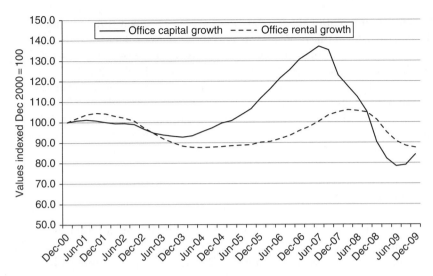

Figure 4.7 Quarterly capital and rental value growth in the office sector 2000–2009. *Source:* MSCI/IPD (2014b). Reproduced with permission.

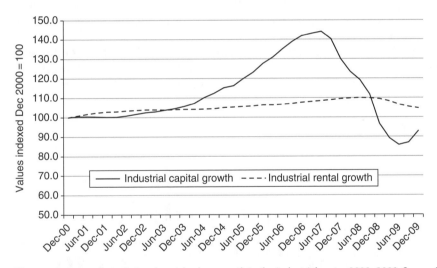

Figure 4.8 Quarterly capital and rental value growth in the industrial sector 2000–2009. *Source:* MSCI/IPD (2014b). Reproduced with permission.

debacle. It was also supported by lower interest rates (see Chapter 3). The boom gathered pace from 2004, but there were signs that the market had begun to correct before the onset of the GFC. Overall commercial property capital values were still increasing up to June 2007, but quarterly growth had slowed from 4.6% in Q4 2006 to 1% in Q2 2007.

It was at this point that the fallout from the sub-prime crisis was emerging as the mortgage-backed bonds issued by banks became impossible to sell (mainly to other banks in the wholesale market) as explained in Chapter 1. There was a consequent loss of bank liquidity as international wholesale markets closed down from August 2007. The first British casualty of this problem was the Northern Rock Bank; its difficulties in refinancing its bonds led to the bank seeking support from the Bank of England. The uncertainty this created resulted in the first run on a British bank since 1878. Queues formed outside its branches as investors sought to retrieve their funds on 14 September 2007. After the Bank of England provided a loan/temporary guarantees and failed in its attempts to sell the stricken bank it was nationalized in January 2008 (Jones, 2012b). The financial storm clouds were gathering. The end to the commercial property boom came in the third quarter of 2007 when capital growth turned negative.

UK Investment Trends

The renewed attractiveness of commercial property as an investment asset class at the beginning of the millennium was reflected in the weight of money being invested in the property market as discussed in Chapter 3. We now look at the time path of the expansion in these funds. A good indicator of these investment trends is net investment on a quarterly basis by financial institutions, as measured by the MSCI /IPD database. As Figure 4.9 demonstrates, net investment by these institutions was particularly strong from late 2003/early 2004 through to quarter four of 2006, when it peaked at £3.895 billion. This period is the height of the boom, and as investment fell away so did the rise in capital values.

The pattern shown in Figure 4.9 also demonstrates the cyclical nature of property capital flows and shows that in the years from early 2004 net institutional investment was strongly positive and stayed that way well into the first half of 2007. Net investment

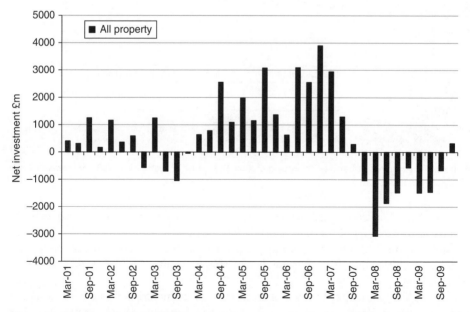

Figure 4.9 Net quarterly institutional investment into commercial property, 2001–2009. *Source:* MSCI/IPD (2014b). Reproduced with permission.

was still positive at the end of Q3 2007, by which time there were clear indications of the beginnings of financial turmoil. This continuing confidence on the part of financial institutions was echoed in the *Financial Times*, which was reporting in July 2007 that the American bank, Citigroup, stated it was 'still dancing', but added that 'the party would end at some point but there was *so much liquidity* at the moment, it would not be disrupted by the turmoil in the US sub-prime mortgage market' (Nakamoto and Wighton, 2007). It was not until the fourth quarter of 2007 that net institutional investment became negative.

Again there were granular differences between the main property sectors, as shown in Figure 4.10. From December 2003 to September 2005 the net institutional investment was dominated by the retail sector but then investment switched predominantly into offices until June 2007. This pattern pretty much reflected the total returns derived from the respective sectors. Retail property showed by far the better returns over the three years 2002/3/4 while offices achieved the better returns in the subsequent two years. Post 2007 the large flows into the office sector were quickly reversed and net disinvestment was subsequently strongest in this sector. Interestingly investment in the retail sector also came back strongly in late 2009 and was the first sector to do so.

The analysis so far has focused only on net institutional investment by considering flows into and out of the MSCI database. Jones, Livingstone and Dunse (2016) decompose these net statistics, and their indices of the real value of sales and purchases based on 1981 as 100 are reported in Figure 4.11 and Figure 4.12. These graphs show the dramatic rise in both the real value of sales and purchases to unprecedented levels in the boom. It demonstrates the sudden rise in market transactions by institutions in the heat of the boom. This finding is endorsed by examining a more broad-based alternative data source, Property Data, based on property transactions involving a wider range of investors, notably from outside the United Kingdom. The Property Data database also suggests a substantial rise in the value of transactions volumes as

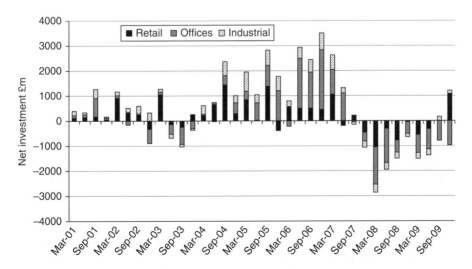

Figure 4.10 Net quarterly institutional investment in the UK property sectors, 2001–2009.
Source: MSCI/IPD (2014b). Reproduced with permission.

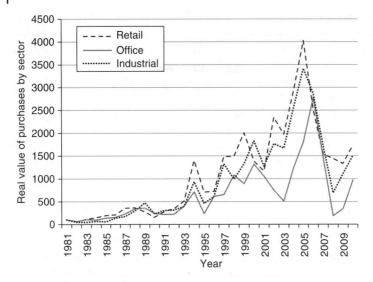

Figure 4.11 Indices of the annual real value of institutional purchases by property sector 1981–2010. *Source:* Jones, Livingstone and Dunse (2016). Reproduced with permission of Taylor & Francis. Figures deflated by the Retail Price Index.

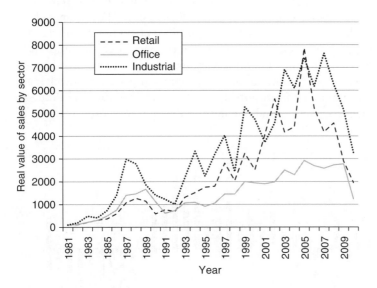

Figure 4.12 Indices of the annual real value of institutional sales by property sector 1981–2010. *Source:* Jones, Livingstone and Dunse (2016). Reproduced with permission of Taylor & Francis. Figures deflated by the Retail Price Index.

the boom accelerated. While this data should be heavily caveated because the data set itself was expanding, the transactions recorded *doubled* in value between 2002 and 2006, as shown in Figure 4.13.

Property Data enables the identification of investor types in transactions, while net investment overall in this transactions database is zero (total purchases equal

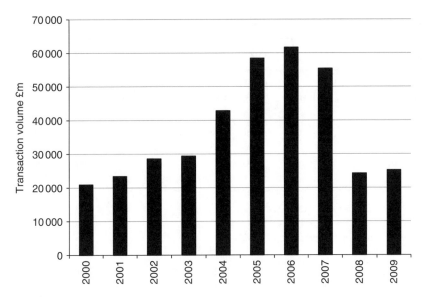

Figure 4.13 Value of commercial property transaction volumes, 2000–2009. *Source:* Reproduced with permission of Property Data.

total sales). The Property Data investor classification used in Table 4.3 and Table 4.4 is as follows:

- *Institutions* — non-bank financial institutions are defined to include pension funds, insurance companies, unit trusts, property unit trusts and limited partnerships;
- *Property Companies* — including listed under Real Estate on the London Stock Exchange, the Alternative Investment Market (AIM) and the Off Exchange (OFEX), and unlisted (non-quoted UK registered companies);
- *Overseas Investors*;
- *Private Investors* — including private syndicates;
- *Other, including banks* — banking organizations that have taken an equity interest in a property investment;
- *Occupiers*.

Looking at these different types of investors, property companies were the largest purchasers of commercial property over the boom but they were also net disinvestors over the period (see Table 4.3 and Table 4.4). This fact reinforces the observation that transaction activity (as they must have been selling too) increased substantially during the boom. In line with the MSCI/IPD data, according to Property Data the institutions increased their purchases from 2003 until a peak in 2006 (property companies a year earlier). It was overseas investors who continued to expand their sales through 2007 and help sustain the boom when there were the indications of a credit crisis looming.

Foreign purchases increased threefold in the database between 2002 and 2007, and overseas investors were the most significant net investors over this period. This was part of a long-term trend, with much of this investment focused on London. European and global cross-border investment had been increasing in popularity from the 1980s and throughout the 1990s. So, for example, in the City of London foreign ownership

Table 4.3 Purchases by type of investor, 2002–2007 (£m).

Investor type	2002	2003	2004	2005	2006	2007
UK Institutions	7671	5692	10664	14534	15441	10159
Property Companies (listed and unlisted)	9855	10034	13129	17866	16968	15259
Overseas investors	5820	8307	10423	17105	18262	19566
Private individuals	3514	3617	4184	4776	5971	5986
Occupiers	668	617	1322	1340	1422	1398
Other banks and institutions	1050	1107	3137	2696	3658	3055
Total purchases	28581	29376	42861	58421	61654	55425

Source: Property Data.

Table 4.4 Net investment (£m) by investor type, 2002–2007.

Investor type	2002	2003	2004	2005	2006	2007
UK Institutions	539	−2982	3949	2669	4980	−1914
Property Companies (listed and unlisted)	−1917	−1618	−6769	−824	−3535	−1567
Overseas investors	1417	3956	3746	5947	3822	11816
Private individuals	2503	2773	2314	599	1271	1547
Occupiers	−2984	−1773	−3364	−6938	−4534	−6379
Other banks and institutions	442	−356	124	−1453	−2004	−3503
Net investment	0	0	0	0	0	0

Source: Property Data.

increased from 10% in the mid-1980s to over 50% by 2011 (Lizieri, Reinhartand Baum, 2011). This investment was driven by a number of factors including the lack of product in their own home countries and investors looking to invest internationally. London was seen as a safe haven in which to invest. Examples include Middle East foreign sovereign wealth funds such as the Abu Dhabi Investment Authority and pension funds from around the world (see Baum, 2015). Although much of this investment was London-centric the scale of foreign investment emphasizes the sheer weight of money being invested in commercial property at the height of the boom with inevitable consequences on values.

Overall these investment patterns not only reflect the weight of money going into the commercial property market but also the pressure to make short-term returns as the momentum of the boom quickened. Investment fund managers were looking at buying and selling opportunities, as noted in Chapter 3, to enhance returns and to rebalance portfolios where prices allowed. It is probable that the high values, especially at the peak of boom, encouraged owners to take opportunities to sell to make (excess) profits and occupiers to take lucrative sale and lease back deals from a variety of investors. Many of these sales were to foreign buyers.

All of this raises the question of whether ultimately pricing in the market was being strongly influenced by overseas investors and the property companies simply because of the sheer volume of transactions activity being undertaken relative to the other main

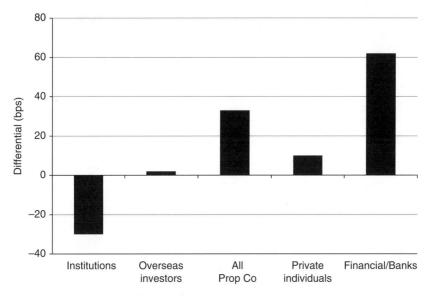

Figure 4.14 Weighted average yield of property purchased by investors compared to the market average in 2006. *Source:* Reproduced with permission of Property Data.

investor types. The evidence from Property Data does not really support this this view. Figure 4.14 plots the differential average weighted yield of purchases for various investor types compared with the all market average weighted yield in 2006 – at the height of the market. The data suggest that the institutions on average were paying lower yields (higher prices) than other investors (possibly a function of the higher quality properties they tend to invest in), but in any case the spread between the highest and lowest yield differential was only just less than 1%, not enough to support the view that certain investor types were driving the market. It suggests that weight of money across the board was causing yields to fall.

The Rise of the Small Investor

Our story so far has looked at broad investment trends. As part of this story we noted how there was a renewed attractiveness to commercial property as an investment asset class at the beginning of the millennium. This was reflected in the weight of money being invested in the property market. This increase was not simply in the money coming into property investment as a result of large institutions and overseas investors moving money into the asset class in the expectation of higher returns and better yields. It was also because property investment became more accessible to the small investors as explained in Chapter 2. To recap, the early 2000s were characterized by changes in the way that small investors regarded commercial property and in the way that property-linked products were created and marketed to this group of investors, and we now turn our attention to the changes that were occurring in this regard.

The number of property funds offered to small investors increased dramatically, from only 5 in 2003 to 34 by the end of 2007 (Investment Management Association, 2010). This ultimately gave small investors indirect access to property investments with some

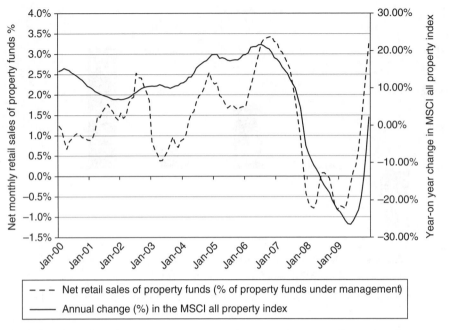

Figure 4.15 Patterns in retail sales of property fund units to investors and commercial property values, 2000–2009. *Source:* Investment Association (2016), MSCI/IPD (2014a). Reproduced with permission.

(relatively small) minimum investment requirements depending on the jurisdiction and fund. With the increasing number of these so-called retail funds (units in these funds sold to individual investors often through investment dealers, independent financial advisors (IFAs) and in open market transactions) came an increasing level of investment by small investors into property in the boom years. By 2006 sales into this type of investment had reached a record annual figure of £3.6 billion, or 3% of the total assets of UK investment funds. By the end of 2007 the total funds under management in retail property funds had reached £12.5 billion (Investment Association, 2016).

Trends in these sales of units in these funds through the likes of the IFAs from the turn of the century to the end of 2008 are shown in Figure 4.15. The level of knowledge these small investors had of the risks of investing in commercial property was probably limited. The chart demonstrates how sales of units into property retail funds more or less tracked the improving total returns coming from commercial property in the early years of this century as reflected in the MSCI/IPD All Property index. Net sales to these retail funds grow consistently through the boom and rose most in 2006.

Lending To Commercial Property in the United Kingdom

At the millennium, the UK economy was almost midway through its long growth phase. Figures from the Building Societies Association show that gross annual lending on residential property in the United Kingdom rose from £221 billion in 2002 to £363 billion at the peak of the housing market in 2007, an increase of 64% in the course of five years

(Building Societies Association, 2008). The outstanding mortgage balance showed an even greater rise – from £675 billion in 2002 to £1.225 trillion in 2007 – an increase of 81%.

In a similar vein, lending on commercial property was just at the beginning of a major growth spurt, as Chapter 3 details. The relatively low interest rates at the beginning of the noughties and the availability of such finance contributed to the demand for these loans at the initial stages of the boom. Low bank lending margins charged by the banks (the difference between the interest a bank pays on deposits and the interest it charges on loans) were an additional factor. The dynamics and logic of bank lending during the property boom are considered in Chapter 6.

It is useful to briefly restate here the vital statistics of this surge in lending as the dramatic increase in debt was primarily used to purchase commercial property. The aggregate value of outstanding debt secured by commercial property increased from £49.9 billion in 1999 to around £250 billion by 2008, when it peaked (Maxted and Porter, 2014). Over the period 2002 to 2007 the annual value of new loans increased from £24.2 billion to £83.3 billion as property became increasingly attractive as an asset class, an increase of nearly 245%! The value of new loans, however, declined rapidly in 2008 with the onset of the GFC.

The peak value of the issue of loans is in 2007, and in this year 52% (around £43 bn) of the gross annual lending was attributable to new loans proper, that is not to loan extensions. Comparing this to the level of annual investment in that year of around £55.43 billion, noted earlier, it suggests that at the summit of the boom around 77% of the total value of transactions were debt financed. Within the context of the boom this 77% debt to value of transactions figure in 2007 represents a step up from the previous years of around 60% and 69% in 2005 and 2006 respectively. There is therefore a clear pattern of increased gearing with higher and higher loan-to-value ratios through the build-up of the boom, and indeed the gearing within new loans increases by more than a quarter between 2005 and 2007.

This vast increase in commercial property lending during the boom reflected the fact that the banks saw it as very lucrative and relatively safe (see Chapter 6) while borrowing was very attractive to investors. First, property investment was arguably often self-financing, as explained in Chapter 3. Second, the fact that commercial property was delivering the strong performance noted above meant that highly geared investors could make astonishingly high returns using readily available debt finance (again see Chapter 3 for quantification). No wonder so many investors were attracted to this new version of easy money.

A Property Boom in an Irrational Market

Our earlier discussions of property market dynamics have suggested clear evidence of irrational behaviour in the property market from 2002 to 2007 with a divergence from pricing fundamentals evidenced by the disconnect between capital and rental value growth. In other words there was a potential investment bubble. In order to understand and quantify this divergence it is important to comprehend the fundamentals of pricing in the marketplace. This involves studying exactly what is being priced and understanding the distinctions between the *price*, *value* and *worth* of an investment. The Royal

Institution of Chartered Surveyors published a paper on this distinction as far back as 1997 (Royal Institution of Chartered Surveyors and Investment Property Forum, 1997), and it is pertinent to consider the differences between these concepts here. In what follows we presume a basic understanding of algebra and financial mathematics that can be found in a standard textbook on investment.

In simple terms *worth* is a specific investor's perception of the capital sum that they would be prepared to pay (or accept) for the stream of financial benefits which they expect to be produced in the future by the investment. Worth can be expressed as the present value of future cash flows calculated using a discounted cash flow (DCF) with a discount rate which is the investor's required rate of return. *Price* is the actual observable exchange price in the open market, while *value* is an estimate of the price that would be achieved if the property were to be sold in the market. Value is calculated using DCF but this time with a discount rate which is the market discount rate. It is useful to note that

- Worth is the value in use.
- Open market value can be considered as the most usual manifestation of value in exchange.
- Price/value is the outcome of the interplay of the respective values in the different uses, (i.e. 'worths') of *actual* market makers.

In practice, in an open and free market there will be no transaction if

$$Value\ in\ use/worth\ (vendor) > value\ in\ use\ (purchaser).$$

In addition, a potential purchaser will not deal where

$$Price > value\ in\ use\ (purchaser).$$

These principles are fundamentally important when considering the purchase/sale decision, as is the way in which each of these interests is assessed. Generally speaking the investors' target rate of return is related to a risk-free rate from a secure investment plus a risk premium (see Chapter 1).

$$The\ required\ rate\ of\ return\ (\%) = Risk\text{-}free\ rate\ (\%) + Risk\ premium\ (\%) \quad (4.1)$$

Clearly, an investor's required rate of return may not match the market rate of return (based for example on market yields). This distinction can be used to identify mispricing in the market or to create decision rules as to whether an investor should or should not purchase/sell an investment at a given price. So, for example, simple decision rules can be derived from a comparison of a property's initial yield (see Chapter 1) with an investor's required return or the worth to the investor with its price. Required rates of return (r_p) are judgements based on the investor's attitude to risk. For example an investor may want a target rate of return that is at least equivalent to the Retail Price Index (inflation) over a defined period. This is not necessarily (almost certainly not?) the market rate of return.

A judgement of whether pricing is right for the investor or not may be made on the basis of whether the initial yield is higher or lower than this rate of return. This can be explained using some straightforward, basic assumptions. In simple terms, the initial yield (k) on a property is a function of the total required rate of return less the net growth in income which is expected (g), that is:

$$k = r_p - g \qquad (4.2)$$

If this condition does not hold then the asset is mispriced as far as the investor is concerned.

Given this condition and given that we have already noted that an investor's required rate of return (r_p) is related to the risk-free rate and the risk premium for property then substituting for r_p in Equation 4.2 we have

$$k = r_f + p - g \qquad (4.3)$$

where r_f represents the risk-free rate and p the risk premium. As Chapter 1 explains, the risk-free rate is usually taken as the redemption yield on a 10-year government issued bond (gilt). If we allow for depreciation (d), this will reduce future net income growth, and the equation becomes

$$k = r_f + p - g + d \qquad (4.4)$$

The allowance for rental growth, g, is the expected average rental growth in perpetuity for continuously new property. Its importance is often underestimated and is as follows:

- growth NOT arising from yield shift as the model assumes that the property is rack-rented (rent is reviewed every year to market level) and there is no expectation of yield change;
- representative of the investor's *expectations* for future rental growth (typically using their own forecasts); and
- given that rental growth will fluctuate it must be considered as an average growth rate and will be strongly influenced by the rate of growth expected in the near future (3–5years).

The allowance for depreciation, d, is the expected average rate of depreciation in perpetuity.

The difference between the risk-free rate of return defined as the redemption yield on government bond (gilt) yields and (All) property initial yields is often referred to as the 'yield gap'. The determinants of the yield gap can be gleaned by rearranging Equation 4.4 as follows:

$$p = k - r_f + g - d \qquad (4.5)$$

From Equation 4.5 the yield gap is dependent on expected rental growth and the risk premium (and expected depreciation, although this can be seen as part of the risk premium). Figure 4.16 plots the relationship between the yield gap and gilt and property yields through the noughties. The falling yield gap through to mid-2007 cannot be explained by substantial rising rental growth (noted above) as this was modest, so it must be the result of investors' perspective of the falling risk premium.

Figure 4.16 is important in as much as it clearly demonstrates the irrational nature of property markets over the period 2003 to 2007. Gilt yields remained steady over this period, while property yields fell, as did the yield gap, which became negative in late 2006. This clearly should have set off warning bells in the market, but despite this money

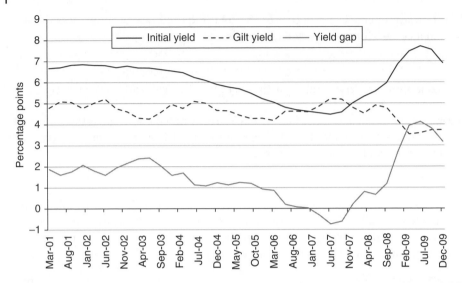

Figure 4.16 Yield gap between yields on gilts* and commercial property, 2001–2009. *Source:* MSCI/
IPD (2014b) and ONS (2016). Reproduced with permission.
*Redemption yield on 10-year government bonds.

continued to be invested in property. The question is why, and to answer this we must
not forget the part that rental growth expectations play in determining risk premium.

We can highlight the irrational behaviour of the market during this period best by
considering what attitudes were just before the GFC erupted. The yield gap between
initial yield and the risk-free rate in June 2007 was negative 0.73 percentage points.
However, at that time the rental growth assumption was for growth of 2.7% over the
next three years (Investment Property Forum, 2007). If we assume a depreciation rate
of 1% per annum, then the implied risk premium at that time based on the yield gap
was a little under 1%. Given that the long-term historic risk premium on property was
assumed to be around 3% (see Chapter 1), although there might have been some concern that the implied risk premium was low, it was still apparently positive. However,
this choice was based on a robust assumption on future rental growth. But these
expectations were far too generous. Over the subsequent three years rents actually
FELL by on average 1.5% per annum. The reality in mid-2007 was that the risk premium was probably nearer -3.2%, and much closer to the reality of what happened in
the markets late 2007/2008! While the risk premium cannot be measured directly, the
negative yield gap suggests at that point it could have been around 6 percentage points
adrift of the long-term average.

The consequence of over-optimism was the growing disconnect between capital
value growth and rental value growth discussed earlier. Capital values were yield
driven – that is, they were being driven by the weight of money coming into property
rather than by rental value growth – and discount rates in our pricing model were
clearly not reflecting a rational required rate of return in the expectation that capital
values would continue to rise to meet the shortfall.

This view is supported by two recent pieces of work (Burston and Burrell, 2015
and Jones, Dunse and Cutsforth, 2014). Jones, Dunse and Cutsforth (2014) looked at

the relationship between property yields and government bond yields. Their work detected a number of structural breaks over the period 1985 to 2010. They suggested that one explanation of an apparent structural break that began in 2005 was probably, at least in part, the boom and subsequent bust in property lending and a re-evaluation of the risk premium or of expected rental growth or both. In other words, it could be investors responding particularly to property upturns and downturns differently, for example being (overly) optimistic about rental growth expectations in a 'boom' and (overly) pessimistic about forecasts in the 'bust'. They note that the flip from one to the other could cause a statistical structural break and that it certainly occurred during the credit crunch. As the GFC began to unfold, investors were still projecting substantial rental growth, only for these expectations to be dramatically and swiftly downgraded.

Burston and Burrell (2015) take a statistical route that assesses the boom in the context of long-run average returns from property. In particular their study looks at the ratio of current rental income returns to capital value in each year and asks whether it is in line with historic experience. To make this comparison, the historic experience is taken to be a 10-year moving average return adjusted for inflation. This 10-year moving average is a variation of Robert Shiller's 'Cyclically Adjusted Price to Earning Ratio' (CAPE). Shiller (2005) applied this approach to compare short-term movements in share prices with long-term movements in their dividends, with CAPE interpreted as a historic mean benchmark to assess fair value. Burston and Burrell (2015) conclude that there was a lengthy period of overvaluation from the late 1990s, *and more significantly so between 2005 and 2007*. In particular during the period 2004 to 2008 property was priced well above fair value.

Overall the evidence from a number of different perspectives agrees that in the heat of the boom, certainly between 2005 and 2007, capital values of commercial property rose well beyond what could be justified by any realistic projections of rental growth. The occurrence of these magnifying speculative effects within the property market is consistent with Shiller's (2005) view on the dynamics of bubbles based on 'irrational exuberance', a term first coined by Alan Greenspan, chairman of the US Federal Reserve Bank in 1996. Shiller (2005, p. 1) notes that 'this term has become a useful name for the kind of social phenomenon … that has happened again and again in history, when markets have been bid up to unusually high and unsustainable levels under the influence of market psychology'. He sees rational causes of this 'irrational exuberance' whereby initial exogenous shocks instigate price increases that in turn encourage further investment demand through adaptive expectations that keep projecting forward capital growth.

In this case, his ideas are consistent with a shock caused by the combination of the dot-com bubble burst and low global interest rates instigating the exaggeration of an existing cyclical upturn. The last stages of the boom can therefore be seen as a bubble, normally defined as a substantial price rise in (financial) asset(s) that is not ultimately sustainable. Usually a bubble is seen to burst when the overblown expectations of future income rewards do not materialize, and with ultimately capital values recognized as overvalued they decline spectacularly. In the boom of the noughties it can be argued that the bubble did not fully follow its full course but was shot down prematurely by the exogenous shock of the GFC. However, this is debatable, and there were certainly signs in 2006 that the market was turning.

Summary and Conclusions

The origins of the commercial property boom can be seen in the upswing in the global economy from the mid-1990s on. As each national economy expanded, the demand for commercial property increased, pushing rents and capital values up (yields fell). Economic growth led not only to a strong increase in the commercial market values but also to a surge in house prices in the noughties.

These phenomena were seen across the globe as many Western countries experienced a long, almost synchronized, and sustained period of positive economic performance stretching over a decade. The scale of the property boom varied with local national market conditions; an extreme was Ireland, where the capital values of commercial properties rose by 70%. In comparison the booms in the United Kingdom and United States were less severe but still historically significant with capital growth of just over 50% and almost 40% respectively.

The boom was not simply a manifestation of a positive macroeconomic environment but also the result of the renewed attractiveness of commercial property as an investment class. At the beginning of the millennium the collapse of the dot-com bubble had skewed investors away from shares, and with interest rates and gilt yields low they turned to the perceived more reliable returns from commercial property. This phenomenon occurred at a global level as significant international investment flows focused on real estate, and the United Kingdom, for example, saw a surge of foreign investors buying commercial property – in London in particular.

Further factors to the large flow of money into property in the United Kingdom at this time were changes in the way that small investors regarded commercial property and in the way that property-linked products were created and marketed to this group of investors. Independent financial advisors to small investors became key wealth managers, yet arguably they did not have the expertise to understand property investment. The number of property funds designed for small investors increased dramatically during the early to mid-part of the decade, giving them access to commercial property investments for the first time. Overall money therefore poured into commercial property, and the inflow was particularly strong from 2003 through to 2006. It was supported by bank lending that was readily available, not only at low interest rates and attractive margins but also with increasingly generous loan-to-value ratios. Investment became more and more highly geared so that returns were magnified while the market was on an upward trajectory encouraging even more investment.

The investment flows inevitably meant capital values rose as yields fell. This led to yield compression across the commercial market as the differences in yields between property types became much smaller. The rising capital values meant that high returns were recorded; it encouraged further investment and contributed to a bandwagon effect. Such herd behaviour was massively important to the operation of the market at this time. But it is also useful to reflect on the words of Scottish journalist Charles Mackay ([1841] 2003, p. viii), who stated, 'Men, it has been well said, think in herds ... they go mad in herds, while they only recover their senses slowly, and one by one'.

The crux of the long-term problem that was building up over this period was that while rental growth was continuing with macroeconomic expansion it was not rising by some way as fast as capital values were. This in turn meant that there was a market disconnect seen between capital value growth and rental value growth. This undoubtedly occurred because the money coming into property had to be invested. To a degree this was masked by the nature of some of the investment vehicles, for example the true gearing of some of the property funds was perhaps opaque. Such wider practices inherent in increasingly deregulated markets prompted Elliot and Atkinson (2008, p. 5) to reflect on the free market economy that promised

> a 'transparent' future in which all costs and prices would be clearly laid out, allowing people to make informed choices in their lives. They have delivered a world of bizarre, occult financial knowledge, one in which everything from the true cost of a mobile phone package to the real value of billions pounds worth of securitised debt is impossible to gauge.

In the United Kingdom, not only was the boom represented by rising capital values but the period was exemplified by a dramatic increase in transaction volumes as investors bought and sold as an opportunity based short-term investment culture took hold. Investment was all driven by improving total returns. The underlying basic economics became lost as there was a continuing perception that property returns would continue to be higher than other types of assets. At best investment behaviour can be said to have presumed an over-optimistic expectation of rental value growth.

In a rational market long-term capital growth ought to be determined mainly by rental value growth and pricing by the income streams generated by the investment. This has been generally true over the bulk of the last 40 or so years. However, the early years of the new millennium were heavily influenced by the exceptionally high liquidity in world financial markets and trends in property investment mirrored, and they were shaped by conditions in other investment markets. A global 'hunt for yield' and the sheer weight of investment money coming into the property market drove yields down and capital values up, and the behaviour generally post 2001 was completely different from that in the years 1981 to 2001. Whereas pre-2002 capital growth could be mainly attributed to rental growth, as one might expect in a rational market, from 2002 it was yield driven, and the evidence is that trends were heavily influenced by behaviour in a UK market that had become increasingly irrational.

Irrational behaviour contributed to a market that was detached from fundamental pricing, arguably a bubble that was ultimately unstable. The flow of cheap money into commercial property assets in the four to five years leading up to the GFC ultimately affected the overall stability of the property market system, and when the financial downturn came it exacerbated the falls in values experienced. It can be argued that a basic ignorance of property market behaviour on the part of some investors contributed both to the large flow of money into property in the boom years, distorting the fundamental relationship between rental value growth and capital valued growth, and to the large outflows of capital when the crunch came.

This analysis puts speculative investment flows (and their interaction with other financial markets) at the heart of shaping the scale and timing of the boom. A long-term global economic upturn was a prerequisite but only a platform for the boom. The increasing availability of investment finance magnified the boom. The combination of readily available finance and adaptive expectations that projected continuing rises in capital values fits very well into the bubble model set out by Shiller (2005). The eventual and almost certain downfall and its ramifications are considered in Chapter 5.

5

The Global Financial Crisis and its Impact on Commercial Property

The US sub-prime market in the early years of this century was in retrospect a disaster waiting to happen. And yet despite, or perhaps because of, the sophistication of mortgage products together with derivative products such as mortgage-backed bonds it was the action of the most basic of economic tools available to any government, that of raising interest rates, that brought about a major correction in the market. Just as importantly, it caused a significant fall in the value of many of the derivative products that had been created on the back of it. A liquidity crisis resulted and with it a full-scale global credit crunch that would spell the end of many an institution, cost thousands their jobs, forced many out of their homes and usher in a decade of austerity across the world. Commercial real estate performance is closely linked to the overall performance of a nation's economy for both the occupier (rental) and investment markets (see Chapter 3), and this dual susceptibility was amply demonstrated in the period 2007 to 2009 as the global financial crisis (GFC) unfolded. Poorer economic performance and a lack of available credit significantly affected the performance of both investment and occupier markets.

In this chapter we undertake a detailed analysis of the initial causes of the GFC in the sub-prime residential markets in the United States and the timeline of subsequent events. This includes the unravelling of banking liquidity and its impact on lending and ultimately on commercial real estate investment markets globally. Financial deregulation and global economic integration has caused property markets to be influenced by international economic trends and capital flows, as we saw in Chapter 4. In particular, increased harmonization of global economies has resulted in a synchronization of property market behaviour/cycles in many parts of the world. As a consequence many national commercial property markets suffered as a result of the global economic impact of the credit crunch. However, the implications were not universally consistent, mediated by national economic specialisms, property market valuation practices and characteristics, and a country's banks exposure to (worthless) mortgage-backed securities.

The chapter starts by looking at the series of financial events that were to become known as the GFC and examines the scale and timing of the impacts on commercial property markets worldwide. The chapter then focuses on the detailed consequences for the UK property market in the turmoil of the post-2007 bust. It quantifies the fall in capital values across the market. This UK analysis is placed in the context of the dysfunctional market and the irrational behaviour discussed in Chapter 4 and noting the continuing

Property Boom and Banking Bust: The Role of Commercial Lending in the Bankruptcy of Banks,
First Edition. Colin Jones, Stewart Cowe, and Edward Trevillion.
© 2018 John Wiley & Sons Ltd. Published 2018 by John Wiley & Sons Ltd.

mismatch between capital value growth and rental value growth. The chapter also assesses the role of net investment, forced sales and the scarcity of loan finance in reducing the level of transactions and the imperative of falling capital values. Finally, it examines the market decline in value in the context of changing perceptions of property risk.

A Crisis Unfolds

The first evidence that the problems of the US housing market were extending beyond individual house buyers to the banking system occurred in April 2007 when New Century Financial, one of the country's largest sub-prime lenders, filed for bankruptcy protection. It was initially believed that this problem was confined to the company itself, but soon it was realized that New Century was not alone and the problem was spreading to other sub-prime lenders. Even so, the early prognosis was that any fallout could be contained, and indeed, six weeks after New Century's bankruptcy, the chairman of the Federal Reserve, Ben Bernanke, suggested that he didn't believe the growing number of mortgage defaults would seriously harm the economy, and he also noted (prophetically) that banks share significant risks when financing private equity deals (Bernanke, 2007). Facing criticism from members of Congress about lax regulation, Bernanke also promised that the Federal Reserve would do everything possible to crack down on abuses that 'have put millions of homeowners in jeopardy of defaulting on their mortgages'.

Two months later, as the problem spread, Bernanke had to admit that the crisis would cost up to $100 billion. At the time that figure caused investors some concern, but the reality was that the full cost of the crisis was to eventually be significantly higher. Over the summer of 2007 it became clear that mortgage-backed securities, notably bonds, were tarnished because no one knew whether their promised income streams were supported by sub-prime loans or not. And the problem was not just one for the United States as many of the bonds issued by American financial institutions had been bought by banks around the world. Banks across the globe had issued similar bonds, and these too were tainted with the possibility that they also were supported by sub-prime mortgages. In quick succession, many hedge funds and other funds built around these securitized products announced that they were either worthless or that they were required to control those investors wishing to exit.

The first signs of the problem in the United Kingdom came in September 2007, when it was announced that the mortgage bank Northern Rock had been granted emergency financial support from the Bank of England (see Chapter 4). The Northern Rock's problem was not one of sub-prime (or even poor) lending but one of liquidity, where it was unable to obtain funding to replace its maturing funds in the wholesale markets (Jones, 2012b). This was early evidence of the beginnings of a UK credit crunch.

Table 5.1 provides a summary of the immediate stages in the unfolding crisis over 2007–2010, primarily in the United States and United Kingdom. Further detail is given in Chapter 6 and Chapter 7. Global regulators were unprepared for the problem. At first, they acted in a piecemeal fashion, lowering interest rates and injecting money into the money markets, but by December 2007 they had agreed to coordinate policies with more effective results. The year 2007 ended on a dismal note. In a coordinated approach, the Federal Reserve in the United States, the European Central Bank and central banks

Table 5.1 A summary of the key events of the financial crisis in the United Kingdom and United States 2007–2010.

Stage	Timeframe	Description
1: Start of the liquidity crisis	August 2007	Severe liquidity issues affect financial markets after fears over the US sub-prime housing market. Sharply exacerbated by the decision of BNP Paribas to freeze three funds exposed to the stumbling US sub-prime mortgage market. In September the UK bank Northern Rock experiences liquidity problems and has to resort to asking the Bank of England for support.
2: Banks face mounting losses	Autumn 2007	Following the problems in the US sub-prime mortgage market, banks across the world report large losses, weakening their capital positions.
3: Bear Stearns and mounting problems	Spring 2008	Bear Stearns requires emergency funding from the Federal Reserve before being bought by JP Morgan Chase. Central banks continue to provide extra liquidity and a number of UK banks undertake rights issues to bolster their capital positions.
4: Solvency crisis (Lehman Brothers collapses) and near meltdown	September 2008	US bank Lehman Brothers files for bankruptcy sparking by the end of the month a frantic round of consolidation in the global banking sector. Merrill Lynch is taken over by Bank of America, and JP Morgan Chase buys Washington Mutual. In the UK, Halifax/Bank of Scotland is acquired by Lloyds and the Bradford & Bingley mortgage bank is nationalized. The US Government intervenes to prevent American Insurance Group (AIG) collapsing.
5: Emergency support	September 2008 to March 2009	Recapitalization of banks by governments. Additional measures to ensure general financial market liquidity are undertaken by central banks. Governments provide additional guarantees for bank deposits. Financial regulators ban the short selling of shares of financial companies. Monetary policy support, includes a coordinated rate cut by central banks. Fiscal policy support.
6: Partial relapse	January 2009 to March 2009	Renewed concerns about the stability of banks, as macroeconomic conditions worsen, in particular, negative economic growth in many countries including the United Kingdom. Stock markets fall. The concerns prompt second wave of financial support from governments.
7: Slow recovery	April 2009 onwards	Confidence begins to return to financial markets, with asset prices rising aided by central bank support through quantitative easing. Banks continue to repair their balance sheets and seek to increase their capital. The recovery in global stock markets assists their profitability.

Source: Adapted from Edmonds (2010).

of the United Kingdom, Canada and Switzerland announced that they would provide billions in loans in an attempt to lower interest rates and ease the availability of credit (Edmonds, 2010). Notwithstanding that, just before Christmas, as explained in Chapter 1, the credit ratings of several monoline insurers (those companies which insure against the risk of default) were cut. There was a general belief that these insurers had insufficient reserves to settle the expected massive scale of default claims.

The financial news in 2008 remained bleak. On 21 January global stock markets, including London's FTSE 100 index, suffered their biggest falls since 11 September 2001. At the end of that month a major US monoline insurer, MBIA, announced its largest ever three-month loss of $2.3 billion, attributing its problems to its commitment to sub-prime mortgages. In response, the US Federal Reserve chairman, Ben Bernanke, expressed his anxiety about monoline insurers, noting that he was watching developments carefully, 'given the adverse effects that problems of financial guarantors can have on financial markets and the economy' (Guillen, 2012, p. 3).

Despite the granting of government guarantees to depositors, Northern Rock remained in difficulty and the UK government announced its temporary nationalization ('temporary public ownership') in February. In the United States the Federal Reserve attempted to ease banks' liquidity, but despite receiving emergency funding, Bear Stearns, a large US investment bank, was forced to sell to another bank, JP Morgan Chase, in March. In the United Kingdom swathes of mortgage products were being withdrawn, and in April Abbey Bank announced the ending of the country's last remaining 100% mortgage (Guillen, 2012).

The sheer scale of the problem was now beginning to be apparent. In a headline report, the IMF warned that the potential losses from the credit crunch could amount to $1 trillion and that its effects were spreading from the initial sub-prime mortgage assets to commercial property, consumer credit and corporate debt (Stewart, 2008; Edmonds 2010). UK commercial property values had been falling since July 2007, and events later in the year would send values down further.

April saw the gloomiest report on the state of the UK housing market for 30 years and the Royal Bank of Scotland shocked stock markets by announcing a £12 billion rights issue, the largest in UK corporate history. This was a clear signal to global markets that banks' balance sheets were weak from the effects of lower asset values (both loans on commercial and residential property and on the variety of derivative products they had invested in). The action opened the floodgates with UBS Bank (€16 bn), Barclays Bank (£4.5 bn) and HBOS Bank (£4 bn) amongst others joining the equity raising. However, 92% of HBOS's rights issue was left with the underwriters, a stark warning that investors were becoming concerned about the wider picture (Guillen, 2012).

In the United Kingdom, housing market new mortgage approvals fell to a 25-year low, housebuilders announced cutbacks to planned developments and the Nationwide Building Society reported the first annual house price fall for 20 years. By August 2008 the decline in house prices had risen to over 10%. September 2008, however, proved to be one of the most pivotal in financial history. The US government was forced to rescue both Fanny Mae and Freddy Mac, national quasi-public agencies (see Glossary) that held or guaranteed around $5.2 trillion of home mortgage loans at the time. They were put into conservatorship, the rescues ultimately costing the US taxpayer $187.5 billion.

A series of other events in the United States and United Kingdom highlighted the scale of the crisis. In quick succession

- Lehman Brothers Bank announced a huge loss, then filed for Chapter 11 bankruptcy;
- Merrill Lynch Bank agreed to be taken over by Bank of America;

Table 5.2 National annual GDP growth in selected countries 2007–2009.

Country	2007	2008	2009
Global growth	4.3	1.8	−1.7
Australia	3.8	3.7	1.8
Denmark	0.8	−0.7	−5.1
European Union	3.1	0.5	−4.4
Germany	2.3	1.1	−5.6
Ireland	5.5	−2.2	−5.6
Italy	1.5	1.1	−5.5
Korea (Rep)	5.5	2.8	0.7
Netherlands	3.7	1.7	−3.8
Singapore	9.1	1.8	−1.6
United Kingdom	2.6	−0.5	−4.2
United States	1.8	−0.3	−2.8

Source: Adapted from World Bank statistics.

- HBOS Bank was bought by Lloyds Banking Group;
- Royal Bank of Scotland became another major casualty;
- The American Insurance Group (AIG) was saved from total collapse by an $85 billion rescue package from the US Treasury (Guillen, 2012, p. 3).

The list of (mostly) government sponsored rescue packages across the world continued well into October. Few countries were unaffected, and over the course of three weeks there were announcements of major government rescues or stimulus packages in Ireland, the United States, the United Kingdom, Germany, Belgium, Switzerland, Sweden, South Korea and France.

What subsequently became clear was that this recession was global in nature and massive in size, being the most severe recession since the Great Depression in the 1930s. A consequence of globalization was the fact that virtually all major countries felt the chill winds of recession at the same time – the world's first global recession. Table 5.2 lists annual GDP growth for selected national economies over the period 2007 to 2009 inclusive. Global growth moved from 4.3% per annum in 2007 to −1.7% per annum by 2009. Major economies such as the United States, United Kingdom, Germany and France did not escape, but amongst the worst fall in output of the European economies was seen in Ireland, where GDP growth moved from 5.5% in 2007 to -5.6% in 2009. Although most countries worldwide experienced falls in output, some economies escaped, for example Australia and The Republic of Korea maintained positive growth throughout 2007, 2008 and 2009.

The Impact on Global Property Markets

The effects of the credit crisis, which had originated in the residential property market, was felt in the commercial property markets almost immediately since credit began to dry up. Just as most countries participated in the commercial property boom so most were destined to suffer from the bust in some form or other. An overview is provided by the graphs in Figure 5.1, Figure 5.2 and Figure 5.3 for offices. Figure 5.1 shows the rise in UK and Western European office average quarterly yields (and hence fall in capital values) from 2007 to 2009 (Real Capital Analytics, 2015) with the GFC. The rise was much more dramatic in the United Kingdom than Western Europe as a whole. Office yields in the United Kingdom jumped 2.5% over the period from the middle of 2007 to the beginning of 2010 before falling again. There is then a fall of 1% through 2010, but subsequent drops are more muted, and some eight years on from the peak of the boom yields had still not reached the low experienced then.

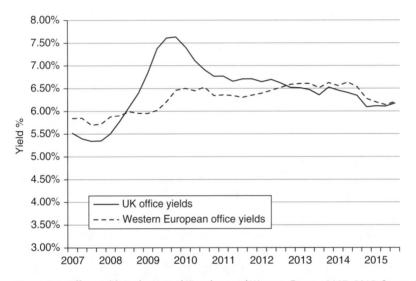

Figure 5.1 Office yields in the United Kingdom and Western Europe 2007–2015. *Source:* Real Capital Analytics (2015). Reproduced with permission.

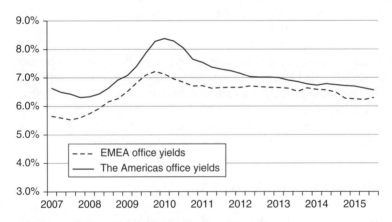

Figure 5.2 Office yields in EMEA* countries and the Americas** 2007–2015. *Source:* Real Capital Analytics (2015). Reproduced with permission.
*European, Mid-Eastern and African.
**North, Central and South America and the Caribbean.

Western Europe (apparently) did not experience anywhere near the same yield shift as UK markets post 2007. This may be a genuine reflection of there being less volatility in some Western European markets, but given the 4.4% fall in economic growth in 2009 in the European Union noted in Table 5.2 it is more likely the result of national valuation practices. These statistics are based on valuations or assessments of yields, and it seems these responded more slowly than actual capital values to the economic downturn in many countries. After a modest increase in yields they remain on a plateau until the middle of 2014. In 2013 the European average yield rises above that of the United Kingdom for the first time since 2008. The European yield pattern as an average also hides considerable variation between countries. Average Irish office yields, for example, experienced a significant increase over the period 2007 to 2012, rising from 3.8% at the end of 2007 to 10.9% by the end of 2012 (MSCI/IPD, 2014c).

Figure 5.2 compares the post-GFC office yield pictures for European, Middle Eastern and African (EMEA) countries and the Americas (North, Central and South America and the Caribbean). This figure emphasizes the global nature of the upward adjustment of yields from 2007. The shift is greater in those of the 'Americas' that are probably dominated by the United States. Finally, yields in the Asia Pacific countries show a very distinctive pattern over the period following the GFC, as shown in Figure 5.3. The immediate impact of the GFC appears less severe than in the United Kingdom and United States with yields only rising by 1 percentage point. This undoubtedly reflects the fact that economies in this region were only moderately affected by the GFC, suffering a pause in general in economic growth rather than a downturn (see Table 5.2).

A greater sense of the bust can be seen by focusing simply on the scale of the decline in capital values from the peak to trough and how long the fall took. Table 5.3 summarizes the falls in capital values in a selection of countries from their respective peaks to their respective troughs, that is, to the point where values began to recover. Capital

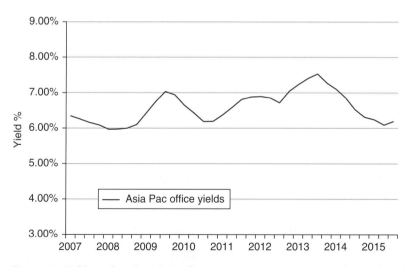

Figure 5.3 Yield trends in the Asia Pacific region 2007–2015.* *Source:* Real Capital Analytics Global Trends Report Q3 2015. Reproduced with permission.
*All parts of Asia (not including the Middle East) as well as Australia, New Zealand, and Pacific islands.

Table 5.3 Peak to trough changes in capital values in selected countries.

Country	Series frequency	Peak to trough years	% Change peak to trough or end of 2013
United Kingdom	Quarterly	Q2 2007 to Q2 2009	42.4
United States	Quarterly	Q4 2007 to Q1 2010	33
Netherlands	Quarterly	Q3 2008 to Q4 2014	20.6
Ireland	Quarterly	Q3 2007 to Q3 2013	67.3
Australia	Annual	2007 to 2009	14.4
Canada	Annual	2007 to 2009	9.2
France	Annual	2007 to 2009	12.5
Germany	Annual	2007 to 2009	5
Italy	Annual	2007 to 2013	13.6
Japan	Annual	2007 to 2012	22.6
Republic of Korea	Annual	No change	NA
South Africa	Annual	No change	NA
Spain	Annual	2007 to 2013	32.7

Source: MSCI/IPD (2014c).

values in the United States and Spain fell by just under a third and in the United Kingdom by 42% from peak to trough. Falls of 20% are not uncommon. The picture is complicated by the fact that the available data is a mixture of quarterly and annual valuations data. Nevertheless, the results suggest that most countries suffered a negative market reaction. There is a group of countries that experienced a relatively short shock over two to three years, whereas some countries take six years or more to recover. This latter group is in the eurozone, including Ireland, which suffered the largest fall of 67.3% from the third quarter of 2007 to the third quarter of 2013. The depth and persistence of the downturn in values in Ireland was quite significantly different to other countries.

Just as in the boom years, the capital values on the way down were mainly driven by these yield shifts rather than by rental value changes (see later for a more detailed discussion in the context of UK markets). Only in the Republic of Ireland is there evidence of a significant reduction in rents accompanying the severe fall in capital values (MSCI/IPD, 2014c). This may explain the greater decline in capital values.

Capital and Rental Values in the United Kingdom Post 2007

The chapter now turns its attention specifically to market response in the United Kingdom in the years of the GFC and its immediate aftershocks. In some ways the period following 2007 was an economic mirror image of the period 2003 to 2007 but events took place over a shorter timescale. Figure 5.4 reprises trends in capital value and rental value growth from December 2000 previously shown in Chapter 4 but extends this out now to December 2014. It emphasizes that while capital values fell through the

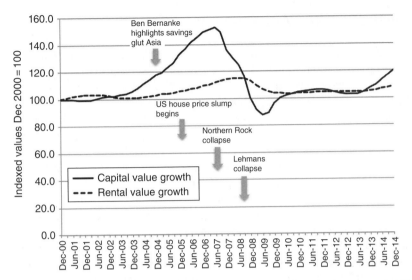

Figure 5.4 Indexed capital value and rental value change in the UK property market 2000–2014. *Source:* MSCI/IPD (2014b) with authors' additions. Reproduced with permission.

GFC, rental growth continued to be positive. The figure also highlights a number of the key events in the progress of the GFC, as points of reference up to when Lehman's Bank failed in September 2008.

There was a 'flip' from investors projecting substantial rental growth and returns at the peak of the boom only for expectations to be dramatically and swiftly downgraded resulting in pessimistic forecasts in this 'bust' period. Thus in May 2007 the Investment Property Forum's consensus industry forecast was suggesting average rental growth over the following five years of 2.8% per annum. By June 2008 the rental growth forecast had fallen to 0.9% per annum (Investment Property Forum, 2009). The respective average total return forecasts were 6% per annum and 5.4% per annum, surprisingly high on both counts. Overall the instability and irrational exuberance in the market in the period 2003 to 2007 was being replaced by perhaps an equally irrational pessimism about where the market could be driven.

From the end of June 2007 until the end of June 2009, when values began to stabilize, average capital values of properties held by financial institutions fell on average by 42.4%. What is interesting when events are superimposed on these trends, however, is that values were increasing even when there were early indications of potential issues in global market trends (as evidenced by warnings of a savings glut in Asia and their potential impact on interest rates and by the slump in house prices in the United States). Presumably this was because of the perception that these problems were too far away to impact on UK commercial markets. Interestingly, though, the market had started to correct before the Northern Rock crisis and, perhaps more interestingly still, there had already been a steep (23.3%) decline in capital values (over half the eventual total decline) by the time of the collapse of Lehman's Bank in September 2008. That rate of decline was the most severe witnessed in the UK commercial property market since meaningful records began in the early 1970s.

But This Time the Bust Was Also Different

These falls in capital values wiped out all the growth in the boom. By June 2009 the average value of properties in all three of the main sectors were lower than they were in January 2000. Offices in 2009 were now more than 20% below their level at the millennium and industrial property over 10% lower. The retail sector had suffered least but was still substantially down in nominal terms with no account taken for inflation over the decade. The real fall in value was much more. Table 5.4 notes that during the 24 months from the end of June 2007 to the end of June 2009 retail values fell by 43.6%, slightly more than the others sectors, although they had increased in value more during the boom years. The capital values of industrial property dropped the least of the three main sectors, by 40.4%. Other minority types of property owned by financial institutions, which includes residential and leisure, did not suffer anywhere near the falls that the three main commercial property sectors experienced.

These falls in capital values wiped out all the growth in the boom. By June 2009 the average value of properties in all three of the main sectors were lower than they were in January 2000. Offices in 2009 were now more than 20% below their level at the millennium and industrial property over 10% lower. The retail sector had suffered least but was still substantially down in nominal terms, with no account taken for inflation over the decade. The real fall in value was much greater.

What was also unique about this 'bust' was the fact that the sectors, *on average* experienced the same timeframe for the period of valuation decline – from June 2007 (plus or minus a month) to June 2009 (plus or minus a month). That level of similarity had not been seen before, but then, neither had the likes of the GFC. Comparing this performance with previous downturns in the UK property market it becomes clear that the 2007 crash differed both in the length of the downturn and its depth.

This difference can be seen by considering the last major UK property recession (and with it major falls in capital values) that occurred at the end of the 1980s' economic boom. The recession resulted from the government's attempt to cool a booming economy (GDP had nudged 5% on an annual basis) and reduce the soaring inflation (which had reached 10%) – using interest rates – prompting valuation falls right across the board for commercial property. From the end of November 1989 to May 1993 average property values fell by 27% – at that time an unprecedented fall. Table 5.5 details the downturns by property sector. Retail assets started to suffer falls in value first, in October 1989, and on average, values fell by 19% over the next three and a half years. It

Table 5.4 Average falls in capital values by property sector, June 2007 to June 2009.

Sector	Fall in value (%)
All Property	42.4
Retail	43.6
Offices	42.7
Industrial	40.4
Other	32.6

Source: MSCI/IPD (2014b).

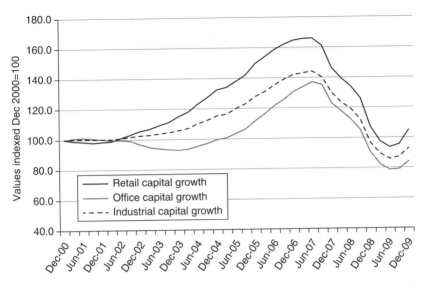

Figure 5.5 Indexed capital value change by sector, 2000–2009. *Source:* MSCI/IPD (2014b). Reproduced with permission.

Table 5.5 Capital value falls November 1989 to May 1993.

Sector	Fall in value (%)	Duration of the fall
All property	27.1	Nov 1989 to May 1993
Retail	19.0	Oct 1989 to May 1993
Offices	38.5	Feb 1990 to May 1993
Industrial	20.9	Dec 1989 to May 1993

Source: MSCI/IPD (2015).

took a few months longer for the average values of industrial assets to begin falling, and they then dropped almost 21% in value. But with offices entering the recession with a significant ongoing development programme, much of which was of a speculative nature, this sector experienced a severe fall in values with average values falling by over 38%. The property market behaved in a relatively rational fashion, in that commercial property lagged that of the wider economy and a variable response from individual sectors reflecting specific circumstances.

The recession/property downturn of the late 1980s onwards can be classified as 'normal', induced by macroeconomic policy designed to dampen a booming economy and rising inflation. In such circumstances the resultant shrinking economy, rising unemployment and (usually) oversupply of new (but empty) commercial property space means falling rents and capital values. The bust from 2007 did not follow the traditional series of dynamics, not least because yields rose before rents fell.

The reaction of the property market to the rapidly deteriorating macro picture in 2007 was dissimilar to anything previously seen in the United Kingdom. It was not just that capital values in retail, industrial and office property all fell to the same degree over a short interval as noted above. It was also broadly true for each region of the United Kingdom: as Table 5.6 demonstrates, all parts of the market started falling in value from June 2007, and ultimately fell by remarkably similar amounts.

There are extremely few outliers, and bar the possibly anomalous figure for Northern Ireland retail and that of central London retail, all of the cumulative declines in capital values recorded in Table 5.6 fall within a narrow range of 7.5 percentage points. Even more curiously, the average falls in capital value across all regions and across all three sectors in England outside central London were within ± 9% of the average fall recorded by all property over that period (42.4%). In fact, all bar three of the returns from the segmentation given in Table 5.5 were within a 10% range around that average.

Given the number of different segmentations of the market in Table 5.6 – geographically not to mention the type of property – and the differences one would normally expect in local conditions with respect to relative valuations at the start of the crash, tenant demand during the crash, the local vacancy rates and the extent of the supply pipeline, the closeness of these regional falls is quite remarkable.

It is also instructive to point out that the best performing segments in Table 5.6 (in relative terms, at least) was central London retail, while the worst performing segments (by the same reference point) were City of London offices. The latter was understandable given the seriousness of the financial collapse, the former less so as much of central London retailing is driven by workers in the financial sectors and tourists, both of which groups would seem to have been at risk given the economic problems being

Table 5.6 Percentage falls in capital value by region and property sector, June 2007–June 2009.

	Retail	Offices	Industrial
London			
City		45.4	
Mid-town		43.7	
City and mid-town	32.8		
West End	28.9	41.3	
Other	43.6		
All London			38.4
South East	43.0	42.2	41.1
South West	43.5	42.4	40.5
Eastern	46.3	40.0	40.5
East Midlands	43.6	38.8	41.5
West Midlands	44.7	43.0	42.3
North West	44.9	42.2	42.4
Yorkshire and Humberside	45.0	42.5	40.9
North East	44.7	41.1	41.1
Scotland	45.0	39.5	32.8
Wales	44.5	38.0	41.1
N. Ireland	34.9	NA	NA

Source: MSCI/IPD (2014b)
NA = Not available.

encountered. And it is therefore all the more surprising that the best performing sectors once the property recovery took root were not only central London offices but also central London shops.

The more this data is analyzed the more it suggests that valuers were paying only cursory attention to property fundamentals and were tending to mark down all assets by almost identical amounts.

This explanation chimes with a breakdown of the causes in the fall in value set out in Figure 5.6. The initial fall in capital value is virtually all the consequence of a rise in yields as rental growth remained positive. Increases in yields in 2008 are even more significant, collapsing values by approximately a further 25% although rents are also now exhibiting marginal negative growth. It is only in 2009 that negative rental growth becomes the main element of falling capital values.

The market bust, like the boom years immediately preceding the GFC, was therefore yield driven as investment valuations marked down commercial property values. In general, the behaviour post 2001 was completely different from that in the years 1981 to 2001, where, apart from the year 1990 and the period 1992/93, capital growth could be mainly attributed to rental growth, as one might expect in a rational market. We have already observed and discussed in Chapter 4 the disconnect between rental value growth and capital value growth in the period 2002 to 2007, and with it the suggestion that something was really different in behaviour this time in the market. However, the changes in market behaviour in this period persisted beyond 2007 and are highlighted in Figure 5.6. It suggests some kind of structural shift in the market post 2001 which has persisted through both the subsequent boom and bust periods and into the recovery period post 2009.

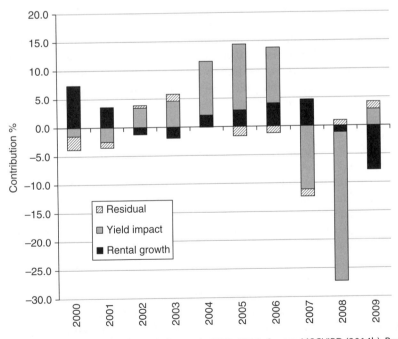

Figure 5.6 Contributions to capital growth, 2000–2009. *Source:* MSCI/IPD (2014b). Reproduced with permission.

While the evidence presented so far is of an almost uniform fall in capital values as yields rose, with little account taken of rental growth, there is evidence of a more subtle response to the crisis that took into account the differential 'quality' of properties. Good investment quality is to a degree subjective but can be seen as a property having a combination of tenants that are financially strong (such as a government department) and the income security from having a long unexpired lease. Similarly a large high-value property is likely to have tenants able to weather the storm of a recession. As Frodsham (2016) notes, the higher the property quality the longer a lease the landlord can negotiate, and he quotes from a Gerald Eve report (2013, p. iv) 'as the quality of assets increases, the proportion of space let to lower value-added occupiers … falls and the proportion let to higher value-added business increases'. However, care needs to be taken with these arguments. In particular this capacity depends on the state of the market; for example, during a recession a landlord may be desperate to let an empty property with any length of lease just to get it let and avoid empty rates, and so forth. Nevertheless a 'good quality' property is likely to have an advantage in a weak market.

Frodsham (2016) assesses whether there were significant differences in performance following 2007 in terms of the degree of fall in capital value between properties when the length of the unexpired lease is taken into account. The hypothesis is that income security is important in the uncertainty of a downturn, although during an upswing investment pricing of an individual property will favour potential rental growth (so long leases with spaced-out rent reviews would be unattractive). High income security is defined as properties in the top quarter of those owned by financial institutions in terms of the length of the unexpired lease (it ignores covenant strength).

Frodsham's research is based on the MSCI/IPD database of properties owned by financial institutions explained in Chapter 1. The analysis differentiates between three retail types – shops, shopping centres and retail warehouses; offices in central London, the South East and the rest of the United Kingdom; industrial property. Property assets in each of these subsets are ranked according to income security and placed accordingly in one of four quartiles. To simplify his presentation, the middle two quartiles are combined and called the 'interquartile range' in the results of the analysis presented in Figure 5.7.

The results show a greater fall in capital values in the downturn for assets with the lowest income security for all property types considered. Figure 5.7 shows there is also a consistent relationship in the decline, with the highest income security having the smallest declines. The impact of (low) income security was most significant for offices outside London and industrial property, while it is least significant for shops. This probably reflects the fact that a prime location is the most important dimension of income security for retail property and central London offices as it could easily attract new tenants at the end of a lease.

Frodsham's analysis is extended here by examining equivalent trends for the same property types differentiated by relative value. A high-value property will almost certainly have well-established companies with solid bank balances as tenants, and even if there is a void it will be well placed to secure a new tenant. The decline in capital values broken down by asset quality measured by relative value for each of the property types reveals a more diffuse picture. In general, as Figure 5.8 shows, the highest value properties suffered the least in percentage terms. However, the bottom quartile only suffered the greatest fall in value for standard shop and industrial property assets. There

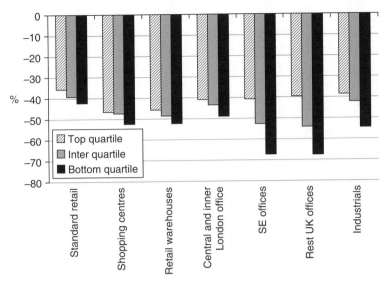

Figure 5.7 Peak to trough change in capital values by length of unexpired lease. *Source:* Frodsham (2016).

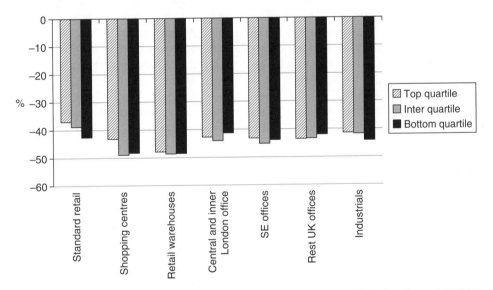

Figure 5.8 Peak to trough changes in capital values by asset quality defined by value. *Source:* MSCI/IPD (2014b). Reproduced with permission.

is little difference in the decreases in value between the different property types and their value compared with the pattern for income security. The most pronounced falls were experienced by shopping centres and retail warehouses, 50% and 48.5% respectively. In both cases, values from bottom quartile properties did not start to recover until December 2013.

Overall the property types in the spectrum most affected by the bust were offices with short terms left on their leases in the South East of England and offices in the rest of the

United Kingdom outside London. Values of both fell by 67% from peak to trough, and the period of this process was much longer than the two or so years for the commercial property market as a whole. It took the value of the offices in the South East six years to stop falling and that of offices in the rest of the United Kingdom as a whole even longer at six and a half years (MSCI/IPD, 2014b). While the research suggests that assets with longer unexpired lease lengths did not experience the same value collapses as other stock, what is perhaps surprising in this regard is that they still experienced falls in values of generally over 40%.

Investment Trends and Capital Value Falls

The chapter now looks in more detail at UK investment trends post 2007 to examine the underlying dynamics of the falls in value. Quarterly statistics from the MSCI/IPD database indicate that net investment by financial institutions actually fell away dramatically after September 2007 as shown in Figure 5.9. The turnaround in investment was very quick. Net investment peaked in the fourth quarter of 2006 at £3.9 billion, i.e. before the onset of the GFC, but fell rapidly to just £254 million by the third quarter of 2007, reflecting the increasing awareness of the scale of the problem facing global markets and falling values in the marketplace. Net disinvestment totalled more than £3 billion in the first three months of 2008 and in all there were eight quarters of disinvestment. It is only in the final quarter of 2009 that the tide changes and net investment by financial institutions resumes and then at a much lower level than at the peak of the boom. Of course for every seller (net disinvestor) there must be a buyer but the magnitude of the disinvestment by key players in the market must have had an impact on capital values.

However, just as on the way up, there was granularity in the market sales on the way down. Net disinvestment by financial institutions post 2007 was deepest for offices. The

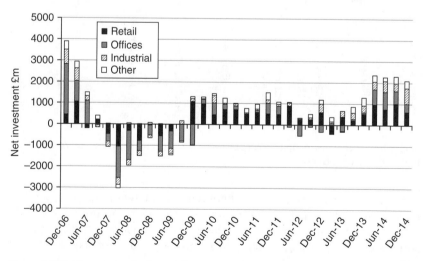

Figure 5.9 Net investment by financial institutions by property sector, 2006–2014. *Source:* MSCI/IPD (2014b). Reproduced with permission.

first sector to begin to recover was the retail sector in late 2009. These statistics relate narrowly to financial institutions based on MSCI/IPD data. This data only covered between 36% and 43% of the investable market in the United Kingdom over the period 2007 to 2009, and between 21% and 23% of the total commercial property stock in the United Kingdom (Mitchell, 2015). A broader market indication of what was occurring is given in Table 5.7 gleaned from the Property Data data set that draws on a wider spectrum of investor types. In theory the Property Data data set encompasses transactions across the whole of the commercial property market in the United Kingdom. The Property Data investor classification (as previously noted in Chapter 4) is as follows:

- *Institutions*   non-bank financial institutions are defined to include pension funds, insurance companies, unit trusts, property unit trusts and limited partnerships;
- *Property Companies*   including listed listed under Real Estate on the London Stock Exchange, the Alternative Investment Market (AIM) and the Off Exchange (OFEX), and unlisted (non-quoted UK registered companies);
- *Overseas Investors*;
- *Private Investors*   including private syndicates;
- *Other including banks*   banking organizations that have taken an equity interest in a property investment.
- *Occupiers.*

Table 5.7 indicates that immediate disinvestment from 2007 was not just by financial institutions but also by property companies and occupiers and banks. As Figure 5.9 indicates, financial institutions came back strongly into the market from 2010 (with a blip in 2012) but the other disinvestors continued to do so for some considerable years. Listed and unlisted property companies divested right through to 2014, and this was actually a continuation of a trend that was established prior to the GFC (see Chapter 4). The banks (included in 'Other') and owner-occupiers divested themselves of property on balance over the whole period post 2007 and until the end of 2015 (discussed in more detail in Chapter 7). These disinvestors were balanced by net investors in the form of private individuals and overseas investors. Overseas investors were the dominant net investors throughout not just the immediate crisis but also in the drawn out aftermath, and so represented a lifeline for struggling investors.

Table 5.7 Net investment (£m) by investor types, 2007–2015.

Investor type	2007	2008	2009	2010	2011	2012	2013	2014	2015
UK Institutions	−1914	−5788	−2350	5464	1438	−767	2885	7802	2657
Property Companies (listed and unlisted)	−1567	−769	−3507	−4058	−500	−2882	−2362	−5534	−6217
Overseas investors	11816	5051	8163	4290	4544	7650	7917	7658	11331
Private individuals	1547	1827	1037	2	433	123	−5	−470	−1152
Occupiers	−6379	−161	−1913	−1930	−2584	−1464	−2943	−2793	−2757
Other banks and institutions	−3503	−160	−1430	−3768	−3331	−2650	−5702	−6663	−3862
Total	0	0	0	0	0	0	0	0	0

Source: Property Data.

Transaction Volumes

As the GFC took hold transaction volumes fell rapidly. Property Data records that transactions peaked at over £61 billion in 2006, but by the end of 2008 annual volumes were down to £24.25 billion, a fall of 60% (Figure 5.10). Expenditure on purchases (not sales) in the MSCI/IPD database, reflecting mainly institutional fund holdings, fell by much more than that: by 73% between its peak in 2005 and 2008, (from £22.1 bn to just £5.86 bn).

Of the six main categories of investor identified by Property Data, the institutions were just the biggest sellers of property over the three years 2007, 2008 and 2009, followed by the property companies (listed and unlisted) at £31 billion and £30.7 billion respectively (Table 5.8). The market was being driven by forced sellers having to accept

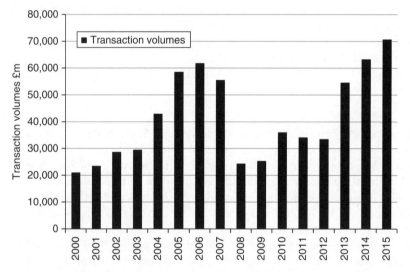

Figure 5.10 Transaction volumes in the commercial property market 2000–2015. *Source:* Reproduced with permission of Property Data.

Table 5.8 Value of sales (£m) by type of investor, 2007–2015.

Investor type	2007	2008	2009	2010	2011	2012	2013	2014	2015
UK Institutions	12073	10077	8863	6122	7933	7379	10549	9751	12328
Property Companies (listed and unlisted)	16826	6342	7504	10419	8983	9978	11773	18284	19262
Overseas investors	7750	2230	1973	7790	7660	8234	17354	12410	23994
Private individuals	4439	893	844	2021	1398	1346	2075	19595	4011
Occupiers	7777	2830	3352	4009	3616	2521	4805	2974	4506
Other banks and institutions	6558	1879	2683	5529	4424	3937	7915	4305	6451
	55423	24251	25219	35890	34014	33395	54471	8406	70562

Source: Property Data.

what the buyers offered because of the need to satisfy the demand of administrators in the case of the banks, liquidity requirements in the case of institutional funds and listed property companies, and covenant breaches by many geared property funds. These issues are discussed more fully in Chapter 7. But the market dynamic was complicated by the fact that although overseas investors were still big net investors, they were still selling large amounts of property albeit at a much lower rate. Total sales by overseas investors over the period 2007 to 2009 inclusive raised £11.95 billion, and by 2010 they overtook the UK institutions as the biggest sellers of real estate in the United Kingdom.

Notwithstanding this picture of investors selling off property in large quantities because of the GFC, the frenzy of deal-making in the boom had gone. The party was over and buyers difficult to come by. The lack of buyers can partly be traced to the paucity of bank funding and the reduced returns from lower gearing. This is discussed in detail in Chapter 3. Bank lending to commercial property peaked in 2007 (see Figure 3.5) as bank interest rate margins rocketed, pushing up financing costs, and the maximum loan-to-value margins they offered fell by more than 10 percentage points (see Figure 3.11). These were only two aspects of the harsher terms imposed on the availability of debt finance, and the lack of credit was a major constraint on demand. Just as the easy accessibility and generous bank lending terms were essential ingredients to the boom so the credit famine was crucial to the narrative of the bust. More details from the banks' perspective are considered in Chapter 6 and Chapter 7.

Total sales, as noted above, fell from £61.7 billion at the height of the boom in 2006 to £25.2 billion in 2009 according to Property Data (and shown in Figure 5.10). Sales in the years 2007 to 2009 according to this data source were actually below the 15-year (2000 to 2014 inclusive) annual average of £39.4 billion. Similarly the MSCI/IPD database reported that institutional sales had fallen overall during the period 2005 to 2009, from £19.16 billion to £12.51 billion in 2009.

These transaction volumes need to be seen in context. First the transactions level recorded by Property Data in 2008 represented around 3.8% of the total commercial property stock in 2008 or 6.7% of the subset of property that can be described as suitable for investment, that is, the investable stock, at that time (using estimates of the stock by Mitchell (2015)). However, the market's interpretation of changes in values and the interpretation of market behaviour have, on the whole, come from the MSCI/IPD databases. Data from this source suggests that 2008 sales (£15.4 bn) were 4.2% of the total investable stock, or equivalent to 2.4% of the total commercial property stock. Neither of these sources therefore report sales percentages that can be considered large, which in turn highlights the relatively small sample available for comparable evidence in valuations.

Interestingly, the *number* of assets sold by financial institutions did not change significantly as a percentage of the total MSCI annual database between 2007 and 2008, 7% compared to 6.8% respectively. This means that with sales by *value* increasing over this period it was the higher value assets that were being sold off. It was probably easier to sell the best assets to raise cash given the state of the market at the time. But it also suggests that even the highest quality properties were being marked down as part of a fire sale. The need to sell is reflected in the fall in the number of purchases by financial institutions, from 7.9% of all assets in 2007 to 1.8% in 2008 compared with the annual average of 6.8% over the period 2000 to 2014.

The market turbulence created by the dramatic collapse in values over a short period represented a huge challenge to the valuation profession. It should be remembered that the falls in value that we have reported above are based on asset valuations that measure the periodic performance of property portfolios owned by financial institutions. The chapter now seeks to analyse more closely what was driving prices during the period following the GFC. To achieve this goal we turn our focus to the yields of actual transactions in the market as these normally form the basis of the comparable evidence used for valuations.

Market Yields

The relationship between the rise in property yield asset valuations for financial institutions and real market yields from 2007 can be seen from Figure 5.11, based on MSCI/IPD and Property Data databases respectively. Yields in the case of MSCI are recorded at year-end and Property Data yields are weighted average yields over the year. Over the period 2007 to 2010, when the market began to stabilize, both valuation and actual yields increased and peaked in June 2009. Market yields then began to reduce. Although the patterns in both sets of data were similar over the period, the actual yields in the Property Data database saw a sharper upward movement (meaning lower prices) during late 2007 and early 2008. This could reflect the broader range of property in that data set but could also represent the market responding quicker than asset valuations.

The potential faster rise of market yields could be because certain types of owners (other than financial institutions) were desperate to sell. Insight into this issue is given by Figure 5.12 which reports the differences between actual yields of properties and the

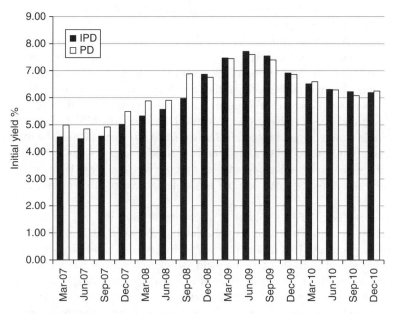

Figure 5.11 Market and valuation yields, 2007–2010. *Source:* Property Data and MSCI/IPD (2014a). Reproduced with permission.
IPD = MSCI/IPD valuation yields PD = Property Data actual yields.

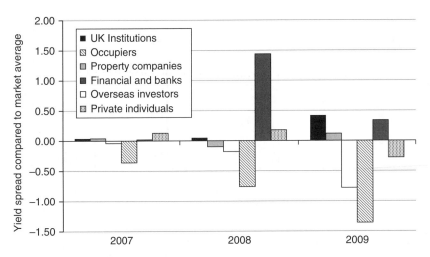

Figure 5.12 Yield Spreads* of Sales by Investor Types, 2007–2009. *Source:* Reproduced with permission of Property Data.
*Difference between actual yield and the weighted average yield for the year.

average market yield sold by different types of investors for the years 2007 through to 2009. At the beginning of the GFC in 2007 there was a pretty much uniform pattern in the sense that no one particular investor was selling especially below market average yields. The one potential exception is occupiers who in fact were selling at an increasingly lower yield differential across the three years, suggesting they were little affected by any imperative to sell. Similarly overseas investors were consistently selling at below the market average, reflecting the fact that they were net investors. The data for the banks in 2008 sales were at a significantly higher yield than the market average, but the value of their sales in that year only amounted to £319 million compared, for example, with institutional sales in that year of £10.1 billion. From this data there is no clear indication that any one particular investor type was selling at sufficient discount (higher yield) and in sufficient quantity to affect market process overall, certainly through 2007 and 2008.

The implication is that yields were moving up across the markets at the same time, consistent with our earlier observation that valuers appeared to be marking property down across the board, but the question remains: What was driving this market revaluation? Financial institutions were selling at slightly higher than market average yields in 2008 and 2009, although interestingly not markedly so. However, it can be argued that it was the large retail real estate funds with big redemption outflows that were driving valuations as a result of forced selling in 2008/2009, not banks or debt backed assets for, as Chapter 7 explains, banks took longer to resolve their problems and initially they were trying to hold assets and work them out.

The dramatic collapse of money into retail funds is shown in in Figure 5.13. After a dramatic increase in inflows in 2006 and the first part of 2007, the reverse suddenly happens. There is a net outflow of £1.2 billion alone in the third quarter of 2007 (following negative headlines about these funds in the press) and this phenomenon continues through to the first quarter of 2009. During the 21-month period from the second quarter of 2007, more than £2.8 billion flows out of these specialist real estate funds. These numbers themselves may be slight underestimates as the figures do not include all such funds.

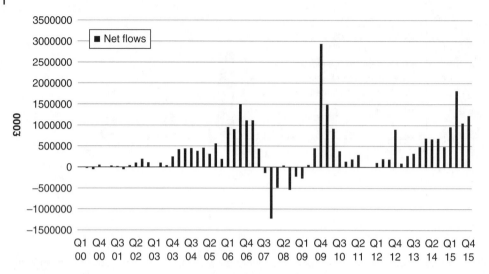

Figure 5.13 Quarterly cash flow into specialist (retail) real estate funds 2000–2015. *Source:* Reproduced with permission of Association of Real Estate Funds.

The value of these retail funds fell rapidly as they were valued monthly (in some cases fortnightly as investment pressure built up) and priced daily, so every new deal completed was the new lower valued benchmark. The need to generate cash and maintain liquidity levels linked to the overall value of the funds, particularly APUTs, necessitated the sale of real estate assets. While these funds were generally part of the MSCI/IPD database, they were only a small element. Given our earlier observation that in 2008 sales from this database accounted for only 4.2% on the total investable stock, it seems it was only a relatively small number of sales that were driving prices down. The retail funds, as the primary forced sellers, may have generated limited sales in proportional terms but these sales brought the general mark down in capital values noted above.

Changing View of Risk

The reaction to the onset of the GFC and the severe lack of credit was a swift readjustment by investors in the form of a rise in the required commercial property yields that in turn brought down capital values. At the same time investors rushed to buy government bonds for 'safety', which resulted in gilt yields falling (as shown in Figure 4.16 and repeated here in Figure 5.14). Both of these processes collectively represented a re-evaluation of relative risk of the different types of assets. Figure 5.14 demonstrates that the yield gap, the difference between commercial property initial yields and 10-year government bonds was negative in the first half of 2007 – unprecedented in modern times. But it was short lived, and at the end of the year the relationship switched round and the positive gap grew and grew through to the middle of 2009.

The growing gap provides a prima facie case that the risk premium associated with purchasing commercial property rose with the GFC. The precise relationship between

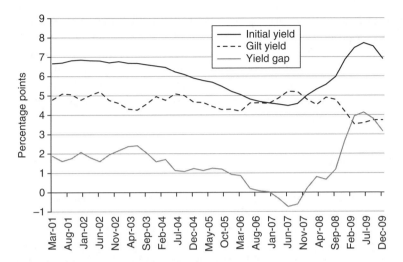

Figure 5.14 Yield gap between gilts* and commercial property, 2001–2009. *Source:* MSCI/IPD (2014b) and ONS (2016). Reproduced with permission.
*Redemption yields on 10 year bonds.

the risk premium, gilt yields and property yields was set out in Equation 4.5. To recap (minus subscript) this stated that

$$p = k - r + g + d \qquad (5.1)\ (\text{from Equation 4.5})$$

where

p is the property risk premium
k is the initial yield
r is the risk-free rate (redemption yield on 10-year gilts)
g is an allowance for rental value growth
d is an allowance for depreciation.

By June 2009 the yield gap had reached 4.2 %, and applying the risk premium formula in Equation 5.1, assuming zero rental value growth in the subsequent three years and a depreciation rate of 1% per annum, gives a risk premium of 5.2%. This is at a historically high level.

Looking at capital values using the Burston and Burrell (2015) approach explained in Chapter 4 offers a different perspective. Their research is based on a comparison of short-term values with long-run average annual returns from property by comparing the ratio of current rental income returns to capital value. To recap, this comparison uses the benchmark of a 10-year moving average return adjusted for inflation. Based on this technique, Burston and Burrell (2015) assess that a lengthy period of over-valuation took place from the late 1990s, and more significantly so at the peak of the boom continued through to 2008. However, during the latter half of 2007 and 2008, rapid downward adjustments to capital values meant that by the beginning of 2009 commercial property was priced below their assessment of fair value. Indeed this brisk 'correction' continued through the first of 2009 so that by the middle of that year values were 7% below fair value. The degree of under-assessment then fell away, but it was not until the beginning of 2014 that there was a significant shift back toward the restoration of fair value.

Overall, the falls in capital value through to at least the middle of 2009 represent a dramatic reappraisal of property investors' perception of risk. Given the implied high risk premiums and the deviations from long-term fair value following the GFC it could be seen as an overreaction. It could be described as irrational pessimism, just as the boom could be seen as irrational exuberance. There then followed a period stretching into the mid-2010s that saw an unwinding process from this extreme. This issue is considered in more detail in Chapter 7.

Summary and Conclusions

The GFC and the world's first global recession resulted in substantial and rapid declines in commercial property values. There were short sharp collapses in capital values in some countries, such as the United States (33%) and the United Kingdom (42%), over two or three years. In other countries the impact was a slow burner as capital values declined over six or more years, many of these countries were in the eurozone. This difference may be because of different valuation practices across countries, so that valuations were in some cases slower to respond to market forces. Ireland experienced by far the largest average drop with a fall of 67.3% from the third quarter of 2007 to the third quarter of 2013. Part of the reason may have been that Ireland was one of the few countries where there was also a significant reduction in rents over this period.

The chapter has focused on the experience of the property market 'bust' in the United Kingdom. A unique feature was the uniform collapse of commercial property valuations across the investment stock of the country. Property values in the retail, office and industrial sectors all experienced a fall by remarkably similar percentages over broadly the same time frame, from June 2007 to June 2009. The decline applied more or less irrespective of region and quality of asset. However, more detailed analysis reveals that the uncertainty of income security during the recession was a key factor in pricing. Those properties with long leases let to financially strong tenants suffered the least.

Notwithstanding the caveat of the role of income security, the evidence implies that valuers were generally paying only cursory attention to individual property characteristics and local property market prospects and were tending to mark up the yields of all assets by almost identical amounts. The fall in capital values, like the boom years immediately preceding the GFC, can be described as almost entirely yield driven. While capital values fell as yields rose, rental growth remained positive, and even though forecasts of future rental growth were downgraded they remained above zero.

Net investment in commercial property by financial institutions went quickly into reverse with the onset of the GFC. While net investment by institutions was at a high of £3.9 billion in the fourth quarter of 2006, by the beginning of 2008 institutions were in divestment mode with net sales of more than £3 billion in the first three months of that year. Net sales continue for two years and then net purchases resume at a diminished level. Offices felt the brunt of the disinvestment and investment in the retail sector was the first to recover in late 2009.

It was not just financial institutions that were selling properties: so were property companies, occupiers and banks (albeit in small numbers). Indeed listed and unlisted property companies were continuing to divest up to 2014. Overseas investors balanced this disinvestment by being the dominant net investors, attracted perhaps by the fact that the institutions and property companies were prepared to sell off their best properties to address their financial difficulties.

However, the picture of investors generally selling off property in large quantities needs to be seen in a broader context of the boom and bust. Total sales actually fell from the peak of transactions activity in 2006 through to 2009. The bust brought a dearth of willing purchasers partly because of the shortage of bank finance and the difficulties of meeting more risk-averse lending criteria by clients of property funds. The deal-making culture of the boom disappeared, and with it market liquidity was significantly reduced. The reduced level of market activity and the trauma of the GFC contributed to the difficulties in the valuation of commercial property given that most of these valuations were for portfolio monitoring purposes rather than as part of a sale.

The main dynamic of the market was the forced sales of the retail funds that suffered large investment redemption outflows. The net outflow began in the second quarter of 2007 but then dramatically escalated in the next quarter. In all, more than £2.8 billion was withdrawn from these specialist real estate funds by the second quarter of 2009. These numbers themselves may be slight underestimates as the figures do not include all such funds. There is a strong case that it was these forced sales that were driving valuations during the downturn.

The market dynamics in the bust can be seen as predicated on a continuation of the type of investment behaviour that also created the boom. There is an apparent structural shift or collective rethink in the market post 2001 which persisted through both the subsequent boom and bust periods and into the recovery period after 2009. This behaviour was (and still is) typified by yield impact dominating changes in capital values rather than rental value growth. It can be characterized as a global 'hunt for yield' by investors, whether it be emerging market debt, corporate bonds or commercial property. It can be argued also that the irrational exuberance of the boom was replaced by the irrational pessimism following the GFC that played havoc with traditional views of the risk premium attached to commercial property. This issue is considered in more detail in Chapter 7, but clearly risks had increased. In historic terms a fair value model suggest that following 2009 property was still priced below fair value and that fair value was only beginning to be restored by early 2015, nearly eight years after the onset of the GFC.

Overall, as the scale of the economic impact of the GFC was gradually exposed during 2007 and 2008, UK commercial property markets experienced rapid and significant rises in property yields/falls in capital values on a historic scale. Credit dried up depriving the market of one of its pillars as banks' lending criteria became more risk averse. At the same time there was falling liquidity with a significant decline in the volume of sales and purchases, together with a re-evaluation of the property risk premium. There was a second 'flip' from investors projecting substantial rental growth and returns at the peak of the boom only for expectations to be dramatically and swiftly downgraded resulting in pessimistic forecasts in this 'bust' period. A collapse in rental growth did not materialize although the market slowed. The instability and irrational exuberance in the market in the period 2003 to 2007 was replaced by perhaps an equally irrational pessimism, driven in part, it appears, by the forced sales of a relatively small segment of investors and by the lack of credit to purchase. Chapter 6 considers the role of the banks through the whole boom and bust cycle.

6

Property Lending and the Collapse of Banks

The headlines reporting the failures of banks during the global financial crisis (GFC) still feel unnerving a decade on. The roll call of banking collapses is still difficult to fully digest. In the United States this encompassed some of the largest investment banks, including the liquidation of Lehman Brothers and the collapse of Bear Stearns (sold to JP Morgan Chase with government support) and Merrill Lynch (sold to Bank of America). Wachovia, the fourth largest bank, was forcibly absorbed into Wells Fargo Bank at the behest of the government to avoid its formal failure. The US government rescued Citigroup, one the largest banks in the world, by taking a 36% equity share. 'Mortgage banks' such as New Century Financial and Country Financial plus savings and loans associations also went bankrupt.

In the UK, mortgage bank failures were led by Northern Rock and quickly followed by Bradford and Bingley and a range of small building societies such as the Dunfermline. Two of the country's major international banks, Halifax Bank of Scotland (HBOS)/ Lloyds and Royal Bank of Scotland (RBS), were taken over and recapitalized by the UK government. Elsewhere in Europe, Fortis, the largest bank in Belgium but with interests in the Netherlands and Luxembourg, was nationalized by the respective countries. Similarly, Anglo Irish bank was nationalized by the Irish government. UBS, the large Swiss bank, wrote off $4 billion bad debts and was bailed out by its government. All this occurred within a relatively short period, spanning 2007 and 2008, but the ramifications continued. In 2012 four failed Spanish banks, including Bankia, were subject to a rescue from a eurozone bailout fund. Bankia had already been previously 'saved' by nationalization in 2010. The 2010–2012 European debt crisis/bailout also embraced Portugal, Italy, Ireland and Greece.

The timeline to the collapse of the banks in the GFC as described and explained in Chapter 1 and Chapter 5 is bound up with the sub-prime mortgage crisis and the role of mortgage-backed securities, that is, wholesale funding. It was the banks' creation and mis-selling of these products globally that actually caused the credit crunch and the consequent lack of banking liquidity. Undoubtedly the combination of these phenomena explains the fall of international investment banks (and sub-prime lending specialists in the United States), but the story of the GFC is also bound up with the role of commercial property lending by banks offering general financial services. The banks used the money raised by wholesale funding to lend to people buying houses, to house builders, to investors to purchase commercial property and to developers

Property Boom and Banking Bust: The Role of Commercial Lending in the Bankruptcy of Banks,
First Edition. Colin Jones, Stewart Cowe, and Edward Trevillion.
© 2018 John Wiley & Sons Ltd. Published 2018 by John Wiley & Sons Ltd.

who built shopping centres, offices, and so forth. There is an important sub-plot as falling commercial (not residential) property valuations hit the capital bases of many banks and ultimately challenged their fundamental economics much more than a short-term liquidity problem. This story is arguably more akin to previous patterns of property market collapse having consequences for the banking system (Herring and Wachter, 1998).

This chapter focuses on why and how this problem emerged, examining the attractiveness of providing loans on commercial property and the impact of falling capital values with the GFC. It reviews the paths to disaster of a number of major banks through commercial property lending in the United Kingdom, Ireland and the United States. In the process it examines attitudes to risk, the failure of predictive models and the impact of banking behaviour on property market trends. It encompasses in-depth case studies of RBS, HBOS, the Dunfermline Building Society and the Co-operative Bank, and Irish Banks. The commercial property lending failings are not limited to the banks considered in this chapter, and indeed equivalent stories can be found across Europe, but the case studies (and the wider content of the chapter) reflect the availability of information in the public domain.

The chapter begins by reviewing the crumbling of the UK banking system, setting it in its historic context and focusing on the significance of the dramatic rise of the use of wholesale funding, with the issue of mortgage-backed bonds, in the lead up to the GFC. Having set the scene, the next part of the chapter looks at why individual British banks/ building societies fell into difficulties from commercial property lending. The anatomy of the parallel Irish banking collapse is then examined. The subsequent section considers the role of commercial property lending in the US banking failures at the end of the real estate booms of the 1980s and noughties. The final section reflects on these international experiences and draws conclusions.

The Crumbling of the UK Banking System

The UK banking system is one of the most mature and well established in the world. The major banks were historically regarded as very secure by savers, investors and customers alike. Before the GFC the last British high street bank to fail was the Bank of Glasgow in 1878, after which a series of banking laws were introduced, underpinned by the establishment of the Bank of England as a lender of last resort. Besides banks, important financial institutions in the property market include building societies. Building societies have a parallel history from the nineteenth century as non-profitmaking 'mutual' institutions owned by their members (savers and borrowers), raising funds from savers and offering mortgages for house purchase. From the 1980s the banks and building societies found themselves in direct competition for the first time as banks were allowed to offer mortgages in the housing market (see Chapter 2).

However, building societies were subject to different and more restrictive legislation. One aspect of this greater freedom was the ability of banks to raise funds on the wholesale market. By law, building societies can borrow only up to 50% of their total funding from the money markets, and very little of this takes the form of mortgage-backed securities (Wainwright, 2010). Banks were seen as being in a stronger position than building societies to meet the perceived growth in mortgage demand, and so, beginning in 1989, as Chapter 2 notes, there was a phase in which the larger building societies converted to banks. These included the Halifax, Bradford and Bingley and Northern Rock.

Banks and building societies were perceived by the public as being conservative, well-run institutions up until the GFC. For some years, beneath the surface, banks had been changing their business models in the pursuit of growth, often into new international markets or to increase market share in the domestic lending market. From the millennium, the loan books of British banks were expanding faster than their deposit bases. As a result they became increasingly (over-)dependent on wholesale funding, in particular by issuing mortgage-backed securities, to support their growing lending activities, as Figure 6.1 indicates. By the end of 2007, what can be described as the *customer funding gap* had reached £700 billion whereas it had been negligible in 2000.

The first to fail was the Northern Rock. During the noughties it dramatically extended its residential mortgage lending aggressively by offering high loan-to-value (LTV) ratios. It tripled its share of the UK mortgage market between 1999 and 2007 from 6% to 19% (Eisenbeis and Kaufman, 2009). Yet it was not the inherent risks of its lending that led to its collapse but its reliance on short-term wholesale funding (House of Commons, 2008). The drying up of this source of funding meant it became the first British casualty of the global liquidity freeze (see Chapter 5). It was nationalized in January 2008. Broadly the same fate befell the Bradford and Bingley, another small mortgage bank which had specialized in providing mortgages for 'buy-to-let' residential landlords (Jones, 2012b).

The collapse of these small banks was the prologue for the emergence of an unparalleled and sudden downfall of Britain's main high street banks in a unique challenge to the financial system. Subsequently the British government took substantial equity stakes in Lloyds/HBOS and the RBS in October 2008, two of the country's largest banks. At the time RBS had notional total assets of over $3.5 trillion, and at the

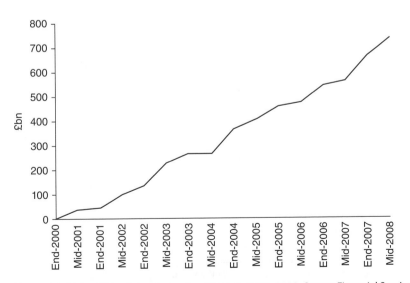

Figure 6.1 Major UK banks' customer funding gap, 2000–2008. *Source:* Financial Services Authority (2014).

beginning of 2008, before the scale of its problems emerged, it was the largest bank in the world by assets and the fifth largest by market capitalization. The UK government's purchase has been described as 'the biggest bail-out in history' as it injected £45.5 billion of equity capital to recapitalize it (Financial Services Authority, 2011). After the nationalizations the British taxpayers owned 43% of Lloyds/HBOS and 57% of RBS (this was subsequently increased to 83%, see Chapter 7). Another large bank, Barclays Bank, addressed its parallel problems by attracting private share capital from Middle East investors.

The explanation behind the problems of these banks is not about sub-prime lending, except in that it had consequences for raising international wholesale funding. To understand how these banks fell to their knees we now look in detail at the workings of RBS and HBOS based on reports by the UK bank regulator. The analysis centres on the part commercial property lending played. Subsequently the section also looks at the Britannia Building Society/Co-operative Bank and the Dunfermline Building Society, which were essentially residential mortgage banks attracted into commercial property lending.

A key issue is the nature and scale of the impairment losses from loans and advances incurred as a result of the downturn in the property market (not just in the United Kingdom) and the global economic downturn. An impairment is a reduction in the value of a bank's loan because the expected repayments will not be forthcoming and the losses are deemed unrecoverable. Before looking at the specifics of these banks it is useful to take an aggregate overview of what occurred in the main UK banks between 2007 and 2013 by reference to Table 6.1. There is a clear cycle to these losses, with dramatic rises through 2007–2009 followed by a modest decline, although the impairments of the Co-op Bank do not escalate until 2012, making it an outlier for reasons explored later. In general, impairments recorded in 2013 are still much higher than in 2007. It is also useful to note that the banks worst affected by losses in absolute terms are Barclays, Lloyds and HBOS, and RBS. The least effected is the Nationwide Building Society, which was most focused on residential mortgage lending (House of Commons Treasury Select Committee, 2014).

Table 6.1 Annual impairment losses on loans and advances to customers at major UK banks, 2007–2013 (£m).

	2007	2008	2009	2010	2011	2012	2013
Co-op and Britannia	116	155	161	97	121	474	516
Barclays	2782	4913	7358	5625	3790	3303	3062
HSBC	1043	1864	3364	1633	1122	1213	1102
Lloyds and HBOS	3733	12732	15783	10727	8020	5125	2725
Nationwide*	106	394	549	359	390	589	380
RBS	2106	6360	13056	9157	7241	5292	8427
Santander	344	348	773	712	501	988	475

Source: House of Commons Treasury Select Committee (2014) Table 4.
*Nationwide is a building society.

Royal Bank of Scotland

The failure of the RBS is complex, bound up with a disastrous decision to purchase a Dutch bank, ABN AMRO, as part of a consortium in October 2007. At the time ABN AMRO was the second largest bank in the Netherlands and the eighth largest in Europe, measured by assets. But the collapse of the combined bank, just one year later, in October 2008, is not simply down to overstretching its corporate empire. The underlying economics of the bank suffered from a long-term reliance on borrowing from wholesale sources and the problems of its lending book once the property market turned. The bank funded the acquisition of ABN AMRO primarily through short-term debt rather than equity and increased its reliance on short-term wholesale funding. It was already highly dependent on such funds, and the acquisition thereby stretched and eroded its capital adequacy position. One impact of the merger was the complicated consortium structure for the bank's accounts, which created a lack of transparency of its long-term lending exposures.

Nevertheless the seeds of RBS's demise stretch much further back in time from before the merger. This section examines its journey to its eventual nationalization based on evidence from Financial Services Authority (2011), an independent report giving an evaluation of what happened and why. Like other banks in the build up to 2007, RBS grew rapidly with an expansion of lending and gearing. Its global banking and markets division was the most rapidly growing area but so was the commercial property loan business sector (they overlapped). Royal Bank of Scotland had had a significant market share in UK commercial property lending and accounted for 28% of the market in 2004. It was of one of a number of banks that had very aggressive lending targets through the noughties. In 2007 its commercial real estate exposure in the United Kingdom was estimated at £60 billion, 30% of the UK lending market. This is commensurate with its share in 2004 but the market had grown rapidly with the property boom as Chapter 4 charted.

In fact, the expanding exposure to commercial property was flagged up by the then bank regulator, the Financial Services Authority, in 2005, but it did not respond to these concerns about this vulnerability. Substantial losses were eventually suffered, particularly in commercial property loans, with the recession and the market downturn. Ultimately, impaired loans and advances summed to £32.5 billion over the years 2007–2010, substantially above losses that occurred in other trading activities such as credit cards. A detailed analysis of these impairments is given Table 6.2 for a shorter period, 2008–2010, over which impairments total £30.4 billion. Unfortunately for our purposes, corporate property covers a wide range of loans, not just commercial property, but speculative property development is at its vast core. It covers activities in the United States, Ireland and around the world and encompasses lending in different divisions that masked the extent of lending to this sector within the bank. The impairments from this source represent *more than a third* of the cumulative losses of the bank between 2008 and 2010 (and while they continued beyond this date consistent statistics are not available). These cumulative impairments represent almost 10% of its assets of this type in 2008, demonstrating the scale of the inherent risk of commercial property lending. In comparison, residential mortgages had an impairment rate of only 1.84%.

To summarize, the losses generated from commercial property lending when property values fell were the most significant contributor to the denuding of the

Table 6.2 Annual RBS impairment losses by lending category, 2008–2010 (£m).

	Gross Loans and advances at end of 2008	2008	2009	2010	Cumulative 2008–2010
Residential mortgages	133451	490	984	983	2457
Personal lending	37395	1443	2006	1193	4642
Corporate property	106633	1398	3995	5029	10422
Corporate other	551834	2733	5430	1517	9680
Other	194623	1047	1726	422	3195
Total	1023935	7111	14141	9144	30396

Source: Financial Services Authority (2011) Table 2.6.

capital base of the bank at a time when it was increasing its gearing to purchase ABN AMRO. Together with a heavy reliance on short-term funding the losses left the bank unviable.

Halifax Bank of Scotland

Halifax Bank of Scotland failed in September 2008 and was taken over by Lloyds Banking Group, which in turn was effectively nationalized the following month. Its downfall seemed sudden. In its annual report for the year ending 31 December 2007 the bank reported a profit before tax of £5.5 billion, yet by the following year the accounts showed a loss of £11 billion. The change in its reported lending losses was dramatic. In its half-year interim results to June 2008 the charge in the bank accounts for impairment losses was only £1.3 billion, but by year-end 2008 this statistic had risen to £12 billion. The following section reviews how this occurred based primarily on a report by the Bank of England (Bank of England, 2015a).

Halifax Bank of Scotland had only been in existence for less than 10 years when it failed. It was formed by the merger of two banks, the Halifax and Bank of Scotland in 2001. This brought together two very different banks. Halifax was at one time the largest building society in the United Kingdom; it had converted to a bank and had an extensive retail branch network throughout the country specializing in lending for house purchase and insurance. The Bank of Scotland was a medium-sized bank that specialized in business customers but also had a significant share of the Scottish retail banking market. The Halifax was formed in 1853 and Bank of Scotland traced its history back to 1695.

The merger appeared at first as a success story generating double-digit profit growth in all but one of the years up to the end of 2006, reflected in a positive stock market performance. The bank's assets grew from £477 billion in 2004 to £690 billion in 2008, giving a compound annual growth rate of 10% over this period. But the bank's growth strategy ultimately led to its demise. There are two important elements to this narrative of short-lived prosperity followed by financial collapse. First, there was the dependence on wholesale funding to support its lending and growth and, second, there was the bank's expansion of lending in the commercial property market. It pursued an asset-led growth strategy that was dependent on an increased scale of wholesale funding. However, the GFC led to the drying up of wholesale funding and the bank was unable to refinance its debts (see Chapter 5). The GFC also led to a substantial downturn in the property market, as we have seen. In this chapter we concentrate on the role of commercial property lending in its downfall, examining the magnitude of its lending in the property boom and the consequences for the bank in the downturn.

From the outset the merged bank set its course on revenue growth and increasing market share in the sectors it was operating in. At the beginning of the merger it had approximately 20% of both the residential mortgage and commercial property lending markets. It was already one of the largest commercial lenders with the RBS and it sought to maintain or grow its market share of this business. Commercial property was identified as offering opportunities for 'quick wins' and an area for an immediate push following the merger (Bank of England, 2015a, par. 268). The commercial property lending business came under the remit of the Corporate Division of the bank that included other property-related businesses, such as construction, hotels and renting, as well as lending to sectors such as manufacturing and transport.

The Corporate Division delivered the returns the bank was looking for. Its assets grew at double the rate of the retail/housing loans sector through the middle of the noughties, as Table 6.3 shows. The profits of the division accounted for a greater share of the bank's profitability as the property boom progressed. By 2007 the division contributed around 28% of overall profits, but this jumped to over 40% in 2007, when it replaced the Retail Division as the largest contributor. The increased competition between banks in the noughties meant lower lending margins so there was limited scope to meet the aggressive income targets set by the bank by just loans. Instead the division significantly increased its non-interest income (commissions, fees and returns from equity interests) from £1.5 billion in 2004 to £2.7 billion in 2007 while maintaining low growth in operating costs to improve its profitability, and the search for return led it to accepting the funding of projects with greater risk.

The result was that there was an increase in the risk profile (across all lending divisions). The Corporate and International Divisions saw the financing of larger deals, encompassing greater complexity, joint equity vehicles and more gearing, while at the same time expanding their property lending into the more risky secondary and tertiary segments of the market. International operations were extended to provide diversification but actually increased the bank's overall exposure to high-risk commercial property. The nominal returns were potentially greater but it was also very cyclical.

Table 6.3 Annual growth of assets in selected divisions, 2004–2008 (£bn).

	2004	2005	2006	2007	2008	% compound growth
Retail (housing)	209	225	243	260	266	6%
Corporate	82	87	97	122	128	12%
International	37	50	61	76	68	16%
Banking divisions	328	362	401	458	462	9%
Total group	477	541	591	667	690	10%

Source: Derived from Bank of England (2015a) Table 1.1.

As the UK housing market slowed, the bank chose in 2007 to turn to the Corporate Division to maintain its revenue growth and increased its asset growth targets. This is at a time when the world economy was on the cusp of the GFC and the gearing and debts of the corporate, household and financial sectors were becoming unsustainable. The bank decided that to maintain its credibility the Corporate Division would continue to lend, with a particular aim of supporting its existing customers. It wished to maintain its avowed mission of 'lending through the cycle' (Bank of England, 2015a, par. 276). As a result, lending continued at well above planned levels throughout 2007 in both the Corporate and International Divisions. Indeed these loans were often provided for new customers, not just existing ones. Consequently, as the scale of the GFC was beginning to emerge, the Corporate and International Divisions grew loans and advances by 22% and 38% respectively in 2007. All of this illustrates in a nutshell the reasons for the demise of the bank, but we now consider in more detail the build-up to this position.

The Corporate Division was created after the merger and operated under the banner, 'Bank of Scotland Corporate'. The division encompassed a long list of activities – management and private equity leveraged corporate buy-outs; specialized industry finance; social infrastructure private finance initiatives; joint ventures providing debt and equity funding for house builders, pubs and hotels; asset finance for leasing and contract hire; debt finance for property investors, developers and house builders; and banking services to very large businesses. Much of this business of the division, in the order of 40%, was focused on commercial real estate, including the provision of equity, mezzanine and subordinated debt finance (see Chapter 3 for definition). The division's property lending formed over 50% of its total portfolio. The objectives of the division included double digit profit growth, partly through a shift towards non-interest income to relieve the pressure on margins.

The division set itself up as a 'relationship bank' that would 'lend through the cycle'. This approach had been followed by Bank of Scotland in the 1990s' downturn and can be seen to a degree as 'counter-cyclical' lending. In other words, the bank would lend to, say, development projects initiated in a downturn not just during a property boom. The division believed that it had a deep knowledge gained over decades of clients and the commercial property markets that enabled it to follow this approach. The strategy was also designed for the bank to support existing customers through difficult times while continuing to lend to those good opportunities that could be found.

In practice, lending continued right through the noughties boom and the beginnings of the bust, so much so that a large part of the bank's property loan portfolio when the credit crunch came had been lent at the height of the economic cycle and was lent to higher risk segments such as construction. By November of 2008, the bank had commercial property or property-related lending of £68 billion in its Corporate Division, and a further £8 billion of undrawn commitments within loan facilities agreed. This lending is broken down in Figure 6.2 and ranges from commercial investment through to development and construction, including funding to housing associations and hotels. Much of this business was with relatively small and regional property companies. In relation to commercial property, £26 billion related to investment (plus £2.5 bn on residential) and approximately £8 billion to development. Only £2.1 billion of this property development was considered purely speculative (i.e. development with no pre-sale to an investor nor pre-let to a tenant (tenants) in place). However, a significant component of

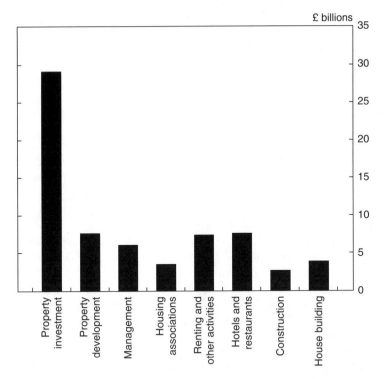

£ billions

Figure 6.2 HBOS property and property related exposures, drawn balances at November 2008.
Source: Bank of England (2015a) Chart 2.36.

HBOS's commercial property lending for investment was against properties that can be regarded as secondary or tertiary in nature. It is difficult to be precise about the figure as these segments of the property market are not easy to define: the Bank of England (2015a) notes that around 65% of the total rental income from these investments was generated by 'sub-investment' grade tenants.

Of more significance were the high LTV ratios, suggesting an inadequate level of security on the commercial property lending. This is fine when the property market is booming but created severe difficulties as the market weakened. In early 2008, the weighted average LTV of the division's property investment portfolio was 77%. But this was only an average, and half of the portfolio had an LTV greater than 80%, with 36% greater than 90% and as much as 14% (or £2.4 bn) greater than 100%. These LTVs can be seen as part of the anatomy of the boom explained in Chapter 3. Unfortunately, as Chapter 5 notes, capital values nosedived in the bust following the GFC, significantly increasing the LTVs on all properties. Capital values in the MSCI/IPD index fell by almost a quarter in the last nine months of 2008, and by the end of 2008 they had fallen by 36% from their high in mid-2007. But these statistics relate primarily to prime (and to a degree secondary) properties owned by financial institutions and large property companies, and the figures for secondary and tertiary properties were probably far worse. The result was that a significant proportion of HBOS's property investments by the end of 2008 was no longer covered by adequate security if the bank needed to recover its outstanding loan or if the borrower found itself in difficulties. And with many property developers in trouble, the bank would inevitably suffer significant impairment losses.

A particular reason why the bank found itself so exposed was that the bank's lending grew faster than the market as a whole as the property boom gained pace. The bank expanded its overall property exposures by 13% in 2006 and then by 31% in 2007 (compared with an 18% average for the industry). The figure for lending to property management and property investment companies increased by more, at just over 40% in 2007, while lending for property development over that year rose by 28%.

This risk position was made worse by the equity investments by the bank through, for example, joint venture vehicles usually with traditional banking clients on secondary properties such as pubs. A typical structure of a joint venture was 15% equity provided by the private investor with an 85% loan from HBOS. Properties were bought by the joint venture with half owned by the bank and half by the investor who managed the assets. The bank received an equity interest plus a premium interest rate on the debt capital. Cash flow took the form of rents and interest payments. It was envisaged that the LTV would fall by 1% per year (as values rose), and the annual return would be the order of 12–15%, greater than that to be achieved simply by lending.

The result was that in September 2008 the bank held equity stakes in 20 of its top 30 lending exposures. There was an excessive depth of exposure through a combination of equity, debt and potentially mezzanine investments in the same company, sometimes in the same property. An extreme example came in March 2007 when HBOS and West Coast Capital, a private investment fund, both invested £50 million of equity in a joint venture to take over the house-building firm Crest Nicholson. In addition, the bank also issued over £1 billion in debt facilities, spread across senior, mezzanine and junior tranches. It was a highly geared package, and yet at broadly the same time the bank also provided hundreds of millions of pounds in funding to West Coast Capital.

Impairments

In the years following the bank's collapse, from 2008 to 2011, the Corporate Division recognized £21.9 billion of loan impairment losses. This sum is equivalent to 18% of its outstanding loan balance at the end of 2008. The financial position deteriorated dramatically in 2008. Prior to the GFC the annual charge for impairment losses had been under 2%. There was then what appeared, at the time, a substantial rise to 3% in 2007, representing £3.2 billion, and a doubling in absolute terms. But the news was about to become much worse with a dramatic jump to 12% in 2008. The overall level of impaired loans up to 2007 as a percentage of loans and advances had been relatively static, even declining a little between 2004 and 2006 (see Figure 6.3). There was no hint of an expected upward trend given the declining level of asset quality. This was because of the benign property market and economic context supporting these funded developments. It also, arguably, lulled the bank into a false sense of security (accounting standards did not require the identification of future losses). In fact, because of the low level of impairments the division reported asset quality as good.

Complacently, the bank at the end of 2007 still thought that most of its problem loans could be recovered. It was not until the latter part of 2008, from September, that losses started to be fully recognized, eventually totalling almost £7 billion for the year (see Figure 6.4). The failure of Lehman Brothers and the subsequent significant deterioration

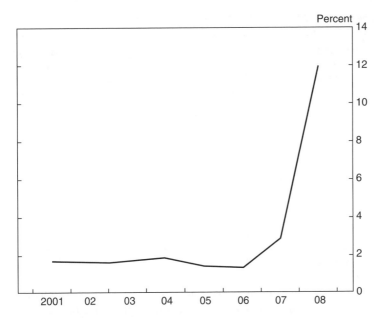

Figure 6.3 HBOS impaired loans as a percentage of year-end loans and advances, 2000–2009. *Source:* Bank of England (2015a) Chart 2.37.

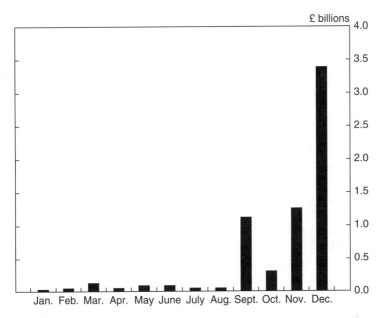

Figure 6.4 HBOS monthly impairment losses charged to the income statement in 2008. *Source:* Bank of England (2015a) Chart 2.38.

Table 6.4 Annual impairment growth 2008–2011 by asset type (£bn).

	2008 gross balance	2008	2009	2010	2011	Cumulative	Loss as % of 2008 balance
Construction and property	52.9	2.8	6.6	1.8	1.4	12.6	24%
Other business services	15.7	0.6	1.6	0.9	0.1	3.2	20%
Hotels, etc.	13.3	1.0	1.5	0.5	0.1	3.1	23%
Financial intermediation	16.6	0.4	0.5	0.1	0.1	1.1	7%
Manufacturing	6.2	0.3	0.4	0.1	0.1	0.9	15%
Other	18.3	1.6	0.5	(0.2)	(0.9)	1.0	5%
Total	123.0	6.7	11.1	3.2	0.9	21.9	18%
Distribution of losses		31%	51%	15%	4%	100%	

Source: Derived from Bank of England (2015a, Table 2.11).

in the financial position of banks finally made the bank address the losses. But the impairment losses were just set to grow much worse in 2009 as the implications of the GFC began to manifest themselves clearly. Losses continued through 2010 and 2011, and the cumulative losses over this period represented 18% of the loan balance at the end of 2008. Table 6.4 shows the breakdown between asset types, and property/construction is the worst performer over this post-GFC period with almost a quarter of the 2008 assets classified as impaired (a higher percentage than RBS). These losses amounted to £12.9 billion and 58% of the division's losses. Overall the scale of losses by the division between 2008 and 2011 more than wiped out its total pre-tax profits of £6.6 billion made in the years 2004 to 2007.

Related Issues

The aggressive asset growth targets were made more onerous by 'churn' in the loan book, with around a third of it redeemed each year. The result was that the division needed to lend £25 billion to £30 billion per annum merely to stand still. Furthermore, although the aim was to grow non-interest income, most revenue came from lending. There were therefore very strong pressures to lend, and inevitably this meant agreeing to larger and riskier projects as the targets increased through the boom. Subsequently a significant proportion of the deals agreed in 2006 and 2007 encountered difficulties.

It also operated an 'originate-to-distribute model' to securitized lending under which the division unusually accepted the full risk of a loan and then sought out partners to share ('sell-down') the loan funding with other banks. In the downturn churn slowed significantly and borrowers increased their draw-down of already committed/contracted loan facilities. Furthermore, as the market turned in 2007 the division found it could no longer sell-down the loans it wanted to. As a result, the division experienced 22% actual loan growth in 2007, well above the 10% planned growth. Indeed the amount lent increased to £109 billion rather than the planned £99 billion. Committed loan facilities also contributed to a continuation of lending through 2008 after the bank had decided to reduce it lending.

The bank actively supported selected entrepreneurs, and many of the associated deals involved large sums and encompassed equity and mezzanine debt with a high level of risk. As the pressures to meet asset growth targets persisted it was seen as easier to grow deal sizes rather than the numbers of deals. In September 2002 the largest loan facility of the Corporate Division was just under £1 billion, with a further four facilities larger than £500 million. By the end of 2005 the division's top 30 exposures totalled £19.2 billion and represented 15% of the portfolio. Nevertheless there were only two facilities greater than £1 billion. At the end of September 2008 the number of facilities over £1 billion had risen to 14, and the top 30 exposures represented 21% (£30.9 bn) of the portfolio. While not all of these facilities were to commercial property, four of the five largest, totalling £6.4 billion, were from this sector, and 15 of the top 30 exposures had clear links.

The size of the deals was exacerbated by the interconnections between the bank and the business partners. At the same time as investing alongside its business partners, HBOS was also lending substantial amounts to them. The consequences were increased potential for contagion within HBOS's portfolio, a significant reduction in the transparency of risks and a further concentration of the risk in the event of a downturn. In the period from 2008 to 2012, 14 of the division's top 30 exposures as at September 2008 – amounting to £15.5 billion – had to have their debt restructured (e.g. by entering into a debt for equity swap), went into administration or otherwise experienced difficulties. Twelve of these exposures were predominantly property or had a significant property component.

In addition, much of the other lending by the Corporate Division was to clients who were severely impacted by the recession following the GFC. Speculative house building saw a dramatic fall, and lending was primarily secured against risky assets in the form of land banks and work in progress. Pubs and hotels were badly affected by the downturn, and a number of large pub chains lent to by the bank got into difficulties. Similarly, three of the bank's healthcare clients subsequently required 'financial restructuring' in part due to the highly geared nature of their operations.

In 2007 40% of the bank's lending was for commercial property against a banking sector average of 23%. This concentration was exacerbated by the bank's large market share, estimated between 20–24% in each year from 2005 to its failure in 2008. Its market share was second only to RBS, and so with a market dominated by only a few banks this was inevitably going to create problems as the property market boom moderated and then fell away. This limited the scope for the refinancing of loans during a downturn and the concentration of impaired or underperforming assets in a small number of banks is probably likely to have exaggerated the depression in capital values, by focusing on the debt problems.

Conclusion

From 2008 the bank's performance fell away dramatically. There was a cumulative loss between 2008 and 2011 of £24.1 billion. The loss was more than the total shareholder equity of £22.2 billion at the end of 2007. The losses were substantially driven by impairments of £52.6 billion during this period. The majority of the losses, £44.7 billion, stemmed from the commercial property lending portfolios of the banking divisions. It is no exaggeration to say that commercial property lending brought down a major UK clearing bank. This is clear from the following quotation from the regulators inquiry into its collapse:

> The growth of the Corporate Division, both in absolute size and in relation to the rest of the Group, combined with the high-risk features of its business model meant that the size of the losses would have been too great for HBOS to withstand if it had not been rescued. (Financial Services Authority, 2015a, par. 399)

Britannia Building Society and the Co-operative Bank

The Britannia was one of a small group of building societies that expanded their lending activities during the noughties outside the traditional prime residential mortgage market that these institutions occupied. The motivation was the same as HBOS, namely during the five to seven years leading up to the GFC in 2007 the lending margins in the mortgage market had been squeezed very heavily. Commercial property loans offered a lucrative alternative. And just like UK banks it had turned to wholesale funding to support its lending growth (within the more restrictive limits explained above). As the impact of the GFC emerged Britannia's losses began to rise as Table 6.1 indicates.

With the GFC in full swing, the Co-operative Bank sought an alliance with the Britannia. On 1 August 2009, these two mutual financial institutions merged under the Co-op banner. The logic of the merger from the Co-op's perspective was to acquire Britannia's large network of branches. However, it also inherited the Britannia's problems, including its reliance on wholesale funding, just as this funding was drying up if not already subject to a drought. In addition, the new bank acquired the portfolio of loans made by Britannia to commercial borrowers, much of it secured on commercial real estate. In retrospect these assets have been seen as of questionable quality, and with growing impairments on its loan book there has been considerable debate as to whether the Britannia was actually a going concern at the time of the merger. By May 2013 it was clear that the (merged) Co-op was itself no longer viable because it had insufficient capital (House of Commons Treasury Select Committee, 2014).

An important cause (the Co-op's IT system also failed and was written off, making matters worse) of the bank's financial collapse was the emergence of substantial impairments on commercial property loans over 2012 and 2013. The majority of these loan impairments, approximately £550 million, were assets acquired from the Britannia in the merger. However, impairments of well over £400 million also stemmed from assets originated by the Co-op itself. These losses materialized much later than those of other banks because the Co-op had a comparatively 'loose' approach to recording impairments. The true scale of the impairments was established in late 2012 following a letter from the bank regulator advising on the criteria for loan loss provisions. At this point too, following on from the GFC, the bank regulator began to require all banks to increase their total capital requirements. The nails in the bank's coffin came from these greater capital requirements and the dramatic rise in capital losses in 2013 (Bank of England, 2015b).

An independent assessment of the Co-op's decisions over this period by the Bank of England (Bank of England, 2015b) concluded that it had failed to take reasonable care to organize and control its affairs responsibly. It stated that it had a culture which encouraged prioritizing the short-term financial position of the bank at the expense of taking prudent and sustainable actions for the longer term. It was especially criticized for not assessing the risks of its loan portfolio properly. This included a lack of recognition of the risks in Britannia's corporate loan book when it merged with it. In particular, out of the Britannia corporate loan book of £3.7 billion the total exposure of the top 10 interconnected borrowers within it was £1.4 billion. There was also a lack of attention to the growing signs of distress as default exposures rose from £1.3 billion in the fourth quarter of 2009 to £2.6 billion in the first quarter of 2013.

Part of its problems lay in the extensive reference to out-of-date collateral valuations on the commercial properties supporting its loans. The bank's policy was to require valuations on performing assets every two years and on 'Watchlist' assets at least annually. Yet in May 2013, just prior to its collapse, approximately £1.4 billion of its corporate lending portfolio had valuation dates before 2010. Much of this property was now overvalued on the bank's books so that any LTV calculations were meaningless, and certainly underestimated the bank's risks. Statistics on impairments were not based on reality but instead were set/massaged to meet the corporate budgets/targets (Bank of England, 2015b).

The story of the Co-op collapse is one of fundamentally profligate lending on commercial property. But it is also a story of poor record keeping, a bank unaware of the risks it was taking and one that deliberately or otherwise refused to recognize the scale of its problems until forced to by the regulator. The bank never recovered from these problems and was put up for sale in 2017.

Dunfermline Building Society

The Dunfermline Building Society was founded in 1869. It was the largest building society in Scotland and the twelfth largest in the United Kingdom with assets of £3.3 billion at 31 December 2007. It had 34 branches and 38 agencies throughout Scotland. But following the announcement of a £28 million loss on 28 March 2009 the Bank of England declared it was no longer viable and would be put up for public sale. Within 48 hours it was 'merged' with the Nationwide Building Society. The causes of the Dunfermline's downfall after 140 years were almost entirely concentrated in its commercial property lending book (BBC, 2009).

At the beginning of the last decade it sought to keep pace with its more aggressive competitors such as Northern Rock Bank (which as previous chapters have noted also collapsed with the GFC) by diversifying into commercial property lending (and social housing) (Scottish Affairs Committee, 2009). While it had no experience of this market, commercial lending was attractive as it offered apparently higher profit margins. It entered the commercial lending market in 2002 and set up a specialist department from scratch; as it had no established expertise it recruited externally. Once this new department was fully up and running it expanded rapidly. The society embarked on a dramatic and accelerating expansion of commercial property lending (Atkin, 2006). Assets grew in five years from zero to £260 million at the end of 2007, making up around 15% of the Dunfermline's total lending by that date. Fee-generation from this lending had amounted to around £2 million.

Besides the head office in Dunfermline, commercial lending offices were established in Glasgow in March 2005 and in Edinburgh the following year, with most commercial lending centred on the central belt of Scotland. By then the commercial lending department had 16 staff and the society had more than 120 investment and development clients. Commercial loans tended to be for investment purposes. Although the society also offered development loans they were usually for large-scale house building. These loans were each for less than £20 million, some of which were in secondary locations and regeneration areas. Loans varied between £500 000 and £20 million, with average deals around £4 million to £5 million. Revolving credit lines were also offered for five to seven years (Mortgage Finance Gazette, 2006).

In the latter phases of the property boom the Dunfermline continued to rack up its commercial lending. Even though capital values in commercial property had already started to fall by the end of 2007 it had expanded its lending to the sector to £650 million. Much of this lending had occurred after 2005 – a sevenfold increase over just three-and-a-half years, seemingly unaware of the risks (Bolger and Pickard, 2009).

One example of failure was a £19.6 million investment and development facility for a joint venture by AWG/WG Mitchell to support the purchase and refurbishment of Shawlands Shopping Arcade in a secondary retail centre in Glasgow (Atkin, 2006). AWG (Anglian Water Group) had expanded into property development and away from its core water services provision. AWG Property bought the arcade, which included offices and a car park, in July 2006, near the height of the boom, for more than £21 million; property firm WG Mitchell was a silent partner. At that time it was in need of substantial refurbishment. Unfortunately plans for refurbishment never came to fruition and a study for the city council in 2010 identified the arcade as a major issue for the wider local shopping area, describing it as an unattractive building (EKOS, 2010). WG Mitchell also went into administration in 2009. The arcade has not reversed its long-term decline and suffered from continuing high vacancies following the recession. In July 2015 AWG put the arcade on the market for around £8 million, less than half the price it had paid for it.

When the end came, the Bank of England took control of the 'toxic' assets including £648 million of commercial property loans – £500 million of which had been made in the last three years of the society's life. These assets were hived off and placed in the Building Society Special Administration Process, where they were managed by an administrator. The administrator gradually reduced this loan book, and sales totalled £255.1 million by 30 January 2014. At the end of December 2014 the administrators decided the commercial property market had recovered enough to seek a purchaser of the remaining portfolio of loans originally valued at £350 million (Montague-Jones, 2014).

A longstanding pillar of the Scottish financial system had been brought down by a brief foray into commercial property lending with its associated risks, exposed by the property bust.

Irish Banking Collapse

The banking sector in Ireland at the turn of the millennium comprised two 'full-service' retail banks, Allied Irish Bank (AIB) and Bank of Ireland (BoI), and a number of specialist institutions. Anglo Irish Bank (Anglo) was a specialist bank providing finance mainly to the commercial property market. The Irish Nationwide Building Society's (INBS) business model concentrated primarily on speculative site finance for house builders. There were also two smaller institutions primarily focused on offering residential mortgages, the Educational Building Society (EBS) and Irish Life and Permanent (IL&P). These banks and building societies had for a century followed traditional banking models.

The context to the build up to the Irish property boom was joining the eurozone and the subsequent disappearance of exchange rate risk and a significant reduction in interest rates, together with unconstrained access by banks to funding from European and other capital markets. The Irish banks therefore gained increased access to relatively cheap wholesale funding by issuing bonds at a low rate of interest. As retail (through branches) and corporate deposits from domestic savers were not sufficient to fund lending growth in the property boom, wholesale funding was employed to meet the demand, but the banks also saw it as enabling them to maintain market share in response to competition. This competition was not only domestic but also from non-domestic entrants such as HBOS. In addition, wholesale funding enabled individual banks to grow balance sheets and earnings, and to help to ensure their independence. However, as the GFC took hold and the availability of wholesale funding on world capital markets dried up, this banking strategy ended in tears. This section charts the process by which this happened, based principally on a study for the Irish government (Commission of Investigation into the Banking Sector of Ireland, 2011).

The timeline for the Irish banking crisis began, arguably, with the first decline in house prices for five years in March 2007. As the GFC gathered pace Anglo Bank's shares dropped by 18% over a week in March 2008. Share prices in Irish banks in general nosedived through 2008, and September saw the pace accelerate until the shorting of bank stocks was banned by the government, as in the United Kingdom. The practice of shorting involves selling shares you do not actually own, anticipating an immediate fall in price at which point you buy the shares you are committed to sell. The ban was designed to safeguard the banks, but as concerns grew about the banks' viability the government also raised its deposit protection scheme for private savers in banks to €100 000. Ireland was officially in recession; bank shares declined 27% on the twenty-ninth of the month, and shares generally on the Irish stock exchange by 13%. The next day the Irish government gave a blanket state guarantee to all savers that it would ensure repayment of all their funds if a bank failed. This decision to act 'unilaterally' was against the wishes of other EU countries. The decision guaranteed €375 billion of the liabilities of the domestic banks for two years, a sum equivalent to *over twice* the country's annual GDP.

It was not enough to stem the crisis. Anglo Bank, for example, was unable to recover the vast amount lost in deposits withdrawn in the run up to the government's guarantee, and other banks suffered from a contagion process. Just before Christmas 2008 the government invested a total of €5.5 billion in preference shares of AIB, Anglo and BoI. In mid-January the government announced the nationalization of Anglo Bank and INBS. The government undertook this nationalization to avoid a bank default that could set off a generalized run on the banks but the reality was the opposite. The nationalization stimulated a flight of deposits in all the other banks greater than that experienced in the build up to the state guarantee. The following month the government announced recapitalizations of AIB and Anglo with €7 billion from the National Pensions Reserve Fund. In 2010 the eventual capitalization costs were estimated to amount to €46.3 billion, involving sums of €29.3 billion into Anglo, €7.5 billion into AIB, €3.75 billion into BoI and €5.4 billion into INBS (Comptroller and Auditor General, 2010). The crisis also eventually led to consolidation in the banking sector with EBS merging with AIB and Anglo with INBS. The National Asset Management Agency (NAMA) was established in 2010 to deal with €74.4 billion of 'toxic assets' of the banks.

How and why did this crisis happen? Reports of the Commission of Investigation into the Banking Sector of Ireland on the causes of the Irish banking collapse collectively blames the financial system, the regulators and Irish society. It summarizes the problem as follows:

> Much points to the development of a national speculative mania in Ireland ..... centred on the property market. As in most manias, those caught up in it could believe and have trust in extraordinary things, such as unlimited real wealth from selling property to each other on credit. Even obvious warning signs went unheeded in the belief that the world had changed and that a stable economy was somehow automatically guaranteed. Traditional values, analysis and rules could be gradually less observed by the banks and authorities because their relevance was seen as lost in the new and different world. (2011, pi)

This verdict encapsulates the fundamental underpinning psyche of the trauma but the detail of the chain of events and decisions is also enlightening and important. The story of the Irish property boom and collapse has focused on the rise and fall of the housing market. However, looking below the surface the banking problems cannot simply be laid at the door of the housing market. The banks took high risks, partly responding to international competition, by providing more and more and larger (percentage) loans for commercial property deals, **and this was a primary reason for the ultimate financial meltdown**. As the Report of the Commission of Investigation into the Banking Sector of Ireland notes:

> neither banks nor borrowers apparently really understood the risks they were taking. Many banks were increasingly led and managed by people with less practical experience of credit and risk management than before. Property-related lending was seen as "really the only game in town" for growth-oriented banking. The purchase of second or more properties by individuals was seen as "a no-brainer". Rapid loan growth could not be funded by retail and corporate deposits; consequently, banks turned to the wholesale market. (2011, pii)

The Anglo Irish Bank was the leading proponent in financing the commercial property sector focusing on a number of long standing customers. This was its main driver of business and profit growth as it sought to grow with its customers, while also diversifying its business internationally to the United Kingdom and the United States. The bank only had a limited number of customers, most of them commercial property developers with whom it had a close relationship. By the middle of the decade the bank was growing rapidly through this 'relationship banking' and was congratulated by many analysts and rating agencies for its business model.

This was its core business with the bank taking the view that a good working knowledge of its customers, the asset security provided by commercial property and the personal recourse of experienced and trusted business men and women would limit the risks inherent in its property lending model. The risk mitigation was seen in the choice of previously successful customers and was very successful as long as property values kept rising. The leadership of the Anglo bank changed in 2005 and this led to an acceleration in lending growth with total loans increasing by over 200% from €23.7 billion as at September 2004 to €72.2 billion in September 2008. To achieve this lending criteria and credit procedures were relaxed at what turned out to be the peak of the property boom, with an inherent accumulation of risk that was neither recognized nor managed.

While the business models of the other main banks were more diversified they too increased their commercial property lending. The reality was that banks in general were accepting lower credit standards as a means of promoting continued growth and that the success depended on the continuing rise in property values. IL&P stood out from the other banks as it did not engage in speculative lending on development with its business essentially concentrated on providing residential mortgages, comprising 84% of its loan portfolio in December 2008.

Over the period 2002 to 2008 net lending in Ireland to the development and the property sectors rose from around €15 billion to over €110 billion. Around 65% of this investment was funded by four of the banks, Anglo-Irish, Bank of Ireland, AIB and IL&P with the rest from international competition. Their lending for speculative development and property projects rose from €3.8 billion in 2002 to €35 billion in 2007. In proportional terms these loans increased from 8% to 21% of all loans by December 2007. Meanwhile the proportion of residential mortgage lending dropped from 75% to 54%, although it had still more than doubled in absolute terms. This was because although residential lending increased by 21% per year between 2002 and 2007, speculative commercial property lending to Irish residents rose by an astounding average of 56.5% per year. In cumulative terms it was estimated that the Irish banks had lent a combined €159 billion to the property and construction sector by the end of September 2008, more than the €149 billion for residential mortgages, and equivalent to 37% of all lending by the banks. There was also an aggregate exposure to land and development of some €63 billion, of which €20 billion was for land that did not have planning permission.

Unfortunately, as noted in earlier chapters, the general tightening in international credit markets through the middle of 2007 and into 2008 led to a drought in wholesale funding on which the banks come to depend. There was the fatal pincer movement of a lack of borrowing facilities for banks and falling property values to support existing loans. As the GFC took hold the banks' recorded combined losses for 2009 of €19.4 billion. These losses for one year were almost as much as the combined after tax profits of €21.1 billion reported for the 2003–2008 period.

The legacy of toxic assets was transferred to NAMA, a special agency set up to unravel the mess. The indicative notional value of the assets/loans owed by borrowers was initially assessed in February 2010 at €82 billion broken down as follows:

- Anglo Irish Bank – €37 billion
- Allied Irish Bank – €23 billion
- Bank of Ireland – €12 billion
- Irish Nationwide Building Society – €9 billion
- EBS Building Society – €1 billion.

Table 6.5 Estimated long-term value of underlying property in 2010 (€m).

	AIB	Anglo	BoI	EBS	INBS	Total
Land (development <30% complete)	2955	2543	1516	96	1413	8523 (24.3)
Residential property for resale	1802	1824	960	173	476	5235 (14.9)
Investment property	4051	8202	2788	151	1072	16264 (46.3)
Hotels	565	1512	502	1	887	3467 (9.9)
Development property (>30% complete)	564	397	423	6	217	1607 (4.6)
Total	9937	14478	6189	427	4065	35096

Numbers in brackets are percentages of column total.
Source: Adapted from Comptroller and Auditor General (2014) Figure 2.2.

The figure was later reduced to €74.4 billion but the above breakdown gives an indication of the spread between banks (Comptroller and Auditor General, 2010). The actual values of these assets were much lower and difficult to quantify as they were dependent on not only the state of the market in the post-GFC meltdown but also future prospects that were particularly difficult to foresee at that time (see Chapter 7). In 2010 the estimated long-term value of the loans as assets was estimated at only €35 billion (see Table 6.5, which gives a breakdown by bank and underlying properties). Completed residential property loans account for only just under 15% of the total, emphasizing the minor role of the housing market in the decline of the banking capital base. Investment property and hotels represent more than half, most of these properties stem from Anglo's loan book. Incomplete development represents almost 30% of the aggregate value, and as such assets are particularly difficult to value it emphasizes the speculative nature of these figures. Of course the lending activities of these banks were not confined to Ireland, so it should be recognized that these properties were also spread across the United Kingdom, Europe and the United States (Comptroller and Auditor General, 2014).

The story of the Irish banking collapse is therefore remarkably similar to that of the UK banks and building societies. To fund the rapid growth of lending the banks turned to wholesale funding that had become readily available at attractive rates for eurozone banks. The commercial property boom combined with increased competition in the residential mortgage market led to falling margins and banks looking towards commercial property lending to make greater returns. The ultimate consequences when the GFC arrived, bringing with it the disappearance of wholesale funding and the subsequent collapse of the commercial property market, was that the banks were left dramatically exposed. The consequences were the Irish government stepping in to recapitalize the banks and the country experiencing a major recession.

US Experience

The US banking system is much less concentrated than other Western countries. Just prior to the GFC there were a small number of large national banks and many smaller local financial institutions. The largest banks were notably Bank of America, Citigroup, JP Morgan Chase, Wachovia and Wells Fargo (Adams, 2012). Although there has been

Table 6.6 Commercial bank failures by year in the United States 1985–1993 and 2007–2015.

Year	Fails	% of Banks*	Year	Fails	% of Banks*
1985	130	0.90	2007	3	0.04
1986	161	1.13	2008	25	0.35
1987	217	1.58	2009	140	2.05
1988	232	1.77	2010	154	2.36
1989	531	4.18	2011	92	1.47
1990	380	3.08	2012	51	0.84
1991	268	2.43	2013	24	0.35
1992	178	1.55	2014	18	0.32
1993	50	0.46	2015	7	0.13

*Number of banks at year end.
Source: Federal Deposit Insurance Corporation (2016).

a long-term trend toward merger there were still just over 6000 'banks' in 2016 whose consumer deposits were insured by the Federal Deposit Insurance Corporation against bank failure. The vast majority of these institutions, 84%, are commercial banks with the rest comprising savings banks, savings and loan associations, or credit unions, and they operate usually within individual states (Federal Deposit Insurance Corporation, 2016). The impact of the latest downturn in the economy/property market on the banking sector is shown in Table 6.6. The peak year for closures was 2010 and almost 400 commercial banks failed during 2009–2011 (the comparison with 1985–1993 is considered later). This does not include the large banks, such as Citigroup and Bank of America, discussed earlier, that did not technically fail as they merged or were bailed out by government funds.

Some argue that the causes of the extensive recent banking failure can be traced in part to the repeal in 1999 of the 1933 Glass-Steagall Act, which had effectively separated commercial and investment banking. The effect of this deregulation is disputed, but it is certainly true that subsequently US banks expanded by seeking funds from wholesale markets. Notwithstanding the problems this created, in hindsight, the role of lending on commercial property has been a longstanding recipe for trouble as the 1980s' property boom illustrates (Cole and Fenn, 2008).

Between the end of 1981 and year-end 1990, outstanding commercial real estate loans at banks increased by a factor of three from $136 billion to $429 billion as part of the commercial property boom that began in 1983. As a percentage of total bank assets, these loans increased from less than 7% in 1981 to 12.7% in 1990. Over this period commercial property loans therefore increased at an annual compound rate of 15% compared to 5% of total bank assets (Cole and Fenn, 2008). These figures include mortgages on completed commercial property and loans to residential landlords and for construction/development/land purchase. As the commercial property boom collapsed the construction/land loans proved particularly problematic to banks. Statistical analysis by Cole and Fenn (2008) reports that the level of construction or development loans issued by individual banks between 1983 and 1985 (rather than on completed properties) was an important factor in explaining failures beginning in 1987 and particularly those occurring between 1988 and 1992.

These banking failures reached a peak in 1989 and remained at a historically high level through to 1991, as Table 6.6 demonstrates. They are traceable to the breakdown of the 1980s' commercial property boom that stuttered in 1988 and then collapsed. As measured by the NCREIF property database, average capital values declined by 44% from 1989 through to the middle of 1993. This figure can only be taken as indicative as it relates primarily just to prime property and includes residential apartments. Nevertheless it is clear that the problem loans were those that supported developments that came to the market just as the property market turned down.

Table 6.7 demonstrates that the level of construction/development loans is highly cyclical, linked, of course, to property booms and busts. Following the market down-turn at the beginning of the 1990s the number of these outstanding loans falls by half between 1990 and 1994. The expansion of these loans subsequently expands year on year before accelerating rapidly from 2004 through to 2007. This mirrors the next prop-erty boom, which sees average capital values rise from 2002 to 2008 by 38% according to NCREIF, with a particular acceleration over 2004 and 2005.

The repetition of the credit cycle and the associated property boom brought the same issues for the banks when the bust arrived. A paper by Cole and White (2012), appropriately incorporating 'Déjà vu All over Again' in the title, undertakes a statistical analysis of the characteristics of banks that failed and survived in 2009. The research

Table 6.7 Construction and land loan balances at year end in US commercial banks.

Year	Construction and land loan balances at year end ($ bn)	Year	Construction and land loan balances at year end ($ bn)	Year	Construction and land loan balances at year end ($ bn)
1976	16.6	1991	102.1	2006	493.0
1977	20.7	1992	78.1	2007	553.2
1978	26.9	1993	65.9	2008	525.9
1979	32.6	1994	64.0	2009	408.0
1980	36.5	1995	68.2	2010	202.1
1981	41.9	1996	75.8	2011	219.1
1982	52.2	1997	87.6	2012	186.4
1983	60.5	1998	105.8	2013	193.9
1984	76.1	1999	134.2	2014	220.5
1985	89.1	2000	180.7	2015	256.5
1986	106.6	2001	191.1		
1987	119.7	2002	205.2		
1988	128.2	2003	229.2		
1989	135.6	2004	288.3		
1990	125.6	2005	387.7		

Source: Federal Deposit Insurance Corporation (2016).

looks back at lending patterns in previous years. The statistical analysis finds that banks with higher loan allocations to construction/development loans, mortgages on commercial properties and loans to residential landlords are particularly likely to fail. On the other hand, greater loan allocations to residential mortgages are either neutral or positive influences on banks' ability to survive. The highly publicized problems of US sub-prime mortgages were therefore focused within a small number of large American financial institutions, but not the smaller banks. The demise of the smaller US banks was primarily from losses incurred from loans to the commercial property market, not from defaults on residential mortgages (Kyle, 2012). This is an important finding that has been crowded out by the hullabaloo about the US sub-prime lending problems.

Comparison of these two American property booms and busts two decades apart reveals a repetition of the issues about the risks of commercial real estate lending. It illustrates how banks appear not to learn from past experience. It is true, as shown in Table 6.6, that the number of banks that failed following the second of these booms is less in absolute and proportional terms but the banking systems are not entirely comparable. The number of commercial banks in the mid-2000s was almost half that in 1985 (Federal Deposit Insurance Corporation, 2016), so while there may have been fewer failures in the latest bust, they were almost certainly suffered by larger banks. The comparative percentages of the scale and number of defaults on commercial property lending are also an unknown.

Discussion and Conclusions

The residential property market collapse and the role of sub-prime lending in the United States has dominated much of the explanation for the international proliferation of banking collapses, but the research here draws out a different narrative. The chapter has considered the significance of commercial property lending in the downfall of banks following the GFC. It has undertaken this through a series of case studies in the United Kingdom and Ireland and an overview of the United States, although the issue is not confined to these countries. The case studies draw on independent reports and articles written about the rise and fall in such lending during the build up to the GFC. While the HBOS case study has been presented in the most depth this does not imply that it was more exceptional than, say, RBS in the United Kingdom, simply that there is more evidence available. Each of these case studies brings a range of in-depth insights into the process and to an extent each highlights a different aspect. The large number of banks in the United States enables more general statistical analysis, but both approaches reveal a number of commonalities.

First, wholesale funding rose significantly after the millennium and this facilitated an expansion of commercial (and residential) property lending. It enabled banks both to meet a demand from the industry and also to fuel the property boom. Second, wholesale funding was seen as a means of banks growing, a strategy that was also viewed as a way of maintaining independence in an era of increased globalization and mergers. The banks became highly geared and very profitable. The accelerated growth of assets and profits led to an expansion of the multiples applied by investors to their earnings, and so their share prices rose. Higher share prices were also a defence against takeover.

The whole process was successful as long as the property boom continued. Third, no one foresaw the abrupt ending of this funding and the subsequent loss of liquidity as international wholesale markets closed down in 2007.

The liquidity crisis on its own created significant problems to those banks heavily dependent on wholesale funding, and it brought down residential mortgage banks such as Northern Rock and Bradford and Bingley in the United Kingdom. A liquidity problem can be potentially resolved if investors believe the fundamentals of a bank are sound. Banks that had depended on wholesale funding and expanded their commercial property lending were caught in a wider pincer movement as funds dried up and property values catapulted downward leaving their loans exposed. These banks saw their capital base disappear as the losses from the commercial property lending added up to ominous numbers, with these losses equivalent to more than the profits made in the good times of the boom. The implications were that these losses alone would have been enough to see the collapse of major banks in Europe and small ones in the United States. In fact a decline of commercial property values had had the same effect at the end of the 1980s in the United States and created the secondary banking crisis in the United Kingdom in the mid-1970s.

At the heart of the underlying problem was the readiness of banks to fund commercial property deals. Their focus was entirely on growth and return with little reference to the inherent risks. Indeed all banks in the case studies seem set on growth with ambitious targets, and that commercial property lending was the key to this goal. The attraction was the high markup on these loans at a time when margins on residential lending were being squeezed partly by competition. The attitude of building societies towards these returns was described by one politician at the time of the Dunfermline Building Society collapse as, 'like little boys in a sweetshop' (Moya, 2009). This quote applies to primary residential lenders seduced into commercial property, but it is has a resonance for the larger commercial banks that were increasingly led not by traditional bankers but managers who had come from a background in retailing.

Remuneration packages for banking executives were also based on growth, that is, lending, with a substantial element in the form of a bonus. It was standard in the United Kingdom (and probably around the world) for these bonuses to be paid in cash, although some were paid in shares, but even then there was no requirement to hold them as an investment. Remuneration in this way is generally accepted as not reflecting an appropriate balance between risk and reward for banks, and hence a contribution to the expansion of lending (Bank of England, 2015a). It is useful to recall a famous saying of Charlie Munger, a long-time business partner of world leading financial investor Warren Buffet: 'Show me the incentive and I will show you the outcome' (see Johnson, 2013). Undoubtedly the incentives encouraged the excesses of lending. Lending continued inexplicably well after the first signs of the GFC and the commercial property market downturn.

It seems that banks comforted themselves that the risk could partly be managed by relationship banking, by issuing loans to a limited number of entrepreneurs with whom they had a track record. It appears there was no awareness that their success may have been built on the long upward swing in property values rather than from their business acumen. It is possible that these investors may also have been encouraged by their profits during this period to seek out riskier projects, now viable because of the spiralling property prices fed by the lending.

Comfort may have also come from the consensus of the herd mentality as banks saw themselves not only competing in the market with domestic but also foreign banks. This consensus seems to have taken no cognisance of the underlying economics of the commercial property market and its underpinning of loan finance. There was no realization of the impact of the banks' policies on property market trends or the potential downside risk. This problem extends beyond just the banks to the property profession as a whole, which was advising the banks, developers and investors. It includes the failure of commercial property market forecasting. A study by Ling (2005) found that consensus forecasts are essentially backward-looking and are therefore little more than the extrapolation of trends. Part of the problem is that published forecasts by property researchers are not pure statistical forecasts but also reflect sentiment and professional judgement (Watkins, White and Keskin, 2012). As a result they are 'tarnished' by their objectives, which were often to present the case for property investment. They also suffered from the same herding problem, which meant forecasts lay in a very narrow range. Papastamos, Matysiak and Stevenson (2015) examine the efficacy of commercial property forecasts by property researchers in the United Kingdom. They find that forecasters did not predict the downturn associated with the GFC despite all the signs recounted in Chapter 4.

There is also the acquiescence of the regulators. The efficient market hypothesis (despite its many assumptions) had a strong influence on the thinking behind bank regulation, with the presumption that self-regulating financial markets tended to remain stable. The spirit of deregulation that engulfed policy makers around the millennium, across the world, meant that bank regulators and the external auditors of banks did little to address the tsunami of funding and risk. It is probable that the prolonged period of economic growth and the growth in capital values contributed to an illusion of stability. Company auditors generally gave out only private warnings to individual banks. Only 'light touch' prudential state regulation of financial firms was deemed necessary as this would stimulate financial innovation and efficiency. In this light the financial expansion based on new forms of debt appeared beneficial. There was little or no recognition that globalization and wholesale funding had changed the standard banking model and brought with it new risks and increased fragility. The tools of the regulators in this low-regulation world proved not fit for purpose in terms of capital adequacy or liquidity.

Looking back, bankers took risks on a quite unjustified scale with a complicit property profession that seemed, inexplicably, to believe the good times would roll on and on, while at the same time there was a lack of regulation. There was no apparent recognition of the banking losses in past downturns of commercial property cycles, such as that reported here for the United States and in the United Kingdom but also as an experience that had been repeated around the world. Bankers perhaps convinced themselves that this time it was going to be different but in the case of the United Kingdom it was worse (see Bank of England, 2015a, par. 384). It is probable that leading decision makers in the noughties boom had not been there the last time round and so they had no memories of what had happened. Whatever the reason, there appears to have been a collective banking amnesia. It all combined to bring about the collapse of banking systems in many Western countries that were ultimately saved by government support. Many banks have been merged as part of survival plans. The longer term consequences and the implications for economies and banks are discussed in Chapter 7.

7

Aftermath and Recovery

In the aftermath of the global financial crisis (GFC) the banks faced massive challenges to their fundamental viability, only part of which was the resolution of the impairments in their commercial property loan book. Many loans were classified as non-performing because repayments were overdue by 90 days or more. Individual investors, too, were faced with restructuring portfolios and/or addressing debt overhangs. Chapter 5 and Chapter 6 chronicled how these problems arose, and in this chapter we consider the steps taken to address these issues. The aggregate task for the banks was daunting, involving an immeasurable number of loans and borrowers, intricate and intertwined investment and occupier interests in different countries with different legal systems, lease restructuring and increased regulatory requirements brought on by the GFC. The nature of the problems is illustrated by the largest UK property company failure: the Kenmore Group managed more than £1.8 billion of property investments and went into administration in November 2009.

The Kenmore Group controlled investments in the United Kingdom, France, the Netherlands, Germany, Belgium, Sweden, Norway, Finland and Dubai. Its assets were spread across a complex web of subsidiary companies and in the United Kingdom they were mostly office blocks and industrial properties in provincial cities and towns. Kenmore had a further £1.5 billion of schemes in the Gulf. It was also heavily involved in development projects. The bank most affected was HBOS. HBOS was a joint venture partner in its £700 million Kenmore Capital Fund, and also a major provider of loans. The company's collapse left the bank being owed approximately £700 million, including £67 million as part of a rescue plan to keep the company afloat in December 2008. Kenmore's property interests also involved other banks, private equity investors and major financial institutions, all of which faced losses (UK Business Property, 2009; *Scotsman*, 2009). This is just one instance, but the problems were replicated not just in company failures but also through impaired loans on individual properties and real estate investment funds.

The backdrop to the banking system's attempts to deal with its overhang of commercial property debt is the macroeconomic environment. This chapter therefore begins by examining the international macroeconomic policy reactions to the GFC, including the recapitalizations/nationalizations of banks, the timing of the recessions in the different countries and the initial international fiscal stimulus followed by austerity policies. It then considers the consequences for the economies of many countries as recession was followed by slow economic recovery, although some still remain in recession at the time

Property Boom and Banking Bust: The Role of Commercial Lending in the Bankruptcy of Banks,
First Edition. Colin Jones, Stewart Cowe, and Edward Trevillion.
© 2018 John Wiley & Sons Ltd. Published 2018 by John Wiley & Sons Ltd.

of writing. The following section reviews the trends in housing and commercial property markets in various countries and the differential impacts of the GFC in the short and medium terms.

The chapter then maps banking strategies to deal with bad debts/non-performing loans, including the practicalities of restructuring debt via the use of retail and wholesale portfolio sales. It examines the degree of success, the role of the property cycle/recovery and the length of time to complete restructuring. It draws on international examples and compares the experience of different countries. The impact of the GFC on UK indirect property vehicles and the medium-term consequences for investors are then considered. The next section focuses on how bank lending to the property market recovered in the context of the impact of banking problems, increased regulation and a changed approach to risk, together with the weak macroeconomic growth resulting from the GFC. In its penultimate section the chapter examines the overall impact on commercial property as an investment class including, in particular, the implications for its risk premium relative to government bonds. Finally, the conclusions draw the various strands of the chapter together.

The Macroeconomic Context

In many ways a decade on the world's economy is still trying to adjust to the international banking crisis of 2007 and 2008. The long period of economic growth for many Western countries culminating in the sudden shock caused by international banking collapses was to have short-term and long-term implications. The ramifications of the bankruptcy of Lehman Brothers Bank in September 2008 demonstrated to world governments that it could not be allowed to be repeated. Governments were going to have to intervene significantly to shore up banking systems. It was therefore not simply the collapse of the banks but also the state funds required to support and recapitalize the banks in Western economies that were the first steps in this process of macroeconomic adjustment to the GFC.

The international scale of state funding fed into the banking systems is difficult to quantify, partly because of the complexities and differences in approaches/schemes between countries. It is also partly because initial announcements and plans were designed to provide signals of surety to the financial markets and savers. Inevitably the sums ultimately required by schemes changed or were not required at all, but they did provide important safety nets. Insurance schemes such as guarantees to savers, relief for impaired assets and liquidity and funding support were particularly difficult to cost. In the United Kingdom three of the largest banks were bailed out at enormous cost in October 2008. Royal Bank of Scotland (RBS) received a capital injection of £20 billion (Financial Services Authority, 2011). The following February RBS agreed to participate in the government's Asset Protection Scheme and received a further capital injection of £25.5 billion (National Audit Office, 2010). Halifax Bank of Scotland (HBOS) received an £11.5 billion injection of capital. Lloyds TSB received a capital injection of £5.5 billion, which also served to facilitate the acquisition of HBOS (Bank of England, 2015a). In return for these capital injections the British taxpayers received shares, making them the dominant shareholders. State ownership of RBS ultimately amounted to 84% of the equity following the additional funds through the Asset

Protection Scheme. These banks had effectively been nationalized at great expense to the country. Another large UK bank, Barclays, avoided such a bailout by refinancing from Middle East investors.

The British banking recapitalization announcement in October was swiftly followed by similar decisions in the rest of Europe; for example, later in the same month France and Germany announced equivalent €40 billion and €70 billion recapitalization funds respectively. The Netherlands had already nationalized that part of the Fortis bank within its boundaries. The same month the US government announced a $250 billion capital injection plan to purchase stakes in up to nine banks. In December the Irish government allocated €10 billion to the recapitalization of domestic banks and nationalized the Anglo Irish Bank (see Chapter 6). The next month France undertook a second round of recapitalization of €10.5 billion. In the United States January 2009 also saw the national residential mortgage insurers Fannie Mae and Freddie Mac stating that they required $51 billion from the government to continue operations. In February, two German states recapitalized the HSH Nordbank, while Italy's €12 billion recapitalization plan was approved (Commission of Investigation, 2011). These international bailouts were only the beginning, and the list above is not exhaustive, but they emphasize the scale of the expenditures required to address the failure of the banking systems.

In parallel, there was a globally coordinated monetary stimulus to address the crisis by a reduction in interest rates and quantitative easing (increasing the money supply). The US base rate rapidly fell from 5.25% in August 2007 to 0% in December of the following year before stabilizing at 0.25%. It stayed at this level until late 2015. In the United Kingdom, bank base rates also began to be reduced from December 2007, falling eight times over 16 months from 5.75% to 0.5% in March 2009. It continued at this level until August 2016, when it was further reduced to 0.25% to address fears generated by the vote to leave the European Union. The eurozone base rate was similarly reduced in stages from the start of the GFC (except for a blip in 2011) to zero in 2016.

Despite the cuts in interest rates, major Western economies went into recession. The US economy experienced a reverse in the first quarter of 2008, and although there was positive growth in the following quarter it then suffered four quarters of negative growth up to quarter two of 2009. The European Union as a whole was in recession from the second quarter of 2008 through to the second quarter of 2009 (as were its major economies). Some countries, such as Ireland and Spain, had longer recessions: in the former the recession began earlier, in the first quarter of 2008, and stretched through to the end of 2009. Recession was not confined to the United States and Europe, Japan had a nine-month recession beginning in the middle of 2008, and the scale of the world downturn can be seen by the fact that the G20, the world's top 20 economies, experienced in aggregate a recession over the six months from the third quarter of 2008 (OECD, 2016).

In response, governments announced plans for fiscal stimulus. A European Economic Recovery Plan represented a modest fiscal stimulus over two years, equivalent to 1.8% of the 2008 EU GDP, comprising 1.1 per cent in 2009 and 0.7 per cent in 2010. The US stimulus package enacted in early 2009 was equivalent to 4.5% of GDP, with 2.1% occurring in 2009 and 2.4% in 2010 (Cameron, 2010). However, in Europe this modest fiscal stimulus was replaced by austerity programmes from 2010 onwards. In some cases this was to resolve subsequent fiscal crises or alternatively it was justified by the scale of the fiscal deficits that had been partly caused directly by the costs of nationalization and recapitalization of the banks.

The result was that the shoots of a global economic recovery were choked off. Even in the United States, where the stimulus had been significant and recovery began in mid-2009, the economy grew at an annual rate of 2.1% through to 2016. It is the slowest US recovery since the stock market crash that began the Great Depression in the early 1930s. Nevertheless GDP per capita increased by 4.4% between 2008 and 2015 (8.1% from 2009), but other Western countries have fared much worse, as Table 7.1 shows. Many countries have experienced very modest growth in GDP per capita or even falls. The UK figure, for example, is only 2.5% up over seven years, which translates into an almost imperceptibly small average increase per year. With negative change for Denmark, Greece, Italy, the Netherlands and Spain balanced by positives in France (just), Ireland and Germany, the eurozone economy has suffered a long-term stutter. These figures are, of course, averages, and many households have seen their long-term real incomes fall.

These macroeconomic trends should be seen in a longer time perspective that encompasses the nature of the build up to the GFC as well as the failure of the banks. Turner (2009) characterizes the processes as follows:

- The global financial system, combined with macroeconomic imbalances, supported an unsustainable credit boom and asset price inflation.
- These characteristics then played a crucial role in reinforcing the severity of the GFC and transmitted banking problems into the real economy.
- Banking failures not only impaired the availability of credit to the real economy, thereby exacerbating the economic downturn, but also sapped the strength of the banking system.

Table 7.1 Change in real GDP per capita in selected countries 2008–2015.

Country	% Change
Australia	6.6
Canada	3.0
Denmark	**−3.9**
France	0.3
Germany	4.8
Greece	**−24.4**
Ireland	8.5
Italy	**−9.6**
Japan	3.0
Netherlands	**−2.3**
South Korea	20.0
Spain	**−5.3**
UK	2.5
USA	4.4

Source: OECD (2016).

The transmission of the banking distress to the real economy progressed rapidly, with credit restraint and business confidence slumping and sapping business investment plans and household demand falling, particularly for consumer durables and housing. Globalization meant that the transmission between countries was all consuming because of the interrelationships between banks in world capital markets, international trade flows of finished goods and also the strongly integrated global component supply chains (European Community, 2009).

Property Market Trends

The impact on housing and commercial property markets varies across countries depending partly on their integration of their banks to world capital markets. As Table 7.2 demonstrates, housing market downturns began in Ireland, Denmark and the United States prior to the GFC, and in the case of Japan house prices had been falling since 1991. However, for other countries house price falls clearly follow the crisis. Irrespective of the cause of the downturn, the subsequent economic cycle undoubtedly influenced the scale of the price falls. These downturns were initially relatively short lived for France and the United Kingdom, but the onset of austerity policies in 2010 brought a further fall. Australia has only a modest, belated house price fall, reflecting the weak impact of the GFC on that country. In general, however, the cumulative decline in real prices was of the order of a quarter for the selected countries.

The prolonged weak macroeconomic conditions in the years following the GFC and policy responses have been reflected in long-term housing market trends. This is despite markets having been supported by interest rates at historically low levels since

Table 7.2 Most Recent Downturns in Real House Prices in Selected Countries.

Country	Most recent downturn	Duration (quarters)	% Change
Australia	2010Q2–2012Q3	9	−8.5
Denmark	2007Q1–2012Q3	22	−28.5
France	2007Q4–2009Q2	6	−9.5
	2011Q3–2015Q2	15*	−9.2
Italy	2007Q4–2015Q2	30*	−26.2
Japan	1991Q1–2009Q2	73	−44.1
Netherlands	2007Q4–2014Q1	26	−25.7
Spain	2007Q3–2014Q4	29	−41.8
United Kingdom	2007Q4–2009Q2	6	−14.7
	2010Q2–2013Q1	11	−5.8
United States	2006Q4–2011Q4	24	−27.1

*indicates incomplete trend.
Source: Adapted from OECD quarterly house price statistics (https://stats.oecd.org/Index.aspx? DataSetCode=HOUSE_PRICES).

2008. In international housing markets, even where the immediate price downturn following the GFC was stemmed, prices had not necessarily recovered the ground lost yet by the end of 2015. Countries in this position include the United States, France and the United Kingdom (Table 7.3). These trends partly reflect continuing falling real incomes for many people, worries about macroeconomic prospects and, until recently, the promise of continuing deflationary macroeconomic policies together with threats/prospect of increases in interest rates.

Over the eight years from 2007 prices fell dramatically in Greece, Spain, Italy and the Netherlands. The percentage fall in Denmark was also in double figures. The rise of 22% in real prices in Germany is an outlier, but it did not participate in the boom leading up to the GFC, and the country's economy has seen modest growth since. Japan also witnessed a modest rise in real prices in this period, broadly in line with economic trends but after decades of decline in house prices.

The consequences of the GFC for international commercial property values are less easy to quantify, partly because of the lack of published data in terms of the range of countries, short time series and the availability primarily of only annual data. Comparison of commercial property trends in different countries is also not straightforward because, as noted in previous chapters, the published indices are based on valuations rather than actual transactions as in the housing market. Different countries have different approaches to valuations (see Chapter 4). The problem is that transaction data may be few and far between or not reliable as a true market price. Indices are based on the regular valuation of portfolios. To complete the task there is a set of rules a valuer is obliged to follow. Guidance by the Royal Institution of Chartered Surveyors, the

Table 7.3 Change in real house prices in selected countries from 2007 to 2015.

Country	Percentage change in real house prices from quarter 4 2007 to 2015 quarter 2
Germany	+22.5
Canada	+19.2
Australia	+18.2
Japan	+4.6
South Korea	+0.4
UK	−5.2
France	−9.2
USA	−9.5
Denmark	−16.6
Netherlands	−23.3
Italy	−26.2
Ireland	−35.0
Spain	−39.0
Greece	−53.6

Source: Adapted from OECD quarterly house price statistics.

largest international property professional organization, is that valuers use previous market values as the basis for current valuations. The result is that there has been a tendency for valuations to undervalue in recessions and overprice in booms (Dunse, Jones and White, 2010).

These difficulties are immediately apparent in the interpretation of international commercial property trends in Table 7.4 (a continuation of Table 5.3), which is based on properties in investment portfolios of large investors. The latest time points in this table are defined by the availability of publicly accessible data. In some countries valuations appear very slow to respond to the market downturn following the GFC and the indices take some years to catch up. It is probable that many of these statistics represent under-estimates of the market falls. Even so, we can see sudden and dramatic collapses in values, often more severe than in the housing markets. Capital values according to these indices fell by the order of a third or more in Ireland, Spain, the United Kingdom and the United States during the bust (and beyond).

The weak recoveries of the national economies noted in Table 7.1 are reflected in the performance of the capital value indices from 2007 to 2013 given in the final column of Table 7.4. The average commercial property capital values in all the major European economies fell, demonstrating only a modest and incomplete recovery from the bottom of their respective downturns. Italy, Germany, the Netherlands and Spain were still on a downward trajectory in 2013 (latest available data). Average capital values in the

Table 7.4 Trends in commercial property capital values for selected countries.

Country annual data	% Change 2007–2008	Peak and trough years	% Change from peak to trough	% Change 2007–2013
Australia	−5.4	2007–2009	−14.6	−6.3
Canada	−2.8	2007–2009	−9.2	16.5
France	−6.2	2007–2009	−12.5	−6.2
Germany	−2.0	2007–2013*	−7.0	−7.0
Italy	−2.0	2007–2013*	−13.6	−13.6
Spain	−7.5	2007–2013*	−32.7	−32.7
Japan	−6.6	2007–2012	−23.0	−21.7
South Korea	−0.8	2007–2008	−0.8	4.2
South Africa	3.4			23.7

Country quarterly data	% Change 2007Q1–2008Q4	Peak and trough periods	% Change from peak to trough	% Change 2007Q1–2014Q3
Ireland	−35.0	2007Q3–2012Q4	−67.3	−57.0
Netherlands	−0.2	2008Q3–2014Q3*	−20.6	−18.0
United Kingdom	−34.0	2007Q2–2009Q2	−42.6	−23.0
United States of America	−7.0	2008Q1–2010Q1	−33.0	−4.0

*indicates incomplete trend based partly on data availability.
Source: MSCI/IPD (2014c).

United States had not recovered the immediate loss in value from the GFC either, and in 2014 were 4% below their level in 2007. However, one word of caution is appropriate that inter-country comparisons, as already stated, are constrained by different valuation practices. Nevertheless these trends are consistent with house prices based on transactions.

More specific detail for the United Kingdom is given in Table 7.5 and Table 7.6 for the annual change in rental and capital values in the aftermath of the bust. There is some variation between sectors but the overall picture is one of rental growth that is stagnant or negative from 2008 through to 2013. After these six years some rental growth occurs in 2014, particularly in the offices sector but also to a lesser extent in industrial property. In terms of the capital values, after three years of falling values there is a short-lived bounce in 2010/2011 before values decrease again in 2012. Capital values then begin to recover with rises in double figures in 2014 for the offices and industrial sectors.

These trends in capital and rental values reflect underlying issues about the balance of supply and demand in the property market, and in particular depressed demand. In the United Kingdom, for example, the recession following the GFC in particular brought high vacancy rates in town centre shops, especially in secondary centres. The level of vacant shops was exacerbated by the unprecedented number of insolvencies of large multiple retailers in the comparison goods sector and the beginnings of Internet sales (Jones, 2010). The vacancies in shopping centres provided a very explicit visualization of the scale of the economic downturn. In percentage terms empty shops more than doubled over the five years from 2008. Voids in shopping centres rose from 7% in 2008 to a peak of 16.3% in 2012, before turning downwards as the recovery in the economy began to take shape; and decreasing marginally to 15.1% by the end of 2013 (Wrigley and Lambiri, 2014). In the second half of 2015 the vacancy rate was still as high as 12.7% (Local Data Company, 2016).

Table 7.5 Annual commercial property rental value percentage change in the United Kingdom 2007–2014 by sector.

Property Sector	2007	2008	2009	2010	2011	2012	2013	2014
Retail	2.1	0.2	−5.6	−1.3	−0.1	−0.5	−0.2	0.9
Office	9.6	−3.7	−13.5	1.6	3.1	1.9	3.4	7.4
Industrial	1.8	−0.1	−4.5	−1.6	−0.9	−0.7	0.7	2.9

Source: MSCI/IPD (2014a).

Table 7.6 Annual commercial property capital value percentage change in the United Kingdom 2007–2014 by sector.

Property Sector	2007	2008	2009	2010	2011	2012	2013	2014
Retail	−10.1	−26.7	−2.4	9.3	1.3	−3.2	2.6	8.5
Office	−4.8	−26.6	−5.9	9.0	3.1	−0.7	8.3	17.3
Industrial	−8.4	−26.0	−3.6	3.3	0.4	−3.6	5.9	16.3

Source: MSCi/IPD (2014a).

Prior to the recession, retail vacancy rates had been very low, and so the recession had been the catalyst for a significant step change in the tenant demand for shops with implications for values. Many traditional high street shops were obsolete as they no longer met the demands of retailers and investors in terms of size or location (Jones, 2010). These developments in the retail sector were mirrored by similar obsolescence issues, if less magnified, within the other sectors. In addition, many owners were unable to undertake capital investment because of the lack of viability created by the lower capital values and the constraints placed on further borrowing by banks (discussed in the property lending post GFC section below). This was especially true if they had an existing loan that had a loan-to-value ratio that was now classified as distressed because of the market fall in capital values. The collapse in values therefore contributed to increased obsolescence and accelerated depreciation (Clarke, 2014).

Bad Bank Debts and Impairments: The Road to Redemption

Chapter 6 charted the growth of impairments on the lending of UK and Irish banks that gradually accelerated as the impact of the GFC hit. While the losses began in the United States with the sub-prime crisis, the write-downs of banks are estimated to have been considerably larger in Europe, notably in the United Kingdom and the eurozone, reflecting the magnitude of losses in the commercial property market in these countries (European Community, 2009). However, it is also true that the figures are subject to a degree of massage or interpretation. This was most evident in the approach of the Co-operative Bank, which sought to keep reported impairments to targets it had itself set. In theory an impairment is a reduction in the value of a bank's loan because the expected repayments (including interest) will not be forthcoming. If the original loan book value exceeds the value of anticipated capital cash flow then it is written down accordingly. The losses are deemed unrecoverable. In the case of a default on a development/construction loan then the value of the incomplete development would be its revised valuation for the bank's accounts. This valuation will be much lower than a finished development with tenants.

The process of impairment assessment incorporates a degree of judgement as it is based on expectations and, for example, a bank might classify a loan as impaired if it is in arrears or it might wait until the loan recipient files for bankruptcy. In addition, an impairment could occur where the (completed) value of a property falls below the value of the bank loan. Given the scale of the decline in commercial property market values shown in Table 7.4 this was likely to be very prevalent after the GFC, and given the pace of collapse it will have happened very quickly. Many loans will have been in breach of their required loan-to-value covenants or conditions. However, recognition of this problem depends partly on the frequency of valuation of the underlying assets, and as Chapter 6 shows, the Co-op's policy, for example, was only to revalue every two years (compared with the international standard of one year (Phillips, 2009)). As a result, in 2013 the Bank of England decided that the Co-operative Bank had not made sufficient allowances for impaired commercial property lending (House of Commons Treasury Select Committee, 2014). The Co-op was probably not alone in turning a blind eye. Recognition of a loan default, as prescribed by the Basel II international accounting rules, also required a bank to set aside additional capital to cover the expected losses (Phillips, 2009).

The timing of announced impairments were almost certainly also a function of the nationalization of banks and the introduction of government schemes to protect banks around the world from the collapse of property values. Examples include the Asset Guarantee Program in the United States, the Asset Protection Scheme in the United Kingdom, Royal Park Investments in Belgium (linked to Fortis Bank), SAREB in Spain (but not until 2012) and the National Asset Management Agency (NAMA) in Ireland (see Chapter 6). Governments were concerned about the lack of confidence in financial institutions from distressed or illiquid assets and that by failing to lend, especially to businesses, banks were not oiling a potential recovery of the economy. Instead banks were seen as retaining cash to meet their own capital/liquidity requirements and still carrying large undisclosed losses. Governments were therefore keen to accelerate identification and quantification of bad debts so that banks could start rebuilding their businesses with the bad debts administratively hived off. In doing so they would provide reassurance to investors in capital markets and personal savers

The US Asset Guarantee Program only operated briefly. It involved supporting the value of certain assets held by the Bank of America and Citigroup by agreeing to absorb a portion of any losses on distressed assets (as Chapter 6 notes these were not generally related to commercial property). In January 2009 the scheme agreed to support potential losses of $118 billion and $301 billion of financial instruments owned by Bank of America and Citigroup respectively. However, in May of that year the Bank of America decided to withdraw from negotiations and pay a termination fee to the government to reflect its temporary guarantee (through the initial statement of intent). In the case of Citigroup, while it paid a fee to join the scheme for five to ten years it chose to exit it after only a few months in December of 2009; instead it elected to raise $20 billion of private capital as a better solution. Citigroup made no claims for losses to the government and the scheme is now closed (US Treasury, 2016).

The United Kingdom's asset protection scheme was launched in January 2009 as a government insurance scheme designed to help RBS and Lloyds (including HBOS) address impaired loans and was seen as a temporary 'sticking plaster'. Essentially, the future value of impaired assets, once the economy and property market recover, is unknown. Nevertheless there is the potential for some of these losses ultimately to be recovered, if some way in the future. Only RBS eventually participated in the scheme, although Lloyds entered into negotiations to do so. Instead, in November 2009 Lloyds undertook a rights issue to raise extra capital, and the government charged it an exit fee of £2.5 billion to cover the financial support the scheme had given over almost a year. Royal Bank of Scotland placed assets valued at £286 billion, of which only £39 billion was in the form of commercial property loans, within the scheme. The arrangement was that RBS would bear the first £60 billion of losses from these assets with the government responsible for the subsequent 90% of losses incurred. In return RBS paid £700 million a year for the first three years.

The scheme required RBS to manage the assets covered by the scheme to minimise losses, and the £60 billion was set as a sum that was seen as achievable (i.e. a fall of 21% in value from the £286 bn) by the bank. The logic was that RBS would strive to keep losses below this £60 billion as up to this ceiling each £1 of additional loss was borne 100% by the bank. The bank was therefore incentivized to reduce losses. With RBS liable for 10% of any further losses this was an extra incentive to manage the assets to minimise further losses above the £60 billion. In addition it was required to manage the covered assets in line with detailed requirements set out in the scheme's complex rules designed both to protect the taxpayer and to ensure that its customers were fairly treated (National Audit Office, 2010).

Overall the object of the Asset Protection Scheme in the short term was to isolate problem assets in a 'bad bank' in which the toxic assets were insured by the government. These assets were on the balance sheet of the bank and were managed by the bank. An Asset Protection Agency was set up by the government to monitor the scheme and support RBS restructuring of these assets and consent to disposals. Royal Bank of Scotland was also required to appoint external advisors in order to speed up resolution of the problem assets.

On 18 October 2012 RBS exited the Asset Protection Scheme. The government adjudged that RBS had been able to stabilize and manage down non-performing assets and so the scheme was no longer needed to support the bank's financial position. There had also been a modest, if fragile, recovery in the global economy so that many asset prices had begun to stabilize at least. Over the three years of the scheme losses had amounted to only £36 billion, and with recoveries of £3 billion only 55% of the £60 billion benchmark at which losses were insured by the government had been spent. Given the fees paid by RBS the British taxpayers made a profit (Asset Protection Agency, 2013).

The closure of this scheme in 2012 should not be interpreted as meaning that the restructuring of bank bad debts had been resolved or evenly nearly addressed. In fact in many ways it was almost at the beginning of the journey of resolving bad property loans. As owners of impaired loans, the banks had control of the associated properties. Deleveraging commercial property exposure was to be achieved through a combination of loan repayments, write downs on loans and sales. The loan disposal process by UK banks started in 2009 with the property market still in a precarious state. The task was intimidating, with RBS for example having around an £80 billion exposure to property loans across the world and Lloyds/HBOS having an even higher total; to tackle the mission banks set up special divisions/units.

The collapse in property values meant that many loan amounts borrowed were greater than actual values on which they were then secured (i.e. loan-to-current-value ratios well over 100%). These borrowers therefore had negative equity in their investment. Many of these owners would be content to walk away, for example if the loan covered an incomplete development or an empty property with no rental income, and pass ownership to the bank involved. However, some, such as owner-occupiers of hotels, were prepared to continue repaying the loan instalments because they had sufficient cash flow and took a long-term perspective on capital values. The initial deleveraging strategies of the banks encompassed running down loans to maturity, restructuring of debt facilities with lower loan-to-values ratios, repossession and the 'retail' sell-off of individual assets on the market, or the appointment of receivers to dispose of a non-performing loan portfolio in conjunction with asset managers. However, enforcement is very expensive compared to a consensual approach (Clarke, 2014). In the case of loan-to-value breaches, many banks worked with the existing borrower to revise the terms of the permitted level of debt or offer an extension to the loan term, although a fee was charged (Phillips, 2009).

A specific example of a forced sale was Silverburn Shopping Centre, a 93 000 m^2 prime out-of-town regional shopping centre in Glasgow. With the property company in negative equity HBOS called in liquidators who sold the property. The property received

40 bids and it was sold in December 2009 to a joint venture of the REIT Hammerson and a financial institution, Canada Pension Plan Investment Board (Hammerson, 2009; Phillips, 2010). Royal Bank of Scotland also actively enforced on some loans, pushing recipients into receivership/administration and repossessing/acquiring/transferring the properties to its internal property company (West Register). This approach brought some public criticism of RBS that it was being over-zealous, and it faced legal claims that it was defrauding customers.

The deleveraging process was hampered by the weak macroeconomic and property market environment. This meant that rental and capital value growth could not in the short-term 'automatically' resolve the breaches to loan-to-value ratios. Much of the vacant property had little prospect of relative immediate occupation, especially retail units. This affected not only existing borrowers who owned these properties but also the potential resale value for creditors. Even properties that were occupied represented threats because many tenants were suffering financially and there was a distinct possibility that they would not renew their lease. Properties with short terms remaining to their leases were blighted in this economic climate, as discussed in Chapter 5.

Initial sales were primarily of prime properties, such as Silverburn, and were in a sense the easy wins, and the real challenges were bad debts on secondary and even tertiary properties (Phillips, 2010). From 2011, banks in the United Kingdom began to sell portfolios of non-performing loans. A collection of non-performing loans was packaged into a new fund to sell on to an external investor with the expertise to, usually, profitably asset strip by piecemeal disposal. This can be regarded as 'wholesale' as the debts are not being sold individually directly in the market. The underlying assets of these funds required active management (beyond a bank's expertise) because property lot sizes were small or in secondary locations, and often loans were complicated by debt shared between banks/investors as a result of initial securitization when a loan was issued (see Chapter 6).

The first such fund proposed was put forward by RBS in 2010: a £2.6–£3 billion portfolio sale called Project Monaco. However, it proved difficult to sell and was ultimately downsized into 'Project Isobel' by removing properties with the highest risk profile, such as car parks. The composition of this loan portfolio was 29 loans with an original value of £1.36 billion, derived from a mixed portfolio of UK secondary and tertiary properties predominantly outside London, including offices, a data centre, hotels, pubs and shopping centres.

Project Isobel was eventually sold to a joint venture with Blackstone, a US private equity investor/asset management company, and RBS itself in an arrangement set out in Table 7.7. It was renamed Avestus. Blackstone itself was funded by investors including the Chinese sovereign wealth fund CIC. The portfolio was valued at a 30% discount to the original value at £952 billion. Even with the paring down of the original portfolio it was difficult to finance, and RBS had to provide the debt capital of £550 million for the purchase (from itself) as no other banks were willing. The loan-to-value ratio was 56%. Blackstone purchased 25% of the equity and was also to receive a percentage fee for managing the portfolio. Part of the deal was a complex formula to incentivize the generation of sales at a higher value (than the base value) so that it could make more than a 25% profit share if returns were better than planned. Project Isobel was one of the largest international loan sales in 2011, which CBRE reported amounted to €20 billion by European banks (Estates Gazette, 2012).

Table 7.7 Structure of Isobel joint venture sub-performing loan fund.

	£m
Book value	1360
Market value	
(30% discount)	952
Total equity	402
Blackstone	100.5
RBS	301.5
Loan from RBS	550.0

Source: Wallace (2011)

At the same time Lloyds/HBOS was also developing its first non-performing loan package known as 'Project Royal'. It was sold in the same month as Isobel. Project Royal involved the sale of £923 million of property loans to Lone Star, another US private equity company, at a 40% discount to this value. It was backed by loans from other banks (unlike Isobel) (O'Connell, 2012). Useful insights on the nature of these deals can be gained in the next paragraph by looking at the detail of some subsequent sales examples that are referred to as projects by banks.

In 2013 Marathon Asset Management, a US hedge fund, paid €400 million cash for the Project Chamonix loan portfolio from Lloyds. The nominal value of the portfolio of 18 loans was €850 million, so the price was equivalent to a 52.9% discount. The loans were on 250 properties, comprising mainly supermarkets in regional towns in Germany together with DIY stores (Wallace, 2013a). In the same year Project Thames was sold by Lloyds for £325 million to the US private equity company Cerebus Capital Management. The gross assets of the fund were £527 million – comprising the total unpaid principal loan balance of £495 million plus mark-to-market swap liabilities of around £32 million – so the sale price represented a discount of 38.3%. The portfolio was composed of 50 loans secured against around 180 secondary properties throughout the United Kingdom (Wallace, 2013b). Similarly, in 2015 RBS sold a package of non-performing Irish commercial property loans from its Ulster Bank subsidiary to a joint venture composed of Deutsche Bank and Apollo Global Management (another US private equity company) for £400 million. It was secured by around 1200 commercial properties with a gross unpaid loan balance of approximately £1.137 billion. The sale price for the portfolio therefore gave a discount of around 64.8%, reflecting the greater fall of values in Ireland.

These examples are part of a new approach to deleveraging across Europe that began with the UK portfolios of Isobel and Royal in late 2011. These sales of portfolios of non-performing commercial property loans were mirrored by equivalent packages of residential mortgages and consumer and corporate debt that were not necessarily non-performing. In 2015 such European loan sales amounted to a total of over €104 billion across 30 European countries (although £13 bn of this total was the sale of legacy residential loans from Northern Rock and Bradford and Bingley sold by the British government, many of which were not non-performing). Just less than 30% of the total values was accounted for by commercial property loan portfolios with the rest, as noted above, backed by a range of other debt. As shown in Table 7.8 these sales were backed by properties across a range of countries but focused in particular in Ireland (42%) and then the United Kingdom (14%). Banks in these countries had led the way in terms of deleveraging in Europe. Spain was the next most important country with 11% of sales volume in 2015, some way ahead of Germany (7%), Italy (5%) and the Netherlands (5%). These statistics demonstrate that mainland European banks were now seeking the same path to deleveraging. There were also limited sales in Eastern Europe (KPMG, 2016).

In Ireland non-performing loan portfolio sales were only €2 billion in 2013. There was a dramatic step change in activity in 2014 with over €27 billion of non-performing loans sold, although about €20 billion stemmed from the liquidation of the Irish Bank Resolution Corporation (IBRC) in 2013 (BTG Financial Consulting, 2015). The IBRC was set up in 2011 as a merger of two nationalized financial institutions, Anglo Bank and the Irish National Building Society (see Chapter 6). The decision to liquidate it led to the sale of its loan assets in a series of portfolios. The result was that €20 billion worth of portfolios, approximately €17.5 billion of which were commercial property loans, were sold off in 2014 in tranches (Irish Bank Resolution Corporation, 2016). As Table 7.8 demonstrates, over €12 billion worth of Irish non-performing commercial property loan portfolios were sold in 2015. In fact by the end of 2015 banks such as RBS and Lloyds had substantially completed their Irish deleveraging of commercial property loans. The National Asset Management Agency sold four 'Irish' commercial real estate portfolios worth €3.66 billion in total (including properties in Europe and United States) and two exclusively in the United Kingdom too. Overall NAMA had sold €18.7 billion

Table 7.8 Number and value of European commercial property loan portfolio transactions in 2015.

Country	Number of portfolios	Total value (€m)*
Central and Eastern Europe	1	185
Croatia	1	217
Czech Republic	1	20
Germany	6	2188
Ireland	10	12399
Italy	7	1582
Hungary	1	180
Netherlands	6	1493
Romania	1	433
Slovenia	1	156
Spain	9	3221
United Kingdom	10	4273
Ireland/United Kingdom	1	467
Pan Europe	2	3000

*Some portfolios also included residential loans.
Source: KPMG (2016, Appendix: Transaction Tracker 2015).

of assets by the end of 2015, not just commercial property loans including 42% (€7.8 bn) of this total alone in 2014. By the end of 2015 it had disposed of 39% of its assets, and NAMA plans to wind down completely by 2020 (KPMG, 2016).

The pace of deleveraging in different countries was a function of the characteristics and maturity of the property market, legal frameworks, banking systems and the state of the macroeconomic recovery from the GFC. The slower the recovery in the macro-economy, the weaker the upswing in property values and the lower the scope for the disposal of assets. On the other hand, increases in GDP often mean that the repayment capacity of borrowers improves and so leads to an overall reduction in non-performing loans. There can be legal barriers to the sale and purchase of distressed loans. For example, the Spanish Insolvency Act 2014 gave added protection to a borrower who became insolvent as a court-appointed receiver became responsible for obtaining a valuation for the underlying real estate and then revising the loan to its fair value. The intention was to prevent creditors from using enforcement as an unfair workout strategy, and it will certainly slow the process of dealing with distressed loans. Similarly, in Italy legal procedures mean that the average foreclosure time is three to five years, in comparison to one to two years in most Western European countries. The quality and availability of property on the market can constrain the pricing of non-performing loan portfolios (KPMG, 2016).

The sales of non-performing loan portfolios are also linked to the securitization of performing loans and so are influenced by sentiment towards the latter. By the end of 2015 this asset-based securities market has not recovered to its level of activity before the GFC. This is partly because of the tighter financial regulation (Basel III and Solvency II) that was introduced after the GFC bringing higher capital requirements for banks (KPMG, 2016). However, the issuance of bonds is increasing, and at the same time the level of non-performing loans held by banks across Europe has been increasing, not falling, as banks have been forced to acknowledge hidden debt problems. Stress tests of banks by the European Central Bank completed in October 2014 encompassed assessments of asset quality and revealed an additional €135.9 billion of non-performing loans in the eurozone (BTG Financial Consulting, 2015).

The growth in the sale of portfolios has been underwritten by a demand coming predominantly from US private equity companies, which have the advantage that they are not subject to the same strict regulations as banks (Clarke, 2014). There has been keen competition to purchase with each sale invariably receiving a number of bids (BTG Financial Consulting, 2015). Part of the reason is the scale of the discounts to nominal value. In the United Kingdom the figure has been the order of 40%, but in Ireland it has been over 60%. Even some regional portfolios in the United Kingdom have had a discount of 50%. It should also be remembered that these sales are not of the very worst property, as illustrated by the initial attempts, noted above, to construct the Isobel loan package. It had to be pruned of the least attractive properties. A useful bi-product is the transparency in the write-offs that the banks have been required to accept to remove these loans from their balance sheets.

Despite the transparency of these deals, the overall picture remains muddied. The high-profile nature of the portfolio sales is only part of the process of deleveraging, and the balance between retail and wholesale sales and loan repayment is unclear. For example, the wholesale fund Royal raised £923 million for Lloyds in 2011, but the bank also achieved cash retail asset sales in that year of £4.8 billion (Estates Gazette,

2013). The process will be unique in every country, each of which is at different stage of the deleveraging process. The scale of the write downs is hidden in aggregate bank accounts, but it is undoubtedly true that banks have made substantial write offs of loans. The precise figures will never be known outside the boardrooms of the banks themselves.

It is part of a more general predicament for European banks that continue to make losses year on year as a result of the overhang of bad debts, commitments from legal judgements such as the repayments of payment protection insurance and increased capital requirements from tighter regulation. They have some way to work through their bad debts (not just those related to commercial property lending). The banks in general have not been in a rush to offload their property loans, and they are content to suffer short-term pain to benefit from the expected, albeit muted, recovery in property values. In some cases development projects were taken over and completed by banks. The banks have taken a medium-term view on asset recovery, avoiding too many fire sales in a weak market at knockdown prices. The deleveraging process has turned into a marathon. The effective nationalization of many banks has shielded them from market concerns. The long-term governments' plans to offset the cost of nationalization by receiving dividends from their shares, and ultimately selling them after a market recovery, is still some way ahead in the future. Nevertheless there is a growing background political pressure to bring the deleveraging processes to a completion (whatever the cost) and clear the losses from the balance sheets to enable privatization.

The Response of Property Investors, Property Funds and Property Companies

Like banks, large property investors also experienced a chastening time in the immediate aftermath of the GFC. Many had witnessed either all of or at least much of their equity wiped out as a direct result of the use of debt to gear up to maximize investment returns in the boom, only to see the losses magnified with the fall in capital values. But even those who did not use debt were also affected. The property market saw not just the rapid reduction in values but also a sudden lack of liquidity. While commercial property assets were traditionally seen as illiquid, in the heady times pre-crash liquidity had risen dramatically (Jones, Livingstone and Dunse, 2016). After the GFC there was a very different illiquid market environment (see Chapter 5). The response to these challenges varied depending on the types of investors, and these are now considered.

Looking first at institutional investors linked to life assurance and pension funds it is important to note that there has been a major upheaval over the last decade or so in pensions, with a dramatic shift from defined benefits occupation schemes to those based on a defined contribution. This is referred to in Chapter 2. Defined benefit schemes guarantee a percentage of the final annual salary based on years of membership or the career average (more recently) of the employee. The final salary is an unknown for the pension fund, and the risks all lie with the fund. In the defined contribution funds the ultimate pay out to an individual is linked to the money paid into it and the performance of the money invested. Despite their current popularity at the time of the GFC, these defined contribution schemes were still very much in the minority.

During the crash, most of these funds, whether defined benefit or contribution, would have not have had cash flow problems so will have suspended any planned property sales, awaiting better conditions. The state of the financial markets did not affect the rate of life/pension policy maturities driven by demographic forces. However, the subsequent recession also brought many early retirements in the labour market shakeout, and as the workforce reduced so did the premium income. All these funds were subject to falls in regular and one-off contribution income in the economic downturn as real wages fell and unemployment rose. Regular pension contributions to life funds in the United Kingdom as a whole fell by more than a quarter between 2007 and 2011 before beginning to recover. Life assurance premium income fell by two thirds over the same period. Pension funds experienced similar problems to the life funds, and both experienced a downturn in assets of the order of 13–14% in 2008 (Office of National Statistics, 2016b).

At the individual fund level these reductions may have required sales of assets. However, while institutional investors own a substantial proportion of the property stock in the United Kingdom they were shielded from the fallout from the collapse in values and liquidity by the relatively small percentage, less than 5%, of property in their investment portfolios. Funds' actuaries were able to take a pragmatic approach to finessing the size of the property component of the overall fund, giving the property manager time in which to initiate any sales of assets required. There were unlikely to have been forced property sales. Nevertheless the overall value of net institutional investment in property fell in the aftermath of the GFC, through 2008 and 2009, before bouncing back in 2010 and then became positive in subsequent years (see Chapter 5).

Greater challenges were faced by the specialist real estate unit-linked and unit-trust (retail) property funds. These funds suffer from 'hot money' and are potentially vulnerable to sharp swings in money flows, particularly the mass withdrawals of funds. This occurred on an unprecedented scale from the third quarter of 2007 through to the first quarter of 2009, as detailed in Chapter 5. Such funds do not have the leeway of the more general mixed portfolios of property, shares and gilts. These latter funds are partially protected from rapid outflows by strategic altering of the asset mix, which helps in the short term. Funds that invest only in property assets do not have that luxury, and it is therefore these unit-linked funds (and unit trusts) that have seen most radical changes in the way they have operated as a result of the bust.

Chapter 2 explains the changes to fund guidelines/mandates of Authorised Property Unit Trusts from 2002 that permitted property investment of up to 100% of a fund's assets. This enabled them to take full advantage of the boom. It is surely ironic that in the immediate aftermath of the crash, the first change these retail fund managers made was to revert to a similar template to that of the previous APUT – the template that was deemed not fit for purpose as (among other reasons) it did not provide adequate investment in property assets. Many funds changed their investment mandate, with unit-holder approval, to one which reduced the maximum amount permitted to be invested in direct property assets and increased the amount permitted in more liquid assets. In some cases, the maximum amount allowed to be invested in bricks and mortar was cut to 60%.

This revision created a potential conflict, given the overriding goal of unit holders in these funds to invest in real estate. Investing in REITs, property company bonds, property derivatives and cash improved a fund's liquidity – but at a cost to performance. None of these additional assets necessarily perform in line with direct property in the short term. Property derivatives are the closest, but this very much depends on the price one pays for exposure and the price at which one exits. Shares in REITs have been seen to follow the stock market rather than the property market in the short term. The extent to which shares in REITS meet an objective to invest in the underlying real estate market is questionable (Kroencke, Schindler and Steininger, 2014). Consequently, in order to improve the liquidity of these funds, investors have to settle with a short-term fund performance which is potentially different from their logical desire for real estate exposure. On the other hand, international research finds that REITs follow property returns on a long-term horizon (Hoesli and Oikarinen, 2012).

The offshore property unit-trust field (most noticeably the JPUT market) was arguably the part of the market most affected by the property crash. Many entered the downturn in an over-extended position, utilizing relatively high levels of borrowing. Negotiations with their unit holders on recapitalizing the fund often proved extremely time consuming as the range and type of investor often had differing views on the way forward. But given the (at times) tortuous negotiations that were required, it would seem clear that the fund managers and investors involved will not wish to go through the process again. As a result post-crash gearing levels have settled down to levels much lower than those at which they were previously, reducing from, say, around 60–70% to around 25% to 30%.

But the more dramatic change has been the move away from these commingled funds to 'club deals'. The changing investor base of many JPUTs/LPs often brought about conflicts in how the funds should be run: some looking to the longer term, some with shorter term horizons; some wishing higher levels of gearing, some wishing lower and so on. Many investors are going back to investing jointly with partners they know, trust and understand. It may be a life fund partnering another life fund or a pension fund, but it will be one they have worked with before possibly, or at least one whose modus operandi they understand. These so-called club deals are often, but not exclusively, conducted between two partners; sometimes a formal entity is formed (such as a limited partnership), but mostly these deals are merely conducted informally between the two parties. These arrangements include legal documentation setting out the details on how the venture is to be run, which party is to manage the asset and so on. In some cases, the structure used is a throwback to the early days of property investment when life funds partnered developers in joint ventures.

Property companies (including REITs) were severely impacted by the fall in property values, as discussed previously. As the crisis proceeded not only were capital values falling but rental income was also in decline because of the recession. Entering a sharp stern downturn with high gearing was a recipe for losses. While liquidity for them was not a factor in terms of meeting exiting shareholders' demands it was in seeking sales (even at a 'discount') to address the scale of their borrowing and gearing and breaches in borrowing covenants. Some companies were also exposed to an inability to roll over maturing debt. As discussed earlier, many companies could not successfully address these problems as the net equity was worthless and they consequently collapsed, which left their lenders with the problem of having to sell the assets. For others, repairing the weakened balance sheet was an option.

For listed companies and REITs a rights issue was a possibility. In the wake of the recession there were five rights issues by UK REITs in 2009, including issues from four of the largest REITs – Hammerson, British Land, Land Securities and Segro, covering all the major sectors of the commercial property market. These rights issues raised £2.65 billion in total, virtually all from existing shareholders. The funds were primarily used to pay back debt and reduce gearing, and to remove the threat of the distressed sale of assets. For example Hammerson's gearing (in terms of its ratio of debts to equity capital) more than doubled from 57% to 118% during 2008, and the rights issue reduced this down to 81% (Robbins, 2009). Such was the scale of the bailout by the rights issue that these new shares were equivalent to more than half (58.3%) of Hammerson's enlarged capital base (Ruddick, 2009). Given that these rights issues were used principally only by very large REITs it is likely that this route to salvation was only practical for a few.

Property Lending Post-GFC

As observed in previous chapters, banks typically lent up to 75% of development costs with low markups over base rates in the boom, and finance was readily available for speculative projects. With the bust that followed the GFC banks turned volte-face as they sought to rebuild their capital bases and address their impaired loans. There was limited lending for development or investment in commercial real estate. This was exemplified in the United Kingdom, where the value of new loans originated against all commercial property in 2010, both investment and development, was only £20 billion (Morris, 2011). This figure was also low because demand for finance was depressed by the state of the economy. Debt finance was not available at all, or only under strict conditions: notably that the development was substantially pre-let with tenants waiting, and even then banks offered less generous sums based on a lower loan-to-cost ratio, of the order of 55–65%. Fees and margins charged by banks also rose, making finance (prohibitively) expensive and inaccessible given the health of the property market. These constraints meant that active developments at that time were primarily financed through access to corporate funding such as internally generated profits, corporate banking facilities or the issue of company bonds. A small minority of developments was financed by financial institutions through a forward purchase arrangement with a property company (Morris, 2011).

Annual bank lending to real estate fell by over £50 billion between 2009 and 2013 (Clarke, 2014), but by 2015 there has been a marked increase in the availability of development finance in the United Kingdom. The total value of new lending secured against all UK commercial property in 2014, both investment and development, had more than doubled since 2010, to approximately £45 billion (Gimblett, 2015). Banks were mainly interested in financing investment purchases, and the availability of development finance was still predominantly for pre-let developments. The loan-to-cost ratio ceiling had increased by five percentage points to normal levels of 60–70%, although margins on loans had fallen as a result of competition (Gimblett, 2015).

The continuing requirement for pre-lets is driven by new UK 'Supervisory Slotting' regulations. In December 2010, as a consequence of the impact of the GFC, the bank regulator decided that all UK banks were to use 'slotting' to calculate their risk-weighted capital for real estate loans. The precise amount of regulatory capital a bank is required to hold against a development loan is calculated by reference to its risk-weighting slot. This in effect requires a commercial development loan to be 'de-risked' through pre-lets. The minimum level of pre-lets is set so that the rental income ideally covers interest payments on the loan. The absence of the funding of speculative development by banks has to a limited extent been met by non-bank debt funds (discussed below), which are not subject to the banks' regulation regime (Gimblett, 2015).

The terms of these development loans have meant that large REITs/property companies continue to prefer to fund development via internally generated capital or raising funds on capital markets through the issue of bonds or via revolving credit facilities from banks. Debt raised on the basis of their corporate balance sheet is not subject to the strict regulation of development finance and it is cheaper for these large companies (Gimblett, 2015). Nevertheless bank lending has (finally) become available as the economy has recovered from the recession and banks have wound down their bad debts. This is illustrated by the fact that Lloyds Bank provided approximately £9 billion of loans on UK commercial real estate in 2015, of which an estimated £2 billion to £3 billion was syndicated to other banks. However, the conservative nature of this lending is indicated by the fact that less than £1 billion of this total was development finance and the average loan to value (not costs) was 60% (Wallace, 2016).

The trends in the aftermath of the GFC in the United Kingdom are almost certainly reflected in similar banking operations across Western economies. The increased regulatory requirements on lending in the United Kingdom are also part of a wider global trend, but there is no common approach across Europe. However, there are consultative moves towards standardization. In the United States the capital requirements underpinning lending were tightened at the beginning of 2015 (Gimblett, 2015).

The constrained availability of debt from the traditional banking sources has spawned new providers of debt. Some are opportunist funds obtaining shareholder funds with which to lend to suitable projects. These are called 'debt funds' and they now account for around 5% of all loan originations in the United Kingdom (Maxted and Porter, 2014). The other new source of debt comes from the life funds of financial institutions. Chapter 2 recalls the early days of commercial property investing, when it was the life funds that provided most of the long-term finance. As the banks moved into this space and the life funds themselves shifted direction into the ownership of property itself, this form of finance evaporated. But since the crash, more and more life companies are offering loans to property investors or developers. Technically, these loans form part of the funds' fixed-interest (bonds) portfolio and not the direct property portfolio, but these areas of the life company's operation will work together on assessing and managing the loan. For the life companies, it is very much back to their roots. Loans issued by the life funds now account for as much as 10% of all loans granted.

Implications for the Pricing of Commercial Property and Investment

The GFC wrought a sharp shock to economies and commercial property markets around the world. The dramatic collapse of commercial property values, subsequent high numbers of vacancies, weak rental growth, the debt overhang and weak bank lending together with the tighter regulation of banks stunningly contrast with the long-standing property boom that preceded it. The reverse in fortunes was spectacular and raises a question about its impact on commercial property investors. To what extent has the chain of events caused a reappraisal of commercial property as an investment class whether in terms of the prices investors are prepared to pay or of their search for alternative investments? This section considers the implications by summarizing Jones, Dunse and Cutsforth (2015).

A key government policy response in the major economies to the GFC has been the significant lowering of interest rates to almost zero with concomitant falls in government bond yields. At the same time, commercial real estate yields (capitalization rates) rose globally, that is in the opposite direction to yields on bonds. As Chapter 1 notes, property is usually priced in a country by reference to the yields on long-dated 10-year government bonds (i.e. with 10 years until they mature) plus a 'risk premium', so the divergence is an important phenomenon. This leads to questions about whether this is a temporary phase in a property cycle, as detailed in Chapter 5, that has happened before or whether it is a fundamental change in the assessment of the risk premium demanded by investors.

To begin to answer these questions it is useful to recap on the pricing of real estate based on the fundamental equation which explains the yield gap between real estate capitalization rates and government bond yields (commonly called 'gilts' in the United Kingdom). This equation features a risk premium for commercial property that has traditionally been linked to the inherent inefficiency in the property market, given, for example, its illiquidity and imperfect information characteristics. This basic pricing equation was set out first in Chapter 4 (Equation 4.3) as:

$$k + g = r + r_p$$

where

k = initial yield
r_p = risk-free rate of return
rp = risk premium
g = expected net rental income growth.

It is useful to repeat what underpins this equation. The essential logic for the real estate risk premium is based on the idea that property and government bonds are competing forms of investment, both seeking funds. To persuade investors to buy commercial property the yields must reflect their different characteristics. Commercial property as an investment has higher transactions and management costs, lower liquidity and marketability, and poorer information about market performance. The redemption yield on 10-year government bonds is taken as the risk-free rate of return as an investor is normally guaranteed this income without any risk. The premium therefore reflects general weak property market efficiency, which by its nature fluctuates very little over time.

In a standard textbook, this risk premium is often quoted as 2% (can be as much as 4%) as a rule of thumb, so that the required rate of return on property is 2% above the redemption yield on long dated (10-year) government bonds (Dubben and Sayce, 1991). In Chapter 1 it was reported that Baum (2015) estimated the expected long-term risk premium for the property market at 3%. However, it is recognized that this risk premium will vary by property type, for example owing to differential risk associated with leases and tenant default (Sayce *et al.*, 2006). Baum (2015) argues that indicative risk premiums differ with property type from 2% for standard shops through to 4% for secondary offices and industrials, as well as by town, lease type and building.

A number of studies have challenged this static perception of the risk premium, including Baum (2015). Blundell (2009), for example, argues that the UK risk premium fluctuates significantly around a 3% level depending on expectations for income growth inflation. Two studies by Jones (2009; 2010) have charted evolving yield differentials within the UK retail real sector that he explains in terms of the risk premium adjusting to changed liquidity and obsolescence. Another study, by Jones, Livingstone and Dunse (2016), quantifies a massive rise in liquidity in the UK commercial property market from the 1980s accelerating in the noughties (see also Chapter 4). Overall there are a number of reasons why the risk premium could change encompassing structural changes to the investment sector such as liquidity, risk of obsolescence and the macro-economic cycle/interest rates, shortening leases structures and greater international capital flows with globalization. Investment sentiment towards property relative to shares is a further potential influence, and the risk premium could be modified by key investment 'events' such as the bursting of the dot-com bubble or the GFC.

With these prerequisites the results of recent research by Jones, Dunse and Cutsforth (2015) on the subject can be reviewed. It must be said immediately that unfortunately risk premiums cannot be identified directly and instead the focus of analysis is on the gap between government bonds and real estate yields/capitalization rates over time for the United Kingdom, Australia and the United States. Although the yield gap between government bonds and real estate capitalization rates, as noted earlier, has traditionally been seen in terms of 10-year government bonds, there is an argument that a more appropriate gap is that between the yields on commercial property and index-linked government bonds. This is because the latter is arguably a truer risk-free rate as it accounts for inflation. Both were used in the analysis by Jones, Dunse and Cutsforth (2015).

In all three countries there has been falling inflation since the 1980s and equivalent trends in bond yields. This trend has led to lower expectations about rental growth and the yield gaps rising. Nevertheless there are cycles and significant changes in yield gaps that are associated with booms, followed by recessions in all three countries. All the yield gaps narrow/disappear in the mid-noughties, just before the GFC, only for the gaps to widen again in the aftermath. The gap rose substantially in the United Kingdom and the United States after the GFC and least in Australia, suggesting that it suffered minimally from the global event (Australia did not suffer a technical recession).

Chapter 4 and Chapter 5 submit that the experience of the boom and bust suggests structural breaks in the way investors behave in the United Kingdom. Jones, Dunse and Cutsforth (2015) find that there are *statistical* structural breaks in these yield-gap time series. In the United Kingdom these occur during the 1990s, the mid-2000s and the late 2000s. There is also a series of potential breaks from the latter half of the noughties and 2012 in the United States. These breaks coincide with periods of extreme change and are either the result of a re-evaluation of the risk premium or expected rental growth or both. In the case of the GFC, Jones, Dunse and Cutsforth (2015) suggest that it occurred because investors react to property upturns and downturns in dissimilar ways, for instance being (overly) optimistic about rental growth expectations in a boom and with (overly) pessi-mistic forecasts in the bust. This point has also been made earlier in the book. The process is like flicking a light switch, and hence the occurrence of a statistical structural break. They point to what happened in the United Kingdom, where even as the GFC was ensuing forecasters were still anticipating significant rental growth (see Chapter 6) and returns only for these expectations to be rapidly shrunk. In the aftershock investors at best assumed no growth in calculating capital values (see Chapter 5).

This is the very short-term explanation but Jones, Dunse and Cutsforth (2015) also posit an alternative explanation that significant property market downturns act to initiate structural change to investment strategies and the property market. This was particularly the case at or around the GFC with the corpus of flux. The mid-noughties saw the increasing adoption of shorter leases, the UK retail sector was profoundly affected by the recession and shopping on line (Jones, 2010), and the office sector was beginning to adopt the green agenda as a marketing tool to let properties (Oyedokun, Jones and Dunse, 2015). Only industrial sheds were perhaps left unscathed from structural change that accelerated obsolescence after the GFC. Liquidity also fell away as the property market collapsed, as Chapter 5 charted (Jones, Livingstone and Dunse, 2016). All these changes logically raised the overall risk premium and a fall in property values and influenced the existence of a structural break.

Econometric analysis by Jones, Dunse and Cutsforth (2015) of the underlying explanatory variables of the yield gap provides further perspective on the changing risk premium over the boom and bust. The statistical analysis forecasts yield gaps based on government bond yields and rental growth and ignoring the risk premium, based on UK monthly data from 1987–2013. Figure 7.1 and Figure 7.2 demonstate the relationship between the forecast values from the regression equations and actual values for both yield gaps over time. The differences between forecast and actual values reflect the changes in the risk premium that are not included in the statistical model. The models particularly overestimate the gap in the lead up to the GFC, implying a lower than average risk premium. And in the aftermath they also underestimate the gap between 2010 and 2013, so the reverse is true. As an example, Jones, Dunse and Cutsforth (2015) note that the index-linked yield gap has the steadiest pattern with a long-term average gap of 5%, and on that basis property yields should be at around 3.2% according to the model in 2014 instead of actually above 7%. The analysis shows that the consequence of the GFC has been a rethink of the risk premium leading to a substantial rise, but it is probably too early to say it is a long-term fundamental change. However, parallel research on fair value of commercial property by Burston and Burrell (2015) explained in Chapter 4

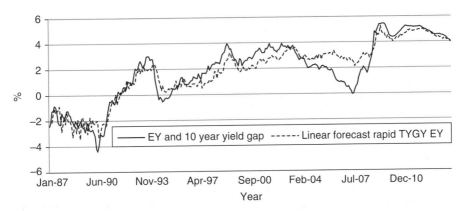

Figure 7.1 Actual and forecast 10-year gilt yield gaps, 1987–2013. *Source:* Jones, Dunse and Cutsforth (2015). Reproduced with permission of Emerald.

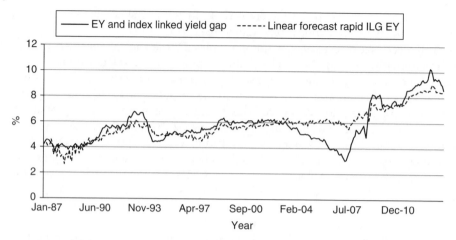

Figure 7.2 Actual and forecast index-linked gilt yield gaps, 1987–2013. *Source:* Jones, Dunse and Cutsforth (2015). Reproduced with permission of Emerald.

and Chapter 5 suggests a reappraisal happening through 2014. Typically these changes in sentiment have lasted up to 10 years.

There are wider questions about the attractiveness of property as an investment in multi-asset portfolios of financial institutions. This issue is complicated by the switch from company pensions based on defined benefits to ones linked to defined contributions noted earlier in this chapter. This has meant that the defined benefit funds are in winding-down mode as employees are changed over to schemes based on defined contributions. This is often achieved by moving new employees over to defined contributions. The implications for property investment is uncertain, and there is an argument that it could be higher in defined contribution schemes than in defined benefit schemes; because the average age of the defined contribution scheme member is younger, and hence they can support greater long-term investment in real assets.

Actuaries have to address the appropriateness of an illiquid property class in a declining defined benefit fund, counterbalanced by the attributes of property in a multi-asset fund, in particular its high and relatively secure yield and the diversification the asset class offers. It is fair to say that currently the latter attributes are seen by many to outweigh the increased problems of liquidity. However, as traditional life assurance funds continue to wind down (with the move to unit-linked defined contribution schemes), there will come a point where it is not viable to include commercial property in its asset mix; and that time has probably been brought forward as a result of the problems recently encountered. The move to defined contribution schemes will expedite the move toward indirect property investment (Harrison, Blake and Key 2013).

Conclusions

The recovery from the bust at the outset was not simply daunting in terms of the mountain of bad debt facing the banks; the GFC had brought a shock to the world economy, unprecedented at least in living memory. There had been a failure of financial regulation that had led almost to an international economic meltdown as the banking systems lay on the brink of collapse. The global nationalization of banks, recessions and the sovereign debt crises that followed meant that banks, investors and policy makers were stepping into the unknown. There was inevitably going to be more financial regulation, but the first need was stabilization. The fundamental key to resolving the ubiquitous bank problems of bad debt was the revival of individual economies within a broader framework of an improving global economy.

With perhaps the exception of the United States, in the major Western countries the subsequent economic upturn has been muted. The upswing was dampened by the wide acceptance across Europe of macroeconomic austerity policies from 2010. The economies in some countries have not recovered at all. The relatively weak macroeconomic context has been a frail platform for the revival of housing and commercial property market values from the lows experienced in the GFC. In many countries house prices were still lower by some margin in real terms in 2015 than they were in 2007. In the commercial real estate capital values were also slow to pick up. In the United Kingdom significant rental growth did not materialize until 2014, and then not in the retail sector, which was particularly affected by the recession and continuing falling real incomes. UK capital values also begin to revive in real terms in 2014, but the retail sector did not experience any rebound as it addressed a quagmire of high vacancy rates.

The huge scale of the non-performing commercial property loans following the GFC could not be resolved overnight. Although banks (and agencies/bad banks such as NAMA) had effective control of the properties involved it was not possible to sell them off immediately without flooding the market and setting off a fire sale of assets. The strategy followed was to incrementally work through the legacy of bad debts but the speed of this process was inevitably slowed by the feeble post-recession economic 'bounce' (although supported by low interest rates). United Kingdom banks were probably nearing the end of this process in 2016 after seven years, although this has required considerable write-offs. NAMA set 2020 as its target to complete its task and is apparently ahead of this timetable. However, banks/bad banks in other countries delayed starting their deleveraging and are almost certainly behind these timescales. The weakest assets were/are inevitably at the end of the queue and the most difficult to resolve.

The deleveraging process has involved a high proportion of consensual (re)arrangements between borrowers and banks, often involving negotiation of loan terms, not simply sales of the assets. There have also been many enforced sales although their numbers have been mitigated by the additional costs involved. As the relatively easy to resolve distressed loans were addressed, banks turned to wholesale sales of secondary properties as complex loan arrangements packaged into portfolios and sold to the highest bidder. Most of the purchasers of these portfolios have been American private equity funds, which were not subject to the same regulatory strictures as banks. They raised capital especially for this purpose and hired relevant expertise, and without the regulatory burden these equity funds were able to achieve a higher return than banks on the assets (Clarke, 2014).

The balance of retail and wholesale sales in this deleveraging is unknown, buried in the internal accounts of banks. It has varied between countries as legal frameworks have influenced the nature and pace of the deleveraging process. There is a general lack of transparency as to the costs and the nature and scale of the risks taken in bank lending in the boom. The result is that there is now greater international regulation of the banks in terms of capital requirements to support lending. In the United Kingdom there have been calls for better information on individual loans to be made available to the regulator (Investment Property Forum, 2014).

The problems facing investors following the GFC were not just falling values but also weak liquidity. This combination made it very difficult to adjust to the dramatic turn of events through sales. Large financial institutions delayed property sales until market conditions improved. But these institutions also had to adapt to the wider restrictive macroeconomic context and its implications for pension/life premiums and expenditures. To some extent they were sheltered from the lack of liquidity by their multi-asset portfolios. Specialist unit-linked property funds and unit trusts were much more susceptible to the exceptional outflow of funds following the GFC. It is therefore the unit-linked funds (and unit trusts) that have seen the most radical changes in the way they operate, and in particular have increased their proportion of liquid assets. To some extent this has changed the underlying nature of these funds. More widely the GFC exposed many flaws/conflicts in indirect real estate investment funds and led to the greater use of club arrangements in the form of, say, limited partnerships/joint ventures to diversify and share risk between a small number of partners.

To survive, many property companies had to seek substantial additional capital. Large REITs in the United Kingdom were forced to undertake very large rights issues whereby existing shareholders were obliged to buy further shares (to shore up their existing investments). The capital raised was in some cases equivalent to more than the previous equity base and was mainly used to pay off debts and reduce gearing.

In the aftermath of the GFC banks have become far more conservative in their lending to the commercial property market as judged by loan-to-value ratios (or ratios to cost in the case of development). It is a classic case of the underlying approach towards risk from banks fundamentally changing from under-pricing risk in the boom to over-pricing in the subsequent initial recovery. This about turn has been reinforced by the financial collapse of the banks and the need for recapitalization, and the more restrictive banking regulation on lending.

The overall impact of the long boom, dramatic bust and slow recovery has shaken investors' attitudes toward commercial property. The sudden swing in fortunes saw expectations about rental and capital values turned on their head. The unprecedented rise in liquidity in the build up to the peak of the boom was spectacularly reversed as the property market collapsed. The events challenged the underlying pricing of commercial property by investors. In particular the impact was a reappraisal of the risks associated with property as the recession exposed its frailties in particular in terms of obsolescence.

8

Conclusions

The boom and bust of the 2000s is the stand-out global commercial property phenomenon of modern times. It still casts a shadow on the market a decade later. The story of the boom is bound up with the role of the banks' lending policies but also investors' arguably irrational exuberance. The boom was experienced across the world although its scale differed with national market conditions. At its extreme, Ireland saw capital values of commercial properties rise by 70%, while in the United Kingdom and the United States capital values grew by just over 50% and almost 40% respectively.

The foundation of the commercial property boom can be traced to the long upswing in the global economy from the mid-1990s on. This long period of synchronized economic growth led many economists, investors and governments around the world to believe that severe macroeconomic cycles were in the past. Economic growth provided the platform for rising demand for commercial property, which in turn saw both rents and capital values increase. It also led to sustained growth in house prices in many Western countries through the early noughties.

The commercial property boom was also supported by a change of investment sentiment. The collapse in share prices as the dot-com bubble burst saw investors turn to the bricks and mortar of commercial property with its secure rental income as its attraction. The establishment of retail investment funds, created partly as a result of taxation changes, was a further important ingredient as they allowed greater access to commercial property investment for small investors. This innovation quickly gained traction and the number of these property funds grew rapidly in the early to mid-part of the decade. Vast investment sums flowed into commercial property in the United Kingdom, especially from 2003 through to 2006, as the boom gathered pace. In parallel, banks expanded their lending for commercial property investment offering more and more generous loan-to-value (LTV) ratios at relatively low interest rates and at ever keener margins. The result was that the commercial property investment market was driven by record levels of investment funds many of which were very highly geared. As the boom proceeded it meant that heavily indebted investors saw their geared returns soar to reach mouth-wateringly high levels.

Rather than worry about the underlying economics, investors were seduced by 'doing the deal' and there began a frenzy of activity with transaction volumes in the United Kingdom and elsewhere attaining record levels. Extrapolation of capital value and return trends drove investment with little, if any, attention to rental value growth. Part of the reason for this may have been ignorance of property market behaviour on the

Property Boom and Banking Bust: The Role of Commercial Lending in the Bankruptcy of Banks,
First Edition. Colin Jones, Stewart Cowe, and Edward Trevillion.
© 2018 John Wiley & Sons Ltd. Published 2018 by John Wiley & Sons Ltd.

part of new investors looking for quick returns. But such was the scale of the investment flows that it is difficult not to conclude that many key players were culpable, including financial institutions and agents/advisors. Capital values were yield driven in a financial environment that became increasingly irrational and detached from fundamental pricing.

In this context, commercial property is a complex investment medium. Unlike equities and bonds, where profit drivers are fairly well understood by investors, commercial property involves much more micro-managing. Successful investment requires a detailed knowledge of the marketplace, the location as well as local economic and demographic factors; understanding of the development process; and the ability to manage internal or external teams in the course of day-to- day work. On top of that, a knowledge of the debt markets, tax and property vehicle structures are prerequisites for the modern property fund manager. The early 2000s were associated with the entry of totally new investors into commercial property, many of whom were ignorant of the minutia described above. At a time when the market was delivering ultra-quick capital profits from yield compression, very little consideration of the minutia seemed necessary.

Investment funds were chasing a stock of commercial property that was virtually static. This resulted in capital values increasing without a concomitant level of rental growth. While rental growth was commensurate with macroeconomic expansion, it was not keeping pace with the rise in capital values. It was, in retrospect, an unsustainable process as investors sought opportunities from the commercial property stock bidding up capital values, encouraging even more investment as investors joined the bandwagon. These dynamics meant that the boom would inevitably collapse. The only questions were when the correction would come and to what extent.

However, when the commercial property market meltdown came it was not initiated by its internal dynamics but from an unlikely external source that at first sight seemed innocuous. The tentacles of the sub-prime residential lending crisis in the United States were to poison the workings of world capital markets, bring banking collapses on an international scale and ultimately bring economic austerity to many Western economies. The domestic American housing market problems arguably first came to international prominence when New Century Financial, a large mortgage lending company (which was not subject to US banking rules), filed for bankruptcy at the beginning of April 2007. Within only a few months the global financial system was teetering on the verge of collapse. A further few months on and residential and commercial property markets around the world had swiftly turned from boom to bust. At the same time world economies were in a tailspin and recession engulfed most Western countries. After an internationally coordinated fiscal and monetary stimulus, policy makers in many countries turned to fiscal austerity to address the problem. A decade on from the global financial crisis (GFC), the world economy and property markets have not yet fully come to terms with the consequences.

To fully understand the phenomenon the book has taken a step back by first examining the evolving investment landscape and the changing lending practices of the banking sector over previous decades in Chapter 2. Subsequent chapters, Chapter 3 through to Chapter 5, examined in detail the build-up to the boom, and the internal dynamics of the boom and the bust. The banks were crucial to the commercial property boom through the support their lending gave to the investment frenzy, and when they turned off this funding tap it was not only the end of the party but the beginning of the down-turn. Chapter 6 considered the detail of why and how this occurred. Chapter 7 reviewed the consequences for the key players and how they extricated themselves from the problems that arose given a stuttering global economy and a muted property market recovery.

The remainder of this chapter considers a number of themes that have underpinned the boom and bust. First, the role of globalization is reviewed, noting in particular the international commonality of macroeconomic cycles and world capital markets that entwined banks in a labyrinth of debt instruments. It also resulted in greater international competition for commercial property lending between banks. The second section draws attention to the fact that the primary quantification of the property boom and bust has been based on valuations rather than actual transaction prices. It considers to what extent the use of valuations biases our understanding. The following section examines the responsibility of banking through the boom, bust and recovery. It assesses the importance of the entrepreneurial spirit that engulfed the banks and the change of business model to one based on wholesale funding. It appraises the general impact of their reckless lending. In the next section the role of irrational exuberance of the property sector is evaluated, including how structural changes to the investment industry contributed first to over-optimism and then to the reverse, over-pessimism, in the bust. The final sections look to the future in terms of could it happen again and what can be done.

Globalization

Since the 1970s globalization, combined with ubiquitous financial deregulation of banks, has brought increasing flows of international financial capital and trade across the globe. It has resulted in a greater synchronization of world economies and of property market behaviour. World economic integration has meant that property cycles can be seen simultaneously in distant cities in different parts of the globe. This is particularly true of cities with a focus on financial services. Importantly, strong user demand for commercial property has been correlated with investor demand for property as an income-producing asset, and so both user and investment markets can be affected by global events.

The late 1990s and early noughties were characterized by a long period of global economic growth. With the national economies of many countries benefitting from this upturn, commercial property markets experienced rising demand, values improved and property yields fell. This was especially so in those countries more intimately integrated into the global capital cycle, and where long-term changes in the nature of cities (especially those linked to financial and business services) resulted in similar property market trends. However, countries have distinct institutions and legal systems which, with different informational efficiencies and transparencies, moderated the outcomes.

From the early 2000s trends in property investment mirrored, and were shaped by, conditions in other investment markets following the international dot-com crash. Central banks around the world cut interest rates to very low levels in historical terms. At the same time, high volumes of savings in the world economy attempted to secure the highest possible returns and a 'hunt for yield' developed which pushed down bond yields. This in turn compressed yields in a range of markets, including corporate bonds and property. Risk premiums were eroded as investors projected conditions of cheap money and low volatility into the future.

These processes all contributed to the parallel nature of the property booms in different countries. The key features of globalization were seen in a world capital market that had created intertwined banking systems and macroeconomies inextricably connected by trade in goods and services. It can be traced back to a globalization that encompassed greater deregulation of banks and international capital flows. World capital markets saw banks internationalize and compete across continents, offering, amongst other services, mortgages and development finance. Yet the globalization that had contributed to the boom would also be the author of its downfall.

The international competition often meant domestic banks offering increasingly generous lending terms to maintain their market share and the adoption of global approaches. These mortgages and development loans were often then securitized through selling bonds backed by these loan repayments. The sale of these bonds on the world wholesale markets supported further lending, underpinning the property boom. Additionally, the banks moved much of this business off balance sheet, a practice which reduced their regulatory capital requirements allowing them to grow their business at a faster rate than otherwise would have been the case. However, this practice contributed to the banking industry's extremely weak reserving position as it entered the downturn. By creating these securitized products that were highly profitable for the manufacturers during the boom years insufficient analysis was conducted by both the originator and the purchaser.

As these bonds were sold on, an international basis, a global spider's web of linkages was created between banks around the world. It was this interweaving of bond sales that ultimately brought the edifice tumbling down as bonds backed by worthless US sub-prime mortgages created a contagion of doubt about all bonds. Unfortunately many banks had bought these bonds on the basis that they were assets that offered high liquidity, believing they could easily be sold as they were backed by reputable international banks. And issuing banks had presumed that they could continue to reissue bonds backed by these securities to support growth of their lending. Both these assumptions proved wrong from August 2007, bringing on the GFC as banks buckled and turned to governments for bailouts.

The GFC represented the first true world recession, whose icy storm was felt by all major countries. At the same time the GFC caused the provision of credit to evaporate almost overnight, impacting on banks' abilities to oil the workings of the macroeconomy. Falling output and rising unemployment and business failures inevitably impacted on commercial real estate (CRE) returns and together with a dearth of available credit brought property market values crashing down.

Globalization therefore contributed to the boom and created the bust. But it also became part of the resolution of the property market consequences. Overseas investors such as sovereign wealth funds were active purchasers certainly of UK properties, especially in London, in the aftermath. Such investment shored up capital values from falling even further. At the same time many American private equity firms, supported by sovereign wealth funds, were buying up property debts from banks across Europe, albeit at discounted prices. The international regulation of banks was also subsequently strengthened through Basel III. This international regulatory framework for banks brought in higher capital requirements for the issuing of loans from 2013.

The Boom and Bust through the Prism of Valuations

The narrative of the commercial property boom and bust has been told in the book primarily by reference to property valuations. Many of the valuations quoted related to those monitoring the portfolios of financial institutions. These valuations do not necessarily relate to market transactions. In addition, valuations are undertaken according to professional rules and practices which vary between countries. A further issue is that valuations that are based on market evidence become less reliable when there are few market transactions as occurred in the property market downturn.

Notwithstanding that there appeared to be a common compression of internal property market yields across many countries during the boom years. Inevitably this pattern was mediated by national market conditions, as well as the operation of financial and legal institutions influencing the transparency of the market.

Certainly some countries, such as Ireland, the United Kingdom and the United States, had sharp downward valuation adjustments as the GFC unfolded followed by a relatively modest upward readjustment that aligned with the macroeconomic cycles in these countries. Elsewhere, for example in Western Europe, values fell less in the downturn but have taken much longer to recover, if at all. This may be a genuine reflection of less volatility in these markets but conceivably may be just a result of different valuation practices or even informational differences. Given that valuation practice is not universally harmonized and there have been some differences in national macroeconomic cycles there was a remarkable coming together of property performance in many countries over the boom, the bust and the aftermath.

It is important to note that the sales of large bank portfolios in the United Kingdom from 2009 onwards were effectively 'off market' in the sense that there is no evidence that they appeared in either the transactional or the mainly institutional data sets maintained by the likes of MSCI and Property Data. Nonetheless these valuations almost certainly impacted on valuers' overall views of the market.

Role of Banking

The emergence of an entrepreneurial banking sector, from its historic staid and conservative approach to business even as late as the early 1980s, sets the stage for the commercial and residential property booms. It could be called a buccaneering spirit, a retreat from traditional financial propriety and responsibility, or a corrupt culture that gave rise to corporate casino banking. It was seen in the United States with the securitization of sub-prime mortgages into bonds given triple A ratings that can be described at best as reckless. It was all supported by incentive-based remuneration packages designed to maximize deals (and do so over the short term). The process was also sustained by governments that placed great faith in the expansion of financial services as a leading sector of the economy and buttressed it by policies of deregulation.

The noughties saw the banks fundamentally change their business model and become overwhelmingly dependent on wholesale funding. The expansion of this funding provided the engine to grow their businesses. It enabled the extension of lending not only for residential mortgages but also for purchase of commercial property. Indeed commercial property was seen as more profitable than residential lending and was targeted particularly for growth. It was also seen as offering secure returns. This misplaced optimism drove higher and higher lending targets for staff. To achieve these goals banks fought off competition by offering more and more generous lending terms to borrowers. In the boom this created high returns for investors and the banks, and the risks complicit with this high gearing were ignored.

There was a blissful ignorance of the scale of the risks or the potential consequences. A prime example is banks in Ireland that accepted personal guarantees from leading developers whose wealth was tied to their real estate empires. These guarantees proved worthless when the property market crashed in 2008. One such developer sued the banks for negligence in funding the company's unrealistic schemes (Murphy, 2012). Similarly, in November 2008, when Deutsche Bank sued Donald Trump after he failed to repay $40 million of a $640 million real estate loan, it was countersued on the basis that the bank had contributed to the global recession that had depressed property prices. He demanded $3 bn in damages (Harding *et al.*, 2017).

When the credit crunch came the result was not simply about the fall in property values. The consequences were effectively terminal for many banks. The initial problems were liquidity related as banks found it impossible to refinance their borrowing through the wholesale funding market which had 'shut down'. It became an existential crisis as the deep falls in commercial property values created a mountain of impaired loans as investors fell into negative equity and many were unable/unwilling to make the required repayments on their loans. All the profits made in the good times of the boom were wiped out by the losses on commercial property lending (but not residential). Even worse, the scale of the losses was such that the capital bases of many banks were completely depleted and they went bust. Many banks were nationalized or bailed out by tax payers, although some closed, and in the years following the GFC the survivors focused on rebuilding their capital. As a result, bank lending collapsed and banks' attentions were on trying to bring their bad debts back to life.

The challenge of impaired loans was complex, and addressing the task has been a lengthy process, still incomplete after a decade. Banks chose to take a long-term strategy to retrieve their losses. The degree of success has been opaque but has definitely been at a cost, with many debts completely written off and others sold on at a considerable discount to their paper value. A particular reason was the subdued property market and muted global economic recovery from the GFC, as governments in Western Europe turned to fiscal austerity policies to solve their fiscal deficits. These fiscal deficits were built up in the main as part of the financial packages required to rescue the banks. The ramifications of the banking collapses therefore stretched out to embrace not just the short-term recession following the GFC but also the long term. In 2016 many countries' real GDP per capita was still lower than at the peak of the boom. In other words, people were poorer than they were in 2008, and this has had inexorable consequences for commercial property values. The banks were pivotal in the stoking of the boom, precipitating the collapse and dampening the recovery.

Irrational Exuberance

The commercial property boom of the noughties was earlier characterized as one in which investors saw dramatic returns supported by banks willing to lend more and more to them. The high returns were partly down to the substantial gearing in a rising market. It was not just individual investors who were heavily geared but also the property investment stock as a whole.

The scale of the investment boom was unprecedented. Previous property booms such as that in the 1980s were also linked to substantial development as a response to rising rents and occupational demand. In this last boom development contributed only a modest addition to the commercial property stock. And as noted earlier in this book, the returns were all yield driven and not supported by adequate rental growth. It is arguably the first commercial property boom that was driven predominantly by investment speculation and possibly irrational exuberance.

How did this happen? There was the long global upswing in economies across the world, the 'Great Moderation' that encouraged commentators to believe that recessions were in the past. Downside risk was too readily discounted. Certainly ready amounts of debt finance helped. Debatably the banks should have known better, but incompetence and inexperience was a factor. In the United Kingdom the larger commercial banks were increasingly led not by traditional bankers but relatively new young managers who had come from a retail background. There was also comfort in numbers as banks from around the world were competing strongly for the same business.

As discussed earlier, it seems the investors, supported by the banks, were simply extrapolating growth in returns and irrationally expecting it to continue. This presumption appears to have been held not just by new retail investors but investment fund managers as well. Indeed the whole property profession, whether employed by financial institutions or by property consultants offering advice, did not foresee any day of reckoning. No property forecasters predicted anywhere near the extent of the downturn.

The result of the over-optimism was that property markets became increasingly irrational. These behavioural patterns impacted on pricing, distorting a proper assessment of price, value and worth. Investment decisions appear to have taken no cognisance of the underlying economics of the commercial property market. In the United Kingdom many fund managers had no option but to focus on buying sufficient property to meet the mandate requirements of their funds as money flowed in. As the decade progressed fund managers were finding it increasingly difficult to source suitable product to invest the wall of money that was arriving at their doorsteps, and increasingly they moved up the risk curve into non-prime property with more uncertain income. The result was that yields fell but risk levels rose, and there was little thought for the management of liquidity. But did these fund managers explain to their clients the necessary change in investment policy? Many funds failed to invest all their cash flow in bricks and mortar during the boom years, the cash drag impacting on performance. The exact opposite would occur during the crash. Again, were their clients made aware of these fundamentally important features of commercial property funds?

The early 2000s witnessed a change in the way that investment products were marketed to retail investors in the United Kingdom. The 'private client' business model, in which firms of stockbrokers or independent financial advisors (IFAs) managed individuals' share portfolios, was subject to significant change. In addition to these IFAs came a new grouping of 'wealth managers'. Their remit was much wider than what they replaced as it now encompassed all asset classes and additionally covered tax planning and other related business. As these wealth managers built up their business, they directed more and more funds to commercial property. Not only were property funds benefiting from this new flow of additional business, they had become a slave to the new asset allocation masters. No longer were individual investors making independent decisions about investing or disinvesting, increasingly these decisions would be taken by the wealth managers. In this new world the management of liquidity was neglected, and yet it had now become paramount in order to cope with the sizeable movements of funds that were now being seen.

When sentiment turned with the GFC came the need to sell to meet redemptions but retail funds, certainly in the United Kingdom, did not have the mechanisms in place to do much more than sell property quickly at fire sale values. Some funds were lucky and had built up substantial cash reserves (not necessarily out of prudence but out of their inability to invest), and they were able to call upon these reserves to pay the first wave of sellers. As that proved inadequate, however, most funds resorted to selling their most liquid assets – usually the most prime – and often at prices well below the latest valuation. It is probable that it was these sales by retail funds that propelled the collapse in market valuations. But given the small number of sales it is likely that these valuations exhibited the reverse of irrational exuberance, irrational panic, and values fell to what might be considered unjustifiably low levels.

Could It Happen Again?

The excesses of the banking system in the noughties were made possible by the weakness of self-regulation. Regulation had been deliberately diluted as governments accepted the industry's arguments that greater freedom would generate innovation and profits. In turn this meant more tax receipts, so everyone won. In the United Kingdom the industry was seen as a core driver of macroeconomic growth. Top bankers were feted and some given knighthoods. Deregulation was also theoretically justified by the efficient market hypothesis, ignoring its many restrictive and unrealistic assumptions, contributing to a belief that self-regulating financial markets tended toward stability. The delusions of the worldwide movement toward deregulation may have been influenced by the protracted period of economic growth.

The residue of regulatory systems was not able to cope with the new entrepreneurial banks, developing new products, expanding dramatically their commercial property lending portfolios and raising vast sums of money via international bond markets. Regulators simply did not have the necessary skills or tools to assess the risks.

So the first issue in considering whether it could happen again is to what extent has bank regulation been improved? Regulation has been tightened up. In the United States the Dodd-Frank Act was passed in 2010 that created a new system of oversight of financial services, including greater transparency of derivatives, consumer protection, more oversight of credit rating agencies, and so forth. The G20 countries set up the Financial Stability Board to increase regulation. The European Banking Authority (EBA) was also established in 2011 with a single set of prudential rules applied to financial institutions within the European Union. In general, while there is now greater international monitoring of banks, national supervisory authorities still remain in charge of supervising individual financial institutions. Banks in the United Kingdom continue to be supervised by the Prudential Regulation Authority (PRA) and Financial Conduct Authority (FCA). One outcome of this monitoring is the stress testing of individual banks around the world to assess their resilience to adverse market developments such as a recession or international banking failure. In the United Kingdom the results of the 2016 testing found that three banks, The Royal Bank of Scotland Group, Barclays and Standard Chartered, demonstrated some capital inadequacies, and they have had to put in place plans to build further resilience (Bank of England, 2016). A further element of the increased regulation was the introduction of 'Basel III' in 2011, or the Third Basel Accord. These international regulations required banks to be subject to 'micro-prudential' assessments that increase their required capital bases for lending and raise required liquidity standards.

There is now, therefore, increased regulation with higher financial standards required. However, there are some signs of a reaction to the increased regulatory regimes. In the United States President Trump has been arguing that the Dodd-Frank Act needs to be abolished. And some reforms proposed in the wake of the GFC have still to be implemented. In the United Kingdom the government expressed a desire to split up the major banks so that their investment and retail arms are separate entities. This ring-fencing has faced resistance from the banks and will not happen until 2019 at the earliest, almost a decade after it was proposed.

Increased banking regulation is not a cure-all for boom and bust property cycles. A key influence is the role of the macroeconomic cycles providing the platform for the variability in demand for property. For a while the optimists believed that the long global economic upswing represented the end of boom and bust, but the 'Great Moderation' became the 'great depression'. Economic and property cycles are here to stay. The emergence of an increasingly short-term investment perspective is likely to reinforce these phenomena. Other factors have not changed. Comparative property valuation approaches, albeit following standard professional procedures, also tend to support cycles by being based on extrapolating the recent past.

Finally there is the question of learning from the past. Going (or almost going) bust, you would imagine, would be a good wakeup call, but banks seem to have well-refined amnesia. This is illustrated by the career of Donald Trump as a serial bankrupt (six times, in all). As noted earlier in the chapter, he defaulted on a loan to Deutsche Bank in November 2008 but subsequently a different division of the same bank has issued mortgages worth $300 million secured on four of Trump's properties (Harding *et al.*, 2017). It seems likely that the allure of the short-term deal will trump any lessons from the past.

This view is endorsed by bankers' remuneration packages, which have not been fundamentally altered since the GFC. The European Banking Authority did introduce a cap that limits bonuses to 100% of salaries or 200% with special shareholder approval. Plans to extend the application of the cap to smaller financial institutions in France, Ireland, Luxembourg and the Netherlands have not yet been put in place (Binham and Odell, 2016). With the inevitability of economic and property cycles all in all there is the potential for another boom and bust. It is simply a question of the amplitude of the cycle.

What Can Be Done?

The irrational pessimism following the GFC played havoc with views of the risk premium that should be attached to commercial property. Property investors' perception of risk increased massively. Clearly though, risks had increased and the risk premium was rightly higher than the long-term historic average. Notwithstanding that, fair value models of the UK property market suggest that after 2009 property was still priced below fair value and that fair value was only beginning to be restored in early 2015, nearly eight years after the onset of the GFC.

What became clear was that forecasting models were inadequate in anticipating the scale of the falls in values that resulted from the GFC, not just property forecasts but economic forecasts too (a fundamental flaw since the latter are used as major inputs to property market models). Consensus forecasts are essentially backward looking and are therefore little more than the extrapolation of trends. Part of the problem is that published forecasts by property researchers are not pure statistical forecasts but also reflect sentiment and professional judgement. In addition, these models take no account of the behaviour that drove yield shift. In terms of the United Kingdom (and elsewhere) the industry needs to consider how we address this aspect of modelling and the irrational behavioural aspects of the market that drove yields, before, during and after the GFC. In this context, the question arises whether there is a way in which an independent body could monitor the risk attached to commercial property. This might take the form of an on-going risk index, for example.

On the plus side, though, the management of risk has moved up the agenda in UK fund management houses since 2007 with a much better appreciation of what constitutes fair value and the building of larger liquidity buffers in retail funds and Property Unit Trusts. Perhaps like Basel III requirements for fund management houses and banks generally there ought to be a basic liquidity requirement specifically for property funds. Due diligence, that in the boom years only received cursory attention from both the banking and property industry, has also moved up the risk agenda but it should not be allowed to become a barrier to business expansion.

Such considerations have been recognized before, but at a business level and in the context of encouraging finance markets to function differently so as to reduce the threat the real estate cycle can pose to the stability of financial systems (Investment Property Forum, 2014). Reflections by an industry-wide working group (Investment Property Forum, 2014) led to the presentation of an overall vision for a commercial real estate market and regulatory regime. These recommendations could protect systemically important financial institutions and the financial system more generally from the commercial real estate cycle, in particular by ensuring that such financial institutions hold sufficient capital to withstand a market crash. This is what the Basel III accord ought to do *per se*, but here we are suggesting protection for property funds at a much more granular level. The 'Vision for Real Estate Finance in the UK' group (Investment Property Forum, 2014) also saw the moderating of the flow of credit to the commercial real estate sector and the establishment of systems to ensure that financial institutions are positioned to support commercial property lending after a market crash. It is important to recognize the significance of the commercial real estate sector to the overall economy and the need to support the availability of debt funding over the cycle.

The Investment Property Forum Vision is focused on loans to the commercial real estate market during the boom years and how a better functioning and better regulated commercial real estate finance market might be delivered over the next 'several' years. Nevertheless there are ideas in the Vision that ought to be applied more widely across the commercial real estate sector, and it is a pity that as yet none of these recommendations have been really taken up by the industry. For example, we support the idea of a committee of senior experts with a duty to interpret all relevant indicators of the market and to communicate its views to the regulator (potentially as a moderator of irrational behaviour). We also support the need for better training on commercial real estate for lending teams and the use of sustainable valuations when assessing LTV ratios.

The use of a long-term sustainable valuation, an approach that underpins Germany's Pfandbrief market, might help mitigate risk when assessing LTV ratios when advancing debt. The rationale here is that the increased risk arising as the market overheats can be mitigated significantly through the use, in addition to current appraised LTV, of a measure that compares the amount of the loan to the long-term sustainable value of the property (long-term sustainable LTV) – being the average value of the property through the market cycle. Under this approach, the most important element of pro-cyclicality would be removed. Although this is based on a significantly more cautious valuation, it allows a better insight into the risks involved. The use of this approach probably explains the different volatility seen in German markets, discussed earlier, and the apparently more stable behaviour. This aspect certainly needs to be considered further as well as whether it ought be used in a much wider context than simply when considering LTV ratios.

The overall impact of the long boom, dramatic bust and slow recovery has shaken investors' attitudes towards commercial property. The sudden swing in fortunes saw expectations about rental and capital values turned on their head. The unprecedented rise in liquidity in the build up to the peak of the boom was spectacularly reversed as the property market collapsed. The events challenged the underlying pricing of commercial property by investors. In particular the impact was a reappraisal of the risks associated with property as the recession exposed its frailties, particularly in terms of obsolescence. Given the turbulence over the period considered in the book it is right, therefore, to ask 'Is property still a good investment?'. We believe that the historical reasons for investing in commercial property as an asset class are still valid. Property is a tangible asset representing rights over land and buildings. In a rational market leases offer the potential for a stable income across economic cycles, if tenants can be kept, and, in the United Kingdom, there is the attraction of upward-only rent reviews (in general, businesses will stop paying dividends before they stop paying rents). For fund managers it still offers diversification benefits in a multi-asset portfolio having good risk–return characteristics compared to other asset classes.

Final Thoughts

We began the book with the parallel between the sub-prime lending crisis in the United States and the little local difficulty of the assassination of the Archduke Franz Ferdinand that led to the First World War. It is widely accepted that unresolved issues at the Versailles peace treaty at the end of the First World War indirectly contributed to the outbreak of further hostilities just two decades later. Many of the bitter and unresolved grievances that Versailles aroused cast a long shadow over interwar Europe that led to political tensions and ultimately to the outbreak of the Second World War. We have yet to see whether the solutions to the GFC agreed by central bankers, politicians and regulators were appropriate, will be effective, or will merely paper over the cracks and whether, like the outbreak of further war, we can expect further stress in global real estate markets in the years ahead. The test will be the next inevitable significant economic upturn and subsequent correction.

References

Adams, R.M. (2012) *Consolidation and Merger Activity in the United States Banking Industry from 2000 through 2010, Finance and Economics Discussion Series 2012–51*, Divisions of Research & Statistics and Monetary Affairs Federal Reserve Board, Washington, DC.

Alonzi, P. (2015) *Structuring Real Estate Funds*, Presentation at Eversheds Real Estate Conference October, London. Available at http://www.aref.org.uk/sites/default/files/LON_LIB1-%2313074986-v3-AREF_slides_6_October_2015.pdf (accessed 13 June 2017).

Anderson, K., Brooks, C. and Katsaris, A. (2010) Speculative Bubbles in the S&P 500: Was the Tech Bubble Confined to the Tech Sector? *Journal of Empirical Finance*, 17, 3, 345–361.

Armstrong, L. (2007) *Delinquencies and Foreclosures Increase in Latest MBA National Delinquency Survey, March*, Mortgage Bankers Association, Washington, DC.

Asset Protection Agency (2013) *Annual Report and Accounts for the Period from 1 April 2012 to 31 October 2012*, House of Commons, London.

Atkin, J. (2006) Dunfermline Punches above its Weight, *Mortgage Finance Gazette*, 1 October. Available at http://www.mortgagefinancegazette.com/commerical-lending/dunfermline-punches-above-its-weight/ (accessed 15 June 2015).

Bank of England, Prudential Regulation Authority (2015a) *The Failure of HBOS PLC (HBOS)*, Bank of England, London.

Bank of England, Prudential Regulation Authority (2015b) *Co-operative Bank PLC Final Notice (FRN 121885)*, Bank of England, London.

Bank of England (2016) *Stress testing the UK banking system: 2016 results*, Bank of England, London. Available at http://www.bankofengland.co.uk/financialstability/Documents/fpc/results301116.pdf (accessed 15 June 2015).

Barras, R. (1994) Property and the Economic Cycle: Building Cycles Revisited, *Journal of Property Research*, 11, 183–197.

Barras, R. (2009) *Building Cycles: Growth and Instability*, Wiley Blackwell, Oxford.

Baum, A. (2015) *Real Estate Investment: A Strategic Approach*, 3rd edn, Routledge, London.

BBC (2009) Nationwide takes over Dunfermline, BBC, London. Available at http://news.bbc.co.uk/1/hi/scotland/7971244.stm (accessed 15 June 2015).

Benson, J. and Burrows, O. (2013) Commercial Property and Financial Stability, *Bank of England Quarterly Bulletin Q1*, 48–58.

Bernanke, B.S. (2004) *Remarks by Governor Ben S. Bernanke at the Meetings of the Eastern Economic Association, Washington, DC, February 20, 2004*, Federal Reserve Board, Washington, DC. Available at https://www.federalreserve.gov/BOARDDOCS/SPEECHES/2004/20040220/default.htm (accessed 15 June 2015).

Bernanke, B.S. (2007) The Subprime Mortgage Market, Speech to Federal Reserve Bank of Chicago's 43rd Annual Conference on Bank Structure and Competition, Chicago, IL, May 17. Available at https://www.federalreserve.gov/newsevents/speech/bernanke20070517a.htm (accessed 15 June 2015).

Binham, C. and Odell, M. (2016) UK Declines to Extend EU Bonus Cap Rules, *Financial Times*, 29 February. Available at https://www.ft.com/content/e67a0630-dee8-11e5-b072-006d8d362ba3 (accessed 15 June 2015).

Blundell, G. (2009) *Repricing Property Risk, IPF Short Paper 4*, Investment Property Forum, London.

BNP Paribas (2015) *Main Investment Markets in Western Europe: At a Glance Q4 2014*, BNP Paribas, Paris.

BNP Paribas (2016) *Main Investment Markets in Western Europe: At a Glance Q4 2015*, BNP Paribas, Paris. Available at https://www.realestate.bnpparibas.com/upload/docs/application/pdf/2016-02/aag_invest_q4_2015_ve.pdf?id=p_1653100 (accessed November, 2016).

Bolger, A. and Pickard, J. (2009) 'Reckless Decisions' sink Dunfermline, *Financial Times*, 30 March. Available at http://www.ft.com/cms/s/0/2f76915a-1cc2-11de-977c-00144feabdc0.html#axzz3jaXIzGPQ (accessed 15 June 2015).

Brown G (2003) The Budget speech in full, *The Guardian*, Wednesday 9 April 2003. https://www.theguardian.com/money/2004/mar/17/budget.budget20044 (accessed 4 July 2017).

BTG Financial Consulting (2015) *The NPL Market – Europe 2015*, BTG-FC, Manchester.

Building Societies Association (2008) *Total Gross Lending (All Lenders)*, Building Societies Association, London.

Building Societies Association (2010) *FSA Mortgage Market Review: CP 10/16 – Responsible Lending Response from Building Societies Association on Interest Only Mortgages and Non-Deposit Taking Lenders*, Building Societies Association, London.

Burston, B. and Burrell, A. (2015) What is Fair Value? *Short Paper 24*, Investment Property Forum, London.

Cameron D.R. (2010) Fiscal Responses to the Economic Contraction of 2008–09. Paper presented to the annual meeting of the American Political Association, Washington, DC, September. Available at https://webspace.princeton.edu/users/piirs/pdf/Cameron.fiscal.responses.pdf (accessed 4 July, 2017).

Carey Olsen (2012) *Jersey Property Unit Trusts*, Carey Olsen, St Helier, Jersey. Available athttp://www.careyolsen.com/downloads/Jersey_property_unit_trusts.pdf (accessed November, 2016).

CBRE (2008) *Credit Crunch and the Property Market*: The Mayor of London's Office GLA Economics, London.

CBRE (2014a) *UK Retail Warehouse Parks in the Pipeline: Market View*, CBRE, London.

CBRE (2014b) *UK Shopping Centres in the Pipeline: Market View*, CBRE, London.

Clarke, P. (2014) *Zombies and Beyond: A Further Update on UK Real Estate Debt, IPF Short Paper 4*, Investment Property Forum, London.

Cole, R.A. and Fenn, G.W. (2008) The Role of Commercial Real Estate Investments in the Banking Crisis of 1985–92. Paper presented at the annual meeting of the American Real Estate and Urban Economics Association, Washington, DC, January 1995. Available at http://ssrn.com/abstract=1293473 (accessed 15 June 2015).

Cole, R.A. and White, L.J. (2012) Déjà Vu All Over Again: The Causes of U.S. Commercial Bank Failures this Time Around, *Journal of Financial Services Research*, 42, 1, 5–29.

Commission of Investigation into the Banking Sector of Ireland (2011) *Misjudging Risk: Causes of the Systematic Banking Crisis in Ireland*, Government of Ireland, Dublin.

Comptroller and Auditor General (2010) *National Asset Management Agency Acquisition of Bank Assets*, Government of Ireland, Dublin.

Comptroller and Auditor General (2014) *National Asset Management Agency Progress Report 2010–2012*, Government of Ireland, Dublin.

Collett, D., Lizieri, C. and Ward, C. (2003) Timing and Holding Periods of Institutional Real Estate, *Real Estate Economics*, 31, 2, 205–222.

Crosby, N. (2007): German Open Ended Funds; Was There a Valuation Problem? *Working Papers in Real Estate and Planning, No.05/07*, University of Reading, Reading.

Daly, M.T. (1982) *Sydney Boom Sydney Bust*, George Allen & Unwin, Sydney.

Davies, R., Richardson, P., Katinaite, V. and Manning, M. (2010) Evolution of the UK Banking System, *Bank of England Quarterly Bulletin*, Q4, 321–332.

Dobbs, R., Lund, S., Woetzel, J. and Mutafchieva, M. (2015) *Debt and (Not Much) Deleveraging*, February, McKinsey and Company, London. Available at http://www.mckinsey.com/global-themes/employment-and-growth/debt-and-not-much-deleveraging (accessed 15 June 2015).

Dokko, Y., Edelstein, R.H., Lacayo, A.J. and Lee, D.C. (1999) Real Estate Income and Value Cycles: A Model of Market Dynamics, *Journal of Real Estate Research*, 18, 1, 89–94.

DTZ (2010) *Money into Property*, DTZ, London.

Dubben, N. and Sayce, S. (1991) *Property Portfolio Management*, Routledge, London.

Dunse, N., Jones, C. and White, M. *et al.* (2007), Modelling Urban Commercial Property Yields: Exogenous and Endogenous Influences, *Journal of Property Research*, 24, 4, 335–354.

Dunse, N., Jones, C. and White, M. (2010) Valuation Accuracy and Spatial Variations in the Efficiency of the Property Market, *Journal of European Real Estate Research*, 3, 1, 24–45.

Edmonds, T. (2010) *Financial Crisis Timeline: House of Commons Briefing Paper Number 04991*, House of Commons, London.

Eisenbeis R.A. and Kaufman G.G. (2009) Lessons from the Demise of the U.K.'S Northern Rock and the U.S.'s Countrywide and Indymac, in F. Bruni and D.T. Llewellyn (eds), *The Failure of Northern Rock: A Multi-dimensional Case Study*, SUERF, Vienna.

EKOS (2010) *Shawlands Town Centre Retail Study: Report for Glasgow City Council*, Glasgow City Council, Glasgow.

Elliot, L. (2016) Greece's Latest Financial Emergency is Both Tragic and Absurd, *The Guardian* 9 May. Available at https://www.theguardian.com/business/2016/may/09/greece-financial-emergency-tragic-absurd-imf-debt-relief (accessed 15 June 2017).

Elliot, L. and Atkinson, D. (2008) *The Gods that Failed*, The Bodley Head, London.

Estates Gazette (2012) *Banks' Loan Sales Top €7.5bn*, Estates Gazette. Available athttp://www.egi.co.uk/news/banks-loan-sales-top-7-5bn/?keyword=bank%20sales%20top (accessed 15 June 2017).

Estates Gazette (2013) Lloyds to Offer Loan Portfolios, *Estates Gazette*. Available at http://www.egi.co.uk/news/lloyds-to-offer-loan-portfolios/?keyword=Lloyds%20to%20offer%20loan%20portfolios (accessed 15 June 2017).

European Community (2009) *Economic Crisis in Europe: Causes, Consequences and Responses, European Economy 7*, European Community, Brussels.

Fainstein, S. (1994) *The City Builder: Property, Politics and Planning in London and New York*, Blackwell, Oxford.

Federal Deposit Insurance Corporation (2016) website: www.fdic.gov (accessed 15 June 2017).

Fergus, J.T. and Goodman, J.L. (1994) The 1989–92 Credit Crunch for Real Estate: A Retrospective, *Journal of American Real Estate and Urban Economics Association*, 22, 1, 5–32.

Financial Services Authority (2011) *The Failure of the Royal Bank of Scotland*, FSA, London.

Fitch Ratings (2007) *Financial Guarantors – Third Quarter 2006 Matrix Capital Model Results Special Report*, Fitch Ratings, New York.

Fletcher, G.A. (1976) *The Discount Houses in London: Principles, Operations and Change*, Macmillan, London.

Forster, S. (ed.) (2013) *Developing Property as an Asset Class*, Investment Property Forum, London.

Fraser, W.D. (1993) *Principles of Property Investment and Pricing*, 2nd edn, Macmillan, London.

Frodsham, M. (2016). *Defining Investment Quality Short Paper 29*, Investment Property Forum, London.

Gerald Eve (2005) *Holding Periods: Analysis for UK Office Investors*, Gerald Eve, London.

Gerald Eve (2013) *Multi-let: The Definitive Analysis of the UK's Multi-let Industrial Property Market*. Gerald Eve, London.

Gimblett, K. (2015) *UK Development Finance Review 2015, IPF Short Paper 27*, Investment Property Forum, London.

Giostra, N. (2011) *The Funding Gap: Is Mezzanine Lending the Solution?* CBRE, London.

Ghosh, C., Guttery, S. and Sirmans, C.F. (1994) The Olympia and York Crisis, *Journal of Property Finance*, 5, 2, 5 – 46.

Goetzmann, W.N. and Wachter, S. (1996) *The Global Real Estate Crash: Evidence from an International Database, Yale School of Management Working Paper*, New Haven, CT.

Gola, C. and Roselli, A. (2009) *The UK Banking System and its Regulatory and Supervisory Framework*, Palgrave Macmillan, London.

Guillen, M.F. (2012) *The Global Economic and Financial Crisis: A Timeline*, The Lauder Institute. University of Pennsylvania. Available at http://lauder.wharton.upenn.edu/wp-content/uploads/2015/06/Chronology_Economic_Financial_Crisis.pdf (accessed 15 June 2017).

Hager, D.P. (1980) Measurement of Pension Fund Investment Performance, *Journal of the Staple Inn Actuarial Society*, 24, November, 33–64.

Hammerson (2009) Acquisition of Silverburn Shopping Centre: Press Release 21 December 2009, Hammerson, London. Available at http://www.hammerson.com/media/press-releases/acquisition-of-silverburn-shopping-centre/ (accessed 14 June 2017).

Harding, L., Kirchgaessner, S., Hopkins, N. and Smith, D. (2017) Deutsche Bank Examined Donald Trump's Account for Russia Links, *The Guardian*, 16 February. Available at https://www.theguardian.com/us-news/2017/feb/16/deutsche-bank-examined-trump-account-for-russia-links (accessed 14 June 2017).

Harrison, D., Blake, D. and Key, T. (2013) *Returning to the Core: Rediscovering a Role for Real Estate in Defined Contribution Pension Schemes*, Pensions Institute, Cass Business School, London.

Harvard University (2008) *The State of National Housing in 2008*, Center for Housing, Harvard University, Cambridge, MA.

Harvard University (2010) *The State of National Housing in 2010*, Center for Housing, Harvard University, Cambridge, MA.

Herring, R. and Wachter, S. (1998) Real Estate Booms and Banking Busts: An International Perspective. Paper presented to Wharton Conference on Asian Twin Financial Crises, Tokyo, Japan, 9–10 March.

HM Treasury (2010) *Building Society Capital and Related Issues: A Discussion Paper*, HM Treasury, London.

Hoesli, M. and Oikarinen, E. (2012) Are REITs Real Estate? Evidence from International Sector Level Data, *Journal of International Money and Finance*, 31, 7, 1823–1850.

House of Commons Treasury Committee (2008) *The Run on the Rock*, Fifth Report of Session 2007–08 Vol. I: Report and Minutes, Stationery Office, London. Available at http://www.suerf.org/download/studies/study20091.pdf (accessed 4 July 2017).

House of Commons Treasury Select Committee (2014) *Project Verde: Sixth Report of Session 2014–15, Volume 1, HC 728-1*, The Stationery Office, London.

Institute and Faculty of Actuaries (2014) Working Party Paper November 2014, *The Management of With-Profit Funds in Run-off*, 9.

Investment Association (2016) *Asset Management in the UK Annual Survey 2014–2015*, Investment Association, London.

Investment Management Association (2010) *Asset Management in the UK 2009–2010: The IMA Annual Survey*, Investment Management Association, London.

International Monetary Fund (2005) *World Economic Outlook*, 2005, IMF, Washington, DC.

International Monetary Fund (2006) *World Economic Outlook* 2006, IMF, Washington, DC.

International Monetary Fund (2007) *World Economic Outlook* 2007, IMF, Washington, DC.

Investment Property Forum (2007) *Consensus Forecast for All-Property, Q2 2007*, Investment Property Forum, London.

Investment Property Forum (2009) *UK Consensus Forecasts, May, 2009*, Investment Property Forum, London.

Investment Property Forum (2014), *A Vision for Real Estate Finance in the UK*, Investment Property Forum, London.

Irish Bank Resolution Corporation (2016) *Progress Update Report 27 May*, IBRC, Dublin.

Johnson, D. (2013) Industry Needs More Carrots than Sticks, *Financial Times*, 12 May. Available at https://www.ft.com/content/ef09271c-b70f-11e2-a249-00144feabdc0?mhq5j=e3 (accessed 4 July 2017)

Jones, C. (1984) The Future of Building Societies, *National Westminster Bank Review*, May, 33–46.

Jones, C. (2009) Remaking the Monopoly Board: Spatial Economic Change and Property Investment, *Urban Studies*, 46, 11, 2363–2380.

Jones, C. (2010) The Rise and Fall of the High Street Shop as an Investment Class, *Journal of Property Investment and Finance*, 28, 4, 275–284.

Jones, C. (2012a) Introduction: The Housing Economy and the Credit Crunch, in C. Jones, M. White and N. Dunse (eds), *Challenges of the Housing Economy: An International Perspective*, Wiley Blackwell, Chichester, 1–24.

Jones, C. (2012b) The UK Housing Market Cycle and the Role of Planning: The Policy Challenge Following the Financial Crisis, in C. Jones, M. White and N. Dunse (eds) *Challenges of the Housing Economy: An International Perspective*, Wiley Blackwell, Chichester, 195–215.

Jones, C. (2013) *Office Markets and Public Policy*, Wiley Blackwell, Chichester.

Jones, C. (2014) Land Use Planning Policies and Market Forces: Utopian Aspirations Thwarted? *Land Use Policy*, 38, 5, 573–579.

Jones, C. (2018) A Historical, Evolutionary and Cyclical Perspective on Models of Development Finance, in G. Squires, E. Heurkins and E. Peiser (eds) *Companion to Real Estate Development*, Routledge, Abingdon, 185–195.

Jones, C. and Livingstone, N. (2015) Emerging Implications of Online Retailing for Real Estate, *Journal of Corporate Real Estate*, 17, 3, 226–239.

Jones, C. and Richardson, H.W. (2014) Housing Markets and Policy in the UK and the USA: A Review of the Differential Impact of the Global Housing Crisis, *International Journal of Housing Markets and Analysis*, 7, 1, 129–144.

Jones, C. and Watkins, C. (2008) *Housing Markets and Planning Policy*, Blackwell, Oxford.

Jones, C., Dunse, N. and Cutsforth, K. (2014). *The Implications for Property Yields of Rising Bond Yields, Short Paper 19*, Investment Property Forum, London.

Jones, C., Dunse, N. and Cutsforth, C. (2015) The Changing Relationships between Government Bond Yields and Capitalisation Rates: Evidence from the UK, USA and Australia, *Journal of European Real Estate Research*, 8, 2, 153–171.

Jones, C., Livingstone, N. and Dunse, N. (2016) The Changing Nature of Transactions Activity and Liquidity in UK Commercial Property, *International Journal of Strategic Property Management*, 20, 4, 384–396.

KPMG (2016) *European Debt Sales*, KMPG, London.

Kroencke, T.A., Schindler, F. and Steininger, B.I. (2014) *Are REITs Real Estate or Equities? Dissecting REITs in an Asset Pricing Model*, European Public Research Association, Brussels.

Kyle, A. (2012) A Commentary on Déjà Vu All Over Again: The Causes of U.S. Commercial Bank Failures This Time Around, *Journal of Financial Services Research*, 42, 1, 31–34.

Local Data Company (2016) *Restructure and Recovery H2 2015: Analysis of Britain's Shopping Locations in 2015*, The Local Data Company, London.

Lewis, J.P. (1965) *Building Cycles and Britain's Growth*, Macmillan, London.

Ling, D. (2005). A Random Walk down Main Street: Can Experts Predict Returns on Commercial Real Estate? *Journal of Real Estate Research*, 27, 1, 137–154.

Lizieri, C. (2009) *Towers of Capital: Office Markets and International Financial Services*, Wiley Blackwell, Oxford.

Lizieri, C., Reinhart, J. and Baum, A. (2011) *Who Owns the City 2011: Change and Global Ownership of City of London Offices*, University of Cambridge Department of Land Economy/Development Securities, Cambridge.

Lizieri, C., Ward, C. and Lee, S. (2001) *Financial Innovation in Property Markets: Implications for the City of London*, Corporation of London, London.

Luck, C. (2011) *Limited Partnerships – An Overview and No More Reform*, Nabarro, London. Available at http://www.nabarro.com/Downloads/Limited_partnerships_overview_and_update.pdf (accessed 14 June 2017).

Lunde, J. (2012) Impacts on Wealth and Debt of Changes in the Danish Financial Framework over a Housing Cycle, in C. Jones, M. White and N. Dunse (eds) *Challenges of the Housing Economy: An International Perspective*, Wiley Blackwell, Oxford, 128–152.

Mackay, C. ([1841] 2003) *Memoirs of Extraordinary Popular Delusions,* reprinted as *Extraordinary Popular Delusions and the Madness of Crowds*, Harriman House Ltd, Petersfield.

MacLaran, A., MacLaran, M. and Malone, P. (1987) Property Cycles in Dublin: The Anatomy of Boom and Slump in Industrial and Office Sectors, *The Economic and Social Review*, 18, 4, 237–256.

Markowitz, H. (1952) Portfolio Selection, *Journal of Finance*, 7, 1, 77–91.

Marriott, O. (1967) *The Property Boom*, Hamish Hamilton, London.

Maxted, W. and Porter, T. (2010) *UK Commercial Property Lending Market Research Findings Year End 2009*, De Montfort University, Leicester.

Maxted, W. and Porter, T. (2014). *The UK Commercial Property Lending Market: Research Findings Year End 2013*, De Montfort University, Leicester.

Mitchell, P. (2015) *The Size and Structure of the U.K. Property Market, End 2014 Update*, Investment Property Forum, London.

Montague-Jones, G. (2014) Dunfermline to Sell £350 m Loan Portfolio, *Property Week*, 19 December. Available at http://www.propertyweek.com/dunfermline-to-sell-%C2%A3350m-loan-portfolio/5072068.article (accessed 14 June 2017).

Morris, E. (2011) *Outlook for Development Finance in the UK, IPF Short Paper 15*, Investment Property Forum, London.

Mortgage Finance Gazette (2006) Dunfermline Punches above its Weight, *Mortgage Finance Gazette*, 1 October. Available at http://www.mortgagefinancegazette.com/commerical-lending/dunfermline-punches-above-its-weight/ (accessed 14 June 2017).

Moya, E. (2009) Fears That More Building Societies Could Follow Dunfermline Collapse, *The Guardian*, 16 April. Available at http://www.theguardian.com/business/2009/apr/16/warning-building-societies-dunfermline (accessed 14 June 2017).

MSCI (2014) *IPD Indexes and Benchmark Methodology Guide*, MSCI, London.

MSCI/IPD, Investment Property Databank (2009) *UK Key Centres Report*, IPD, London.

MSCI/IPD, Investment Property Databank (2014a) *IPD UK Digest*, MSCI/IPD, London.

MSCI/IPD, Investment Property Databank (2014b) *IPD UK Quarterly Digest*, MSCI/IPD, London.

MSCI/IPD, Investment Property Databank (2014c) *IPD Multinational Digest December Digest*, MSCI/IPD, London.

MSCI/IPD (2015) *IPD Monthly Index May 2015*, MSCI/IPD, London.

Murphy, L. (2012) The Rise and Fall of Irish Developers. Paper presented to European Real Estate Society Annual Conference, Edinburgh, June.

Nakamoto, M. and Wighton, D. (2007) Citigroup Chief Stays Bullish on Buy-outs, *Financial Times*, 9 July. Available at https://www.ft.com/content/80e2987a-2e50-11dc-821c-0000779fd2ac (accessed 14 June 2017).

National Audit Office, Comptroller and Auditor General (2010) *The Asset Protection Scheme*, The Stationery Office, London.

O'Connell, B. (2012) Royal in Waiting: Where is the Deluge of Property Loan Sales? *Estates Gazette*. Available at http://www.egi.co.uk/news/royal-in-waiting-where-is-the-deluge-of-property-loan-sales/?keyword=isobel (accessed 14 June 2017).

Office of the Deputy Prime Minister (2004) *Monitoring the 2002 Code of Practice for Commercial Leases: Interim Report*, University of Reading and Office of the Deputy Prime Minister, London.

OECD (2016) *OECD Data*. data.oecd.org (accessed 14 June 2017).

Office of National Statistics (2016a) *Real GDP Growth since 1948*, ONS, London. Available at http://www.ons.gov.uk/ons/rel/elmr/explaining-economic-statistics/long-term-profile-of-gdp-in-the-uk/sty-long-term-profile-of-gdp.html (accessed 14 June 2017).

Office of National Statistics (2016b) *MQ5: Investment by Insurance Companies, Pension Funds and Trusts, Reference Tables, Q2 2016*, ONS, London.

Oyedokun, T., Jones, C. and Dunse, N. (2015) The Growth of the Green Office Market in the UK, *Journal of European Real Estate Research*, 8, 3, 267–284.

Papastamos, D., Matysiak, G. and Stevenson, S. (2015) Assessing the Accuracy and Dispersion of Real Estate Investment Forecasts, *International Review of Financial Analysis*, 42, 141–152.

Peachey, K. (2013) Endowment Mortgages: Legacy of a Scandal, BBC, London.

Penman Brown, W. (2009) *The Decline and Fall of Banking*, Matador Available at Leicester. http://www.bbc.co.uk/news/business-20858236 (accessed 14 June 2017).

Phillips, M. (2009) *UK Real Estate Debt: A Problem for the Borrowers and the Banks, IPF Short Paper 1*, Investment Property Forum, London.

Phillips, M. (2010) *UK Real Estate Debt: An Update Short Paper 7*, Investment Property Forum, London.

Pike, R. and Neale, B. *(2006) Corporate Finance and Investment: Decisions and Strategies*, 5th edn, Pearson Education, Cambridge.

PriceWaterhouse Coopers (2012) *Unlisted Funds – Lessons from the Crisis*, Association of Real Estate Funds, London.

Pugh, C. and Dehesh, A. (2001) Theory and Explanation in International Property Cycles since 1980, *Property Management*, 19, 4, 265–297.

Real Capital Analytics (2015) *Global Trends Report Q3*, Real Capital Analytics, New York.

Reid, M. (1982) *The Secondary Banking Crisis, 1973–75: Its Causes and Course*. Macmillan, London.

Reinhart, C. M. and Rogoff, K.S. (2009) *This Time It's Different: Eight Centuries of Financial Folly*, Princeton University Press. Princeton and Oxford.

Robbins, M. (2009) Hammerson Rights Issue Focuses City on Real-estate Sector and its Need for Equity, *The Independent*, 10 February. Available at http://www.independent.co.uk/news/business/news/hammerson-rights-issue-focuses-city-on-real-estate-sector-and-its-need-for-equity-1605495.html (accessed 14 June 2017).

Royal Institution of Chartered Surveyors and Investment Property Forum (1997) *The Calculation of Worth: An Information Paper*, RICS Business Services Ltd, London.

Ruddick, G. (2009) Hammerson Announces £584.2 m Rights Issue, *The Telegraph*, 9 February. Available at http://www.telegraph.co.uk/finance/newsbysector/constructionandproperty/4568505/Hammerson-announces-584.2m-rights-issue.html (accessed 14 June 2017).

Sayce, S., Smith, J., Cooper, R. and Venmore-Roland, P. (2006) *Real Estate Appraisal: From Value to Worth*, Blackwell, Oxford.

Scottish Affairs Committee of House of Commons (2009) *Dunfermline Building Society, Fifth Report of Session 2008–09 HC 548*, The Stationery Office, London.

Schwartz, G. (1979) The Office Pattern in New York City, 1960–75, in P.W. Daniels (ed.) *Spatial Pattern of Office Growth and Location*, Wiley & Son, Chichester, 215–237.

Scotsman (2009) Firms Could Lose Millions Following Collapse of Kenmore, *Scotsman*, 13 November. Available at http://www.scotsman.com/business/firms-could-lose-millions-following-collapse-of-kenmore-1-767708 (accessed 14 June 2017).

Scott, P. (1996) *The Property Masters*, E&FN Spon, London.

SG Warburg & Co (2000) *Annual Property Review 2000*, SG Warburg & Co, London.

Shiller, R.J. (2005) *Irrational Exuberance*, 2nd edn, Broadway Books. New York.

Stewart, H. (2008) IMF says US Crisis is 'Largest Financial Shock since Great Depression', *The Guardian*, 9 April. Available at https://www.theguardian.com/business/2008/apr/09/useconomy.subprimecrisis (accessed 14 June 2017).

Strachan, H. (2001) *The First World War: 1: To Arms*, Oxford University Press, Oxford.

Scottish Widows Investment Partnership (2003) *U.K. and European Strategic Market Review, 2003*, SWIP, Edinburgh.

Scottish Widows Investment Partnership (2004) *U.K. and European Strategic Market Review, 2004*, SWIP, Edinburgh.

Scottish Widows Investment Partnership (2005) *U.K. and European Strategic Market Review, 2005*, SWIP, Edinburgh.

Scottish Widows Investment Partnership (2006) *U.K. and European Strategic Market Review, 2006*, SWIP, Edinburgh.

Taylor, A.J.P. (1963) *The First World War: An Illustrated History*, Penguin Books, London.

Tiwari, P. and White, M. (2010) *International Real Estate Economics*, Palgrave Macmillan, London.

Turner, A. (2009) *The Turner Review: A Regulatory Response to the Global Banking Crisis*, Financial Services Agency, London.

UK Business Property (2009) *HBOS Funded Kenmore Property Group Collapses into Administration*, UK Business Property, 12 November. Available at http://ukbusinessproperty.co.uk/news/hbos-funded-kenmore-property-group-collapses-into-administration (accessed 14 June 2017).

US Treasury (2016) *Asset Guarantee Scheme*. Available at https://www.treasury.gov/initiatives/financial-stability/TARP-Programs/bank-investment-programs/agp/Pages/overview.aspx (accessed 14 June 2017).

Wainwright, T. (2010) *Looking to Tomorrow: The Past and Future Roles of Securitisation in Residential Mortgage Funding*, Small Business Research Centre, Kingston University, Kingston upon Thames.

Wallace, J. (2011) *UPDATED: RBS and Blackstone Close Project Isobel*, CoStar. Available athttp://www.costar.co.uk/en/assets/news/2011/December/RBS-and-Blackstone-set-to-close-Project-Isobel-in-next-48-hours/ (accessed 14 June 2017).

Wallace, J. (2013a) *Marathon Pays €400m for Project Chamonix as Lloyds Readies Project Thames UK NPL*, CoStar. Available at https://costarfinance.com/2013/02/22/marathon-pays-e400m-for-project-chamonix-as-lloyds-readies-project-thames-uk-npl/ (accessed 4 July 2017).

Wallace, J. (2013b) *Lloyds Confirms Project Thames Sale to Cerberus at £325m*, CoStar. Available at http://www.costar.co.uk/en/assets/news/2013/May/Lloyds-confirms-Project-Thames-sale-to-Cerberus-at-325m/ (accessed 14 June 2017).

Wallace, J. (2016) *Lloyds Bank Closes £9bn New Business In 2015 Including Record Syndication Levels*, CoStar. Available at http://www.costar.co.uk/en/assets/news/2013/February/Marathon-pays-400m-for-Project-Chamonix-as-Lloyds-readies-Project-Thames-UK-NPL-/ (accessed 4 July 2017).

Watkins, C., White, M. and Keskin, B. (2012) *The Future of Property Forecasting*, Investment Property Forum, London.

Wells Fargo (2010) *Economics Group: Weekly Economic and Financial Commentary*, 17 September. Available at http://www.realclearmarkets.com/blog/ WeeklyEconomicFinancialCommentary_9_17_2010Final.pdf (accessed 14 June 2017).

Wheaton, W.C. (1987) The Cyclic Behavior of the National Office Market, *AREUA Journal*, 15, 4, 281–299.

World Bank (2017) *Open Data*. data.worldbank.org (accessed 14 June 2017).

Wrigley, N. and Lambiri, D. (2014) *High Street Performance and Evolution: A Brief Guide to the Evidence*, University of Southampton, Southampton.

Index

Property Boom and Banking Bust: The Role of Commercial Lending in the Bankruptcy of Banks,
First Edition. Colin Jones, Stewart Cowe, and Edward Trevillion.
© 2018 John Wiley & Sons Ltd. Published 2018 by John Wiley & Sons Ltd.